MANAGING CHILDHOOD PROBLEMS

MANAGING CHILDHOOD PROBLEMS

Support Strategies and Interventions

DR. G. NARAYANA REDDY
DR. SUMA NARAYAN REDDY

KANISHKA PUBLISHERS, DISTRIBUTORS
NEW DELHI 110002

KANISHKA PUBLISHERS, DISTRIBUTORS
4697/5-21A, Ansari Road, Daryaganj
New Delhi -110 002
Phones : 2327 0497, 2328 8285
Fax : 011-2328 8285
E-mail : kanishka_publishing@yahoo.co.in

Managing Childhood Problems:
Support Strategies and Interventions
First Published-2003
Second Edition-2012

ISBN: 978-81-7391-533-4

PRINTED IN INDIA

Published by Madan Sachdeva for Kanishka Publishers, Distributors, 4697/5-21A, Ansari Road, Daryaganj, New Delhi-110 002, Typeset by Sunshine Graphics, Delhi, and Printed at Rajdhani Printers, Delhi.

Acknowledgements

This book was researched and written by Dr. G. Narayana Reddy and Dr. Suma Narayan, who are currently working as Experts at the Department of Social Affairs in the Ministry of Labour and Human Welfare, Asmara, Eritrea. Many international agencies such as the UNICEF and the World Bank are making sincere efforts to alleviate the problems of the disadvantaged families and children in difficult circumstances needing special support measures. The authors' engagement in such innovative projects in India and Eritrea made this effort fruitful.

We express our sincere and heartfelt thanks to all the organizations and individuals who were helpful and supportive in this venture. We sincerely wish that the book would be of great use to a variety of professionals, academics, researchers, trainers, project administrators, students in the field of Family and Child Welfare and the parents too.

Dr. G. Narayana Reddy
Dr. Suma Narayan Reddy

Contents

List of Charts, Boxes and Figures

Charts

Boxes

Figures

1

Introduction

Background and Justification

As the title is indicative, the book illustrates the duties and responsibilities of different stakeholders, State, families and children themselves, in shaping children and managing childhood problems; and in bringing them up with a good start in life until they grow up as valuable citizens of our society. Family impact studies are valued in providing inputs to virtually every government programme, such as social security, foster care, employment, taxation etc. Family members are no more secure, due to the deteriorating family bonds and withering care and decaying support systems of the traditional family. Family functions are being replaced by the non-familial institutions, the government and NGOs. Hence, the need to understand the impact of changes in family relations on the social policies and programmes of government is more pronounced. Professionals too need to understand and draw inputs from the family impact studies, in order to provide effective and culturally acceptable services to their clientele.

Managing childhood! What an idea? Many may wonder, why there is a need to know much about the natural process of transformation of childhood through seemingly safe journey to the adulthood. It may also be true that in traditional societies, such a thought may sound absurd. But, the ever-changing modern society is ridden with several maladies, both man-made and natural disasters compounded by poverty and deprivation. A number of professional and medical advancements also contribute to the necessity of knowing what the childhood problems are and how to deal with those problems. If not possible for parents to deal with certain acute problems, they could then seek services of several professionals and institutions, which are now available to one and all.

Changing family environment, value systems and increasing social, communal and political conflicts in society have endangering effects on childhood development. On the one hand family relationships and bonds for care and protection of children are deteriorating; while, on the other hand, materialism is pervading modern and western families. At the macro-level, political instability and racial and communal tensions, armed conflicts, terrorist activities and separatist movements are increasingly driving children and families to vulnerability and distress. The alleged rise in child abuse, childhood crimes and disorder in society, all reflect on the physical insecurity and moral ambiguity of our society. In short, there seem to be a general lack of social, moral and emotional development of children in the contemporary society.

Most of the available literature on childhood development and related psychological issues are predominantly carried out in urban-based well to do family settings. Some studies were also carried out and deal extensively on family violence, broken families, parent separations and their impact on childhood socialization. There is also much literature on children in conflict with law, such as, juvenile behaviour, delinquency and adult-like crimes committed by children.

Similarly, aspects of parenthood have variously been researched and explored by sociologists, psychologists and medical professionals, who have also proposed certain models of what good parenting should contain. However, most of these studies are overwhelmingly concentrated on urban-based children and families, as their subjects of research or at best on the children in institutional settings.

In the context of development of children and their families in need of special protection measures, a lot more issues remain untouched. Eventhough, several programmes are planned and implemented for the benefit of the disadvantaged groups, much of their social and cultural background, the various circumstances that are behind their disadvantage remain unexplored.

The other trend has been the interventions by professionals and change agents in matters of family counseling and childhood issues. More and more professional interventions are becoming common in exercising power on critical decisions about proper parenting and managing childhood, especially in the western countries. It is not limited to medical professionals, but the media, politicians, religious leaders and community play key roles in passing judgments and modifying social behaviour of people in society. Yet the various issues related to childhood are becoming increasingly important for both the modern-western countries as well as the developing countries.

In the contemporary society, the value systems have been changing at a rapid manner, especially the attitude towards parenting and childhood. Currently, a fewer children, more financial and emotional investments for longer duration on children has been the trend. Children are no more the exclusive possession of parents. The rights of children are paramount in the contemporary society.

Viewed in historical and cultural perspective, children have played little part in shaping of their own identities and social position (Corsaro, 1997). While the 'new history of childhood' project children as competent social actors, that suggest a more informed and confident child population. Boundaries between adults and children are indeed more contested and children are becoming less dependent on adults and they are taking responsibility for their own affairs (Wyness, 2000).

Most parents are now under scrutiny. There are several cases of children seeking court judgments in USA and UK about their childhood abuses and deprivations due to the irresponsible acts of their parents (Campion, 1995). Children abandoning parents and running away from homes have become common. There were instances, where children have filed cases in courts for genetically passing on HIV, which could have been avoided, if their parents were responsible. Thus the progression of knowledge on child rights has brought in a flurry of anxiety and trauma for several parents in the western society. The State policing and laws alone can not provide solutions, as the issues involved affect the whole lot of other stakeholders. In this context, several ambiguities and dangers have emerged, which certainly need to be addressed.

Most governments intervene to protect children in emergencies, and have passed child laws, which are bound to reduce the rights of the parents, while at the same time protect children in need of help. Thus both parents and the State need to invest more considered effort in bringing up children, who develop into socially well adjusted, healthy and productive adults. Practically, the burden of managing childhood is so enormous that, even well-intentioned parents find themselves wondering whether they are getting it right and, if not, to whom they should turn to for advice (Campion, 1995).

With regard to shaping of State policies and programmes of childcare, protection and development, there are many significant lessons that we have to learn in dealing with the "childhood crises". For instance, actions and value system of parents and teachers who deal with the socialization process of children are being contested. Political and institutional interventions have become imperative in reconstructing the childhood of the disadvantaged.

Several factors contribute to care, protection and development of children in society. Proper socialization of childhood depends to a large extent on parents and teachers, whose social and moral value systems play a key role. Family relationships and social environment also contribute to a greater extent, in shaping children's cultural orientation. The economic capability of parents is also a key factor, to the extent that they can meet the basic needs of children and reduce their relative deprivations.

The contemporary society has witnessed several new challenges, which have emerged due to the following reasons:

- Recognition of the rights of children, especially, the right of the child to self determination;
- Increased break-up of parental and family relationships;
- Demands for equal rights to parenthood;
- Changing value system that is tuned to achievement orientation, materialistic and commercialization of relationships in society;

- Increased conflicts and political strife resulting in population movements and displacements affecting mainly children and women; and
- Increasing disabilities and disadvantages faced by children due to natural and man-made disasters.

Apart from these, some new areas of concern, such as sexual abuse of children, use of children as soldiers, trafficking of children for sex trade and child labour have become demanding issues for greater intervention of the State machinery and allocation of new resources. There is a need to address policy reforms and development needs within this backdrop of perceived problems. In view of the above mentioned gaps, an attempt is made in this book to unravel some of the untouched issues, and those issues that seem to have an impact on rehabilitation and development of the disadvantaged children and their families in need of special protection measures.

Methodology

The book is a chronological account of the authors' personal investigations and experiences as a result of their involvement in various development projects concerning social affairs, child care, protection and development, over a period of about two decades. However, most of the issues included in this book were researched and written over a period of three years, during the authors' stay in Africa, as Experts in the Department of Social Affairs at Eritrea.

It was exciting and at times challenging to work in various foreign funded projects that were directly concerned with childcare, protection and development. The authors consider that it was a perfect place that exposed them to a variety of issues that were created by man-made emergencies as well as, natural disasters, in an environment of poverty, diseases and deprivations. Such variety of circumstances and experiences has profoundly influenced the writings in this book.

In writing this book, the following sources were utilized, apart from the first hand experiences of the authors':

- Professional and academic researches;
- The media and government sources;

- Parents and children from a wide variety of backgrounds; and
- Views of professional practitioners.

The style of presentation is simple, understandable and the contents are very useful to a variety of persons including parents, professionals, academics, researchers, trainers, project administrators and students in the field of Family and Child Welfare.

Chapterization

The contents of the book are presented in eleven chapters that are chronologically ordered. In the beginning five chapters, a review of various issues concerned with family relationships, disadvantaged families, deterrents and determinants of proper childhood socialization and healthy development of children were discussed and analyzed with the support of existing research findings and appropriate examples. The end chapters were devoted to a discussion of all possible intervention mechanisms and management strategies to solve various problems associated with helping children in need of special protection measures and their rehabilitation. A gist of each of these chapters is presented here.

The first chapter, "Introduction", was devoted to provide an account of the background and scope of the book. Relevant issues, such as, the changing family relationships, conflicting value system, deteriorating political and social environment and their impact on childhood socialization were analyzed. Several factors that characterize contemporary childhood socialization and consequent problems faced by children, parents, State and other stakeholders were briefly discussed and gaps in researches were explored, in order to fill those gaps and provide new dimensions of knowledge on childhood problems and possible solutions. This chapter also narrated the methodology and a brief summary of issues and discussions in each of the chapters that were included in the book.

The second chapter, "Families and Social Environment in Childhood Development" reviewed basic researches on the roles of family and family relationships in childcare, protection and development. It illustrated as to how family and social environment could support and enhance or, alternatively, undermine happy and healthy childhood development and how parents and children could experience emotional competence in the process.

Many researchers have observed that in contemporary society, family protection and security systems are withering and decaying; and many familial functions are being replaced by non-familial institutions. Hence, the need to understand the impact of changes in family relations on the social policies and programmes of government is more pronounced. It is also imperative for professionals to understand the cultural and social backgrounds of disadvantaged families and their children, in order to provide appropriate and effective services. Family impact studies could provide such knowledge and inputs.

The contemporary society is plagued by several changes that have direct impact on family dynamics, childcare and development. Some of these changes are:

- The traditional family roles of caring, nurturing and providing security to all its members, irrespective of their economic contribution, are being altered;
- The sex roles have brought about changes in relationships and institutional norms;
- Personal choices are on the increase and family obligations are less important, and family relations have become voluntary rather than a necessity;
- People are eager to improve their living standards, which drives many couples to live apart for long periods, subjecting their spouses and children to experience isolation and sometimes depression;
- Social networks and institutions are on the decrease; and
- Material prosperity of individuals tends to result in spiritual poverty, subjecting parents and children to experience many forms of stressful situations needing professional interventions.

In view of the above, the following questions were raised and analyzed in this chapter. What are the characteristics of a good family and good parenting? Under what circumstances parents become stressful and subject their children to neglect and abuse? Are parents doing well in disciplining and protecting their children? How could emotional maturity be brought about among parents facing problems with their children? What could be the remedies to fill those lacunae in good parenting and socialization of children?

The third chapter, "Children of Disadvantaged and 'Under Class' Families" was devoted to a detailed discussion on the characteristics and factors viz., social, economic and cultural, associated with the deteriorating nature of family environment and the consequent emotional reactions of children. If children are burdened in their childhood and deprived of basic necessities, their physical and mental growth diminishes. Parents must understand this process and structure their gradual 'coming up of age' (Murray, 1989).

Parents of disadvantaged families are either ignorant or are not capable of providing basic needs for their children. They can not properly structure the processes of childhood due to several disadvantageous factors affecting their livelihood, which include:

- Poverty and deprivation of basic needs such as, food, clothing, housing, water and sanitation, health care and education facilities;
- Nutritional deprivation, resulting in lack of immunity for infections as well as low physical and mental growth;
- Burden of sharing parents' work to sustain families, depriving child's educational development;
- Increased number of children in families, resulting in less attention for children due to heavy burden of meeting survival needs;
- Cultural factors affecting proper parenting of children (control, dependency syndrome, lack of competence, patronage, over protection, etc.).

To add to this phenomenon of disadvantaged families, is the emergence of what is called as the 'under class' culture, representing 'undeserving poor'; and they are culpable in creating a culture of deprivation and crime among many modern families (Murray, 1989; Wyness, 2000).

An attempt was made in this chapter to describe various facets of the disadvantaged and the "under class" families, in reference to childcare and behaviour in society. Behavioural problems that develop among children as a result of deprivations in childhood, changes that have come about in parent-child relationships due to new technological innovations, emotional reactions and experiences of children due to family violence and parental separations were analyzed and discussed in this chapter.

The fourth chapter, "Child Rights and Children in Need of Special Protection Measures" was devoted to a debate on the rights of children, child rights movements and various categories of children under difficult circumstances needing special protection measures. An attempt was made to analyze the various social and structural problems, which children have been facing in contemporary society; and the remedial measures taken at various levels, that is, at parents, community, national and international levels to provide for meeting their needs, safeguarding their interests, protecting them from exploitation and abuse and facilitating harmonious development of every child.

Historically and culturally viewed, children were generally excluded as a unit of reference, because they were not expected to have a stake in the social, economic and political arrangements. They did not have vote, could not claim income and did not have any formalized role in school or at home. There was a notion that children were, in moral and social terms out of position (Wyness, 2000). Hence, parents, institutions and policy makers by and large were expected to decide on behalf of children, assuming to know what was in the 'best interest' of children.

However, the child rights activists have reputed such ideas and have mobilized support to include the right of the child for 'self determination' in the Convention on the Rights of Children (CRC), thus rendering children visible within the public sphere. The social focus on children has been on the increase then on. Providing an environment, which fosters democracy and stimulates emotional, psychological, social and cognitive growth of children is a universal requirement; and for all the countries, which have ratified the CRC, it is mandatory to implement those provisions provided in the CRC.

But, due to various reasons, such as, lack of resources, lack of political commitment and convenience of using children as soldiers and as child labourers, there has been no significant reduction in tackling the problems of the exploited children. This amounted to blatant violation of child rights at every level.

Political strife leads to armed conflicts. Armed conflicts and wars always resulted in displacements and population movements, mainly affecting children and women. Many parents who joined armed conflicts or the army might die leaving behind single parent families. Such single-parent family mothers are economically unable to provide for the basic needs of their children. Discipline of children in single-parent families is often not effective. Added to these, poverty still remained a main challenge affecting the disadvantaged families. Thus, many children lived in vulnerable environment paving opportunities for their exploitation. The above issues were critically analyzed in this chapter; and remedial measures were suggested for preventing child abuse and rehabilitating various categories of children in need of special protection measures.

Issues concerned with a few categories of children in need of special protection measures, such as, refugees, street children, children in sex trade were also discussed in this chapter. There were other categories of children in need of special protection measures, such as those affected by armed conflicts and the disabled children. Since these are very important groups of children facing serious problems that need everybody's attention, we have devoted two separate chapters to discuss these categories of children and their impact on families and society at large.

Accordingly, the fifth chapter, "Children and Adolescents Affected by Armed Conflicts and other Social Problems", exclusively dealt with the problems of children involved in armies and other armed conflict-groups, as well as the distinct socio-psychological problems that they had to undergo as a result of their deprivations and disadvantageous situation in society.

Due to decline of moral and ethical values among human beings and increased propensity to violence as a means to resolve political and social problems, a significant segment of population, especially children and youth have been subjected to unnecessary and unwarranted suffering. The so-called human rights continue to be violated despite many international conventions and commitments.

War destroys the economy, the infrastructure, manufacturing units, school buildings and hospitals in the country. When the soldiers invade towns and villages, they destroy houses and loot their belongings. Villagers loose livestock and stop cultivation due to the danger of land mines planted in their agricultural fields and passages. State-run welfare programmes vanish. In every conflict situation, children who have been separated from their parents are the most sufferers. Break-up of family life, repeated displacements and constant physical threats deprive children of their natural background for their emotional and mental development.

In view of the above, several issues, such as, awareness among public regarding the problems and plight of child soldiers and those affected by war; problems of refugees and internally displaced children in camps; psycho-social impact of armed conflicts on children; social problems that the adolescents face in society apart from war related ones; and some workable solutions to tackle these problems were examined and analyzed in this chapter.

The sixth chapter, "Children with Disabilities: Family Members Meeting the Challenges" was geared to understand and explore those factors that influence the family's adaptation to having a child with a disability (CWD), which served as a base for intervention plans that were suggested in the next few chapters. The basic premise set in this chapter was that, the CWD is not just a child but, part of a complex family network and we can never fully understand it unless we try to understand him/her as a member of the family system he/she is engulfed in! Till recently, only the child's behaviour and development have been studied. The need to explore the environment that surrounds the child is of recent origin starting with Bristol and Gallangher (1982). There are intergenerational factors that influence parental attitude and behaviour and these aspects also can never be ignored, more so in societies like India. There are also larger cultural groups like extended family, church, relatives, friends, community, political systems etc., which influence the family system either directly or through the other social systems.

Some of the factors that are of profound consequence are the meaning of disability to the parents and family members, their problem solving capacities and resources, the characteristics of the child and roles and relationships within the family. Some factors directly affect the children with disabilities (CWD), while other factors show their impact on family members in varying degrees. We tried to examine only some of the factors that have direct implication for intervention, as it is beyond the scope of this chapter to probe in to all the factors mentioned above. Based on this extensive exercise coupled with the author's own experience, a desired paradigm was recommended. The areas discussed include:

- The families of children with disabilities (CWDs);
- Attitudes and responses of family members;
- The phases of accepting disability by the family;
- The impact of disability on significant family members;
- Critical factors influencing family's response to disability; and
- The desired family paradigm.

The single factor that has considerable influence on CWDs is the family climate that has been created and shaped by the attitudes and responses of parents followed by siblings and others. Numerous studies have been undertaken in studying the attitudes and responses of parents of CWDs during the last three decades. The most consistent finding is that attitudes and responses of parents vary widely and it is interdependent on a few critical issues that are discussed in this chapter.

Some of the most common reactions and responses of parents and family members were analyzed and discussed. These responses could be positive, negative or neutral. The presence of a CWD strengthened some families, and it broke some others; while the majority of the families remained without being unduly disturbed or shaken up. What is being implied here is that, if the family has, in the past, been functioning as a healthy unit, it should be able to cope up with the presence of a CWD reasonably well. It has been observed that, most healthy families will meet the problem in a realistic and productive manner, making the family a closer and more meaningful unit (Buscaglia, 1985).

The seventh chapter, "Optimizing Child's Abilities through Parents' Participation" discusses parents as most potent resource in promoting the development of children. After working with parents as a professional social worker and researcher, the author has come to believe that collaborative working relationship between professionals and parents is a key factor in providing the optimum benefits for children in general and children with disabilities in particular. Several incidents occurred during her work that highlighted the importance of having good working relationships with parents and stimulated her interest in learning more about this aspect of parent's role. In this chapter, the author has mainly drawn on her experiences and research findings in order to provide information, which will help professionals, develop the attitudes, knowledge and skills considered essential for working effectively with parents.

Parents' participation is very often overlooked and taken for granted by professionals to realize that they end up paying heavy prices for that. Parents' participation will not occur on its own and it has to be deliberately planned, conducted and harnessed. Guidelines are provided for professionals for improving parental participation in schools and service centers, in order to facilitate the healthy development of children with special needs. The chapter also provides a rationale for establishing effective working relationships with parents and outlines the knowledge, the skills, and attitudes which professionals need to develop. Cooperative planning between parents and professionals may prevent, alleviate or solve many problems that may arise during the rehabilitation process of their children with disabilities. Professionals who recognize their roles as complementary and supplementary, who approach their interactions enthusiastically and not apprehensively, and view their relationships as a partnership, will usually be rewarded with happy outcomes.

Parents can play a range of roles in educational set-ups *viz.* parents, co-therapists, first-hand information providers, resource persons, advocates, assistants, decision-makers, catalysts and as partners. While executing these roles, they can be a 'buffer' or 'trigger', diminish or intensify disability, promote or impede development, and can play supplementary or complementary roles. Factors that promote or hinder their positive role-play are dealt with. Variables that influence levels of participation and typical ways in which they are involved in schools and rehabilitation set-ups are also discussed.

Various strategies for working with parents are considered, and a model for family and parent intervention is suggested. Indications and contra-indications for working with parents are looked in to. It considers different forms of parental participation in children's rehabilitation. These include assessments, setting of education or training goals, follow-up at home, review of progress and so on. Skills for improving parent participation and skills for working with challenging and difficult parents are also considered. These skills can also be generalized into any other set-ups concerned with parents.

The eighth chapter, "Inclusive Education of Children: the Social Face" is concerned with the latest trend in the educational stream of including students with disabilities in typical, general classrooms with the supports and reorganizations they need. The chapter updates the concept of inclusive education, reviews the history of inclusion and then clearly defines the key components of inclusive education. The chapter revisits the rationale for inclusion, reviews the gains of inclusion for all concerned, especially the main actors' viz., children with disabilities, children without disabilities, teachers, and parents.

One of the determining factors of inclusive education is the attitudes and values of the key actors. Inclusive education is a process that has lot to do with acceptance and positive attitude at all levels. It involves a paradigm shift from 'segregation' and 'special education' to children with disabilities to education in general classrooms, as a matter of right, and in the best interest of a democratic society. But, we have grown in a 'segregating' atmosphere, and we are quite comfortable with this environment of having children with disabilities being taught away from children without disabilities. Inclusive education does stir us out of this 'comfortable' position, as it involves welcoming the so far 'segregated group' back, and making them part of the general education.

Resistance is common to any discomforts, so too to inclusive education in the early stages, especially in countries like India, which is in its infancy stages as far as inclusive education is concerned. The common attitudinal blocks have also been explored. It is believed that inclusion will not come about on its own, it needs to be brought about through conscious efforts. The chapter therefore has extensively dealt with the strategies for bringing about this attitudinal change that is very significant for the implementation of inclusive education with positive impact. The strategies mainly center on the key-players viz. children, parents, teachers and education administrators. Tips for facilitating acceptance are also furnished.

Inclusive education is seen as a very difficult but possible reality. It is believed that with appropriate supplementary aids and services, most children with disabilities can be in general education alongside children without disabilities. It is hoped that with proper preparation and attitudinal change, the vast majority will find inclusive education easy and very rewarding. Even the most resistant teachers and parents can find it appropriate, and highly needed for children with disabilities. Based on an extensive research coupled with author's own experience, the desired social paradigm is suggested. However, the core theme remains, when the required attitudinal changes come about, will the required behavioral changes follow.

The ninth chapter, "Win/Win Paradigm—A Powerful Technique for Effective Parent-Child Relationship" is devoted to the strategies of improving and sustaining parent-child relationship, that are most crucial for healthy social, intellectual and emotional development of a child. We have extensively reviewed the possible mediating factors that could influence the family system and relationships, so that the positive influences can be preserved and strengthened and the negative influences can be nullified or replaced with positive ones.

In the contemporary society, though we confront varying opinions as to the efficacy and value of family system, it continues to play an important part in determining human behaviour, building personality, influencing the course of moral, mental and social evolution and shaping culture and its institutions. Irrespective of all criticism, and technological advancements and influences of modernization, family still remains the basic social unit that lays the foundation for development of children. Therefore, the biggest challenge that we face today is building up strong families, and more than that, maintaining it as a healthy, happy and growth-stimulating unit.

Another most powerful conduit that builds or wrecks families/communities is interpersonal relationships. The relationships confront us everywhere be it family, school, office, neighborhood, play ground, friends circle and society at large. With some persons we relate more intimately than with others; with a few it is out of obligation; it is purely functional, and with a few others it is out of our own choice and interest.

The discussions in this chapter were based on the premise that the quality of each person's life *vis-à-vis* family climate is directly linked to the quality of interpersonal relationship one maintains, which in turn is dependent on the quality of communication one experiences. It means that the behaviour, which leads to poor interpersonal relationship, is socialized in early childhood, that is, it is learned. Secondly, that the problem involved in the effects of poor communication and interpersonal relationship is a lack of cognitive meaning in the parent-child communication system. And thirdly, that the growth of cognitive processes is fostered in family control systems which offer and permit a wide range of alternative actions and thought, and that, such growth is constricted by systems of control which offer predetermined solutions and few alternatives for consideration and choice.

We have argued, that the win/win communication, language and behaviour proposed by Covey (1997) shapes the interpersonal relationships and that interpersonal relationships shape thought and cognitive styles of problem solving. The win/win philosophy consists of four paradigms, viz., win/win, win/lose, lose/win and lose/lose. The win-win paradigm is a frame of mind and heart that constantly seeks mutual benefit in all human interactions. It involves interactions, decisions and agreements and solutions that are mutually beneficial. It is implied that the win/win strategy creates a free and flexible system whereas, other strategies promote a constricted family system. These distinctions were clarified by appropriate examples of parent-child communication using win/win and non- win/win strategy in this chapter.

The tenth chapter, "Interventions through Counseling" is all about counseling and how to help people realize their potential to cope with stressful and difficult situations in life; and discovering the path for peaceful and happy way of resolving interpersonal conflicts. The objectives of writing this chapter were the following:

By reading this chapter a person should be able,

(i) to acquire basic knowledge about the types and uses of counseling;
(ii) to learn the utility of various skills in counseling such as, foundation skills, advanced skills and influencing skills;
(iii) to understand various steps and stages in counseling process and the application of various theoretical approaches, such as the psychodynamic, behaviouristic, cognitive and integrated approaches in counseling;
(iv) to identify common blocks in life and learn methods of managing happy and satisfying life; and
(v) to learn coping mechanisms to deal with stress, disappointments and frustration and can discover the purpose of life, that is, leading a happy and successful living.

Development is the aim of counseling: All human beings have immense potential for growth, yet there are many who are stuck, immobilized, and unable to meet developmental challenges. Counseling is all about how to facilitate another person's development. Clients come to counselors to solve problems, to find answers, to discover reasons for patterns of behavior, but always, to develop their own unique potential.

People usually approach counselors for help when they are going through difficult times in their lives. Feelings such as, sadness, hurt, angry, betrayed, afraid, overwhelmed or shamed, are experienced by one and all. An individual may experience a crisis, or a problem that affected relationships may have lost a job, feel isolated, pressured or just wants to find out what is wrong or if life has any meaning.

Stress and unhappiness may be caused by various problems, sometimes the problems may be long standing involving family disputes, injuries caused by accidents, abuse, domestic violence, victimization etc. Stress may also be caused by financial problems such as insolvency and bankruptcy. Stress and trauma in children may be caused due to coping problems with studies, because of fear of punishment by teachers, because of discrimination shown by others, because of teasing or because of war related experiences such as, bombardments, abuses by soldiers on family members etc. Refugees often experience enormous amount of stress, due to loss of property, loss of family members, hunger and distressing environment. Stress could be caused due to long-term illness such as T.B, leprosy, HIV/AIDS etc.

A counselor will listen to the client attentively, supports and helps the person to find his/her own answers to whatever is troubling. The counselor empathizes with the client with an equal relationship. Working this way, the counselor will focus on how the client can live effectively in this society, knowing and honoring his/her own needs and wishes. Counseling is a series of problem solving purposeful conversations. A process and a method of exploring and identifying personal problems and solutions leading to personal growth and development.

The application part of the discussion, in this chapter, includes two major aspects, which are currently serious issues. These are, the psychosocial work focused on children and the behavioural changes that are required among the adolescents to avoid major social problems in community life. The psychosocial work focused on children has two purposes: *(i)* prevention of psychosocial problems, and *(ii)* provision of special care for those who were traumatized and need to recover. Psychosocial impact on the displaced and refugees children may be difficult to assess, but it is an important area needing attention of the doctors, change agents, social workers and the paramedical workers. Child counseling is an essential strategy to help children cope with stress and traumatic experiences.

Regarding behavioural changes that are required among the adolescents to avoid major social problems in community life, experiences have shown that it takes a longer time for behavioural change to occur among the affected persons. Adults must therefore be good role models to provide positive influence to teenage behaviour. Determinants of behavioural change include education and awareness, knowledge, moral values and norms; and more importantly, the correct perception of consequences and negative aspects of problems and positive aspects of change of behaviour. These issues are analyzed and discussed with appropriate examples in this chapter.

Finally, the chapter on "Conclusion and Some Imperatives" provides enriching discussion on the issues that were examined in this book and throws out a few new questions and issues for further consideration of researchers and practitioners in the field of 'Family and Child Welfare'. The chapter also provides some of the imperatives for establishing effective working relationships with parents and families and delineates knowledge, skills, and attitudes which professionals need to develop to bring about positive impact on children and parents in social and functional aspects of life. As mentioned earlier, the book promises to be of great use to a variety of persons including parents themselves, professionals, academics, researchers, trainers, project administrators and students in the field of 'Family and Child Welfare'.

References

1. Bristol, K.M. and Gallagher, J.J., (1982), A family focus for intervention. In C. Ramey & P. Trohanis (Eds.), *Finding and Educating the High-risk and Handicapped Infant*, Baltimore: University Park Press.
2. Buscaglia, L., (1986), "Together with Leo Buscaglia", in Stewart J., *Bridges Not Walls*, (4th Edition), New York: Random House.
3. Campion, M.J., (1995), *Who is Fit to be a Parent*, Routledge: London and New York.
4. Corsaro, W., (1997), *The Sociology of Childhood, California*: Pine Forge.
5. Covey, R.S., (1997), *The Seven Habits of Highly Effective Families*, London: Franklin Covey Company.
6. Murray, C., (1989), "The under class", *Sunday Times Magazine*, 26 Nov., pp. 26-45.
7. Wyness, M.G., (2000), *Contesting Childhood*, London: Falmer Press.

2

Family and Social Environment in Childhood Development

Introduction

Family impact studies are valued in providing inputs to virtually every government programme, such as social security, foster care, employment, taxation etc. Family members are less secure now than before, due to the deteriorating family bonds, withering care and decaying support systems of the traditional family. Family functions are being replaced by the non-familial institutions, the government and NGOs. Hence, the need to understand the impact of changes in family relations on the social policies and programmes of government is more pronounced. Professionals too need to understand and draw inputs from the family impact studies, in order to provide effective and culturally acceptable services.

The imperative nature of the family has been described in one sentence as below:

"A person who has no need to live in a family because he/she is self-sufficient, must be a beast or a God" (cited in Garbarino, 1982:1). The importance of family relationships and their impact on childhood socialization has been variously described. Family environment can support and enhance or alternatively, lack of

good environment can undermine child development. Family is the basic unit for cultivation of interpersonal and intrapersonal interactions and sociocultural orientation to children, apart from the school and their neighbourhood. It provides a network of relationships that connect together children, parents, aunts, uncles, grandparents, friends, neighbours, communities and professional caregivers. Much of what makes us human beings are the social networks and relationships; while families and society provide these for us.

However, as revealed by many researchers (Cherlin, 1981; Garbarino, 1982; Lewis et. al, 1976; Stinnett, 1979; Zimmerman, 1947), the contemporary society is plagued by several changes that have direct impact on family dynamics, childcare and development. Some of these visible changes are:

- The traditional family roles of caring, nurturing and providing security to all its members, irrespective of their economic contribution, are being altered;
- The sex roles have brought about changes in relationships and institutional norms;
- Personal choices are on the increase and family obligations are less important; and family relations have become voluntary rather than a necessity;
- People are eager to improve their living standards, which drives many couples to live apart for long periods, subjecting their spouses and children to experience isolation and sometimes depression;
- Social networks and institutions are on the decrease; and
- Material prosperity of individuals tends to result in spiritual poverty, subjecting parents and children to experience many forms of stressful situations needing professional interventions.

In view of the above, the following questions may be pertinent to be raised and discussed in order to understand and fill the gaps in the existing literature. What are the characteristics of a good family and good parenting? Under what circumstances parents become stressful and subject their children to neglect and abuse? Are parents doing well in disciplining or protecting their children? How could emotional maturity be brought about among parents facing problems with their children? What could be the remedies to fill those lacunae in good parenting and socialization of children? These are some of the issues, which are explored and analyzed in this chapter.

Family as a Unit of Functional Relationships

Family means different things for different people. It is defined as, "a small kinship structured group with the key function of nurturant socialization (Reiss, 1980: 20). Three common elements in family are marriage, childbearing and kinship (Garbarino, 1982: 32). Children completely depend on parents and families in their first few years of life, and this biological fact necessitates protection, nurturing and teaching of children. Family is also described as "headquarters" for human development (Garbarino, 1982: 62). It is a place for love, care, learning and socialization of children. Children, parents and the lifelong kinship make up the family concept.

Families mediate between individuals and society through socialization and social relationships. Families, individuals and society are thus intertwined. However, the balance of power, individualization and meeting of family goals differ across time and culture. For instance, individual freedom is more in "open families" than the traditional "closed" type of families; while the "atomic" family represents an excessive swing away from the domestic closed type. As family bonds weaken, individualism grows or vice- versa. This means either "deterioration" of family bonds, or positively viewed, as "healthy adaptation to changed conditions" (Zimmerman, 1947 cited in Garbarino, 1982: 66).

As we know, family is basically an interacting unit and the family system is characterized by a whole lot of interactions between parents and children, between father and mother, between children themselves and so on. One most powerful conduit therefore, that builds or wrecks families/communities is interpersonal relationships. The relationships confront us everywhere be it family, school, office, neighborhood, play ground, friends circle and society at large. With some persons we relate more intimately than with others; with a few it is out of obligation; it is purely functional, and with a few others it is out of our own choice and interest. But the underlying fact is that we need to relate at various levels as leaders, parents, teachers, friends, peers, colleagues, children, students and so on, and our success in life depends on how well we are trained to do that in our childhood.

Therefore, our basic childhood training is of profound importance. Failing to get that, the outcome will be 'constricted growth'; unable to cope adequately with the outside world as well as within the family resulting in behaviour problems, emotional difficulties, addictions, and other deviant behaviour. This will be compounded by other coping demands of the modern society. The implication is that, families need to prepare children with adequate interpersonal and problem-solving skills to cope with the external demands. The same idea is being put forth by Powell (1969) in simpler terms, "what I am at any given moment in the process of becoming a person, will be determined by my relationships with those who love me or refuse to love me, with those I love or refuse to love".

Thus, families have to play a large role in the process of developing competence among children when they are young. Families can do well in rising their children, when they have good social support systems and network of institutions in their neibourhood. Only those families that have good interactions within their environment and those that have good support systems and means of livelihood could be successful. While the disadvantaged families, lacking these opportunities sink in their struggles to survive. Professionals must be conversant with all such survival strategies and tactics, so as to intervene, when necessary and shape the environment in order to help families that are in crisis.

Characteristics of Strong and Successful Families

Families are unique with their own characteristics, goals, beliefs and satisfaction or dissatisfaction. One can not easily generalize that a particular family is successful and the other is not. According to Garbarino, a family could be considered as successfully working, "when its members feel good, when their needs are being met, and development and relationships flow smoothly" (1982:72).

However, several researchers on family studies (Kanter and

Lehr, 1975; Garbarino, 1982; Lewis *et. al,* 1976; Stinnett *et. al,* 1979) have suggested that families possess certain relationships and characteristics, on the basis of which they could be evaluated as successful or not. These characteristics include:

- Appreciation of each individual's needs and feelings;
- Family members spending time together;
- Being honest to each other and having open communication between members;
- Commitment to family goals rather than self-centered ideas of members;
- A spiritual sense of life and a common belief and values; and
- An ability to deal with crisis in a positive manner (Stinnett *et. al,* 1979).

Lewis *et. al* (1976) have come up with the following criteria, which indicate both positive and negative aspects of a family life:

- An affiliative, as opposed to an oppositional attitude among members;
- Openness in communication as opposed to confusing or distancing communication;
- A firm and solid coalition in dealing with children as opposed to parental competition;
- Encouragement of creative change rather than routine interests; and
- Appreciation for complex human motivation as opposed to controlling outlook.

Studies on family trends have indicated that, the modern families are withering or decaying because of various factors, which include the following:

- Divorces are increasing due to quest for self-actualization and independence; while vulnerability is also increasing in such families (Spanier, 1980);
- The number of children per family is decreasing, which indicates fewer interactions among children;

- The number of adults in families is also decreasing, leaving no scope of support for working couples;
- Single parent and step parent families are on the increase, which result in psychological distress and behavioural problems among many children (Cherlin, 1981); and
- Children are deprived of intimacy and support in such families.

Changing trends in social and economic conditions of families have implications on psychological satisfaction of members and children. The traditional role of "good provider" of male is undermined and women are no more relegated to home exclusively. Each sex is more often identified in opposition to the other in a competitive society. Social institutions that usually support the goals for social and psychological satisfaction of family members are on the decrease. Consequently, children and parents are facing more and more stressful situations leaving vast scope for counseling services and other caring institutions to intervene on behalf of family members, which were once the family functions.

Children as a First Priority in Families

Children and their issues are the first priority in every family. In an ideal family children are loved, cared and their needs are met. Every parent dreams of bringing up their children, who become very important, liked and loved in family as well as in community. Parents work and earn, take risks, put in extra labour, face all types of problems, all for the purpose of developing their children; in bringing them up with a good start in life and keeping them safe until they are old enough to be independent.

What every family expects their children to experience is healthy socialization that constitutes several goals, such as,

- They develop a positive self-concept;
- They become socially and functionally competent;
- They grow up as self-reliant individuals, who can provide for their needs;
- They learn to provide necessary emotional support when required; and

- They learn life skills that are necessary to meet the needs of their children and families, as adults (Garbarino, 1982; Rutter, 1979; Clare, 1998).

Every family recognizes these goals and strives to optimize the child's development in normal circumstances, where there are no conflicts and stress at home and where they have good support systems to cope with child rearing and related problems. A healthy family meets its basic responsibility to bear and rear children successfully. Skills for handling or coping with stressful situations are a primary resource that is generally obtained through experienced members of the family.

Campion (1995) has pointed out three main indicators that are essential for successful parenting: self-esteem, support networks and socioeconomic status of a family. In traditional societies, self-esteem usually came from being a part of a large family, having well defined roles and life. However, due to collapse of extended families, other neibourhood organizations and institutions such as the Church replaced it. Later on, most people believed in employment as a source of self-esteem. As citizens, we have been more valued for our jobs rather than the families that we nurture and guide.

Greater social mobility and greater value given for profession has disturbed the family life and resulted in loosing support networks. State's interventions and welfare costs have increased consequently. In this context, the role of an extended family, kinship, neibourhood and other service providing institutions is very much-emphasized (Garbarino, 1982; Bronfenbrenner, 1975). The availability of multiple caregivers (Korbin, 1977) relieves stress on the primary care givers. However, those families, which are isolated from the traditional primary groups, have to seek help of new social networks such as, friends, neighbourhood families and other service providing institutions that may provide child rearing relief and support.

Social and economic status of a family was correlated to the adequate provision of basic childcare needs: food, shelter and security. The social and economic status is determined by the access of parents to employment and sufficient income; as well as the support structures and resources the family has in its control. However, too much of value given for work and income has marginalized the parenting roles of family members. Yet another category of parents does not find enough income and are unable to care for the needs of their children. This situation works on eroding emotional and psychological well being of parents and children for it signifies the lack of status and control.

In modern society, it is very difficult to balance between various needs of life-material needs, esteem needs, social needs and intellectual needs (Maslow, 1954, cited in Clare, 1998). Every one has to confront a highly competitive situation, winning and excelling at the profession may take priority rather than being at peace with themselves and their conscience. Thus one has to sacrifice one area of life to achieve excellence in another area. However, an emotionally competent adult can actively develop well enough to achieve and maintain considerably successful balance in most areas/aspects of life.

It is learnt from studies that the foundation for such emotional maturity is laid in childhood. Childhood creates a mould and childhood experiences are interpreted to confirm this sense of reality. For instance, if in childhood, material needs are given a higher order of priority than intellectual needs, that will become priority for adult life (Clare, 1998). Similarly, over protection of the child can do lot of harm for their adult life. We may control some aspects of their environment and protect them from life-threatening situations, but the more we control, the more impossible it may become. If children are not allowed to take risks and face difficult situations, they will either withdraw completely and be unable to face challenges or they will become high risk takers and rebellious to prove their independence (Clare, 1998).

Another important aspect is that, the priorities of children keep changing and growing as the circumstances change around them. Parents have to be flexible to the changes in needs and priorities of children through different ages. It is an essential life skill, which is in most cases learnt, in the process of experiencing and understanding life. The most difficult experiences are usually our best teachers, and they are essential to continuing growth and advancement in terms of development of self-knowledge (Clare, 1998).

In this process, sometimes parents make mistakes and the

outcome may not be as expected and it can make it harder for the child to be successful. However, it is a part of the learning process. Parents must be aware of several methods and processes involved in addressing the needs of children; as well as they should know how to address their mistakes that really count. Some parents may not show much importance to the growing child, as they may be busy with their professional obligations or may be away from child; or they may voluntarily neglect and abuse because of family disharmony and breakdown. In any case, parents must know how important children are for them? In life priorities, where do they place children? How much time and energy they are able to devote for their growing children? These are some of the pertinent questions parents must comprehend in the child rearing process.

Supporting Children to Learn from Their Experiences

Development is a continuos process in which contemporary events play a larger role and the content of exchanges between parents and children will vary with the developmental needs of children from time to time. Parents mediate virtually all-social events in childhood. But, we are aware that many well-laid plans for their children have gone awry and or thwarted by their children. Hence it is not just the planning that matters in meeting the needs of children. Other factors such as reciprocity, communication styles, temperament, out-of-home experiences etc., seem to play key role in socialization and meeting needs of children (Garbarino, 1982).

According to studies (Helfer, 1980: Garbarino, 1982; Rohner and Neilson, 1978), some of the basic social and psychological necessities that parents could help children receive through guidance and support are:

- Positive self-regard acquired through parents' acceptance and love;
- Learning how to regulate impulses and necessary process of self-control;
- Moral structure and a set of good values that shape the child's character; and
- Interpersonal skills and socially acceptable behaviour that is necessary for adequate performance in adulthood.

The primary role in facilitating children to cultivate the above mentioned life skills and values rests with parents. Parents must enable children to learn and experience certain good values, wisdom and precautions that will be of great value in adulthood. Some of the good values that children need to learn are:

- The importance of listening to older and younger persons;
- The importance of remembering old wisdom and teachings;
- The importance of being truthful and not following blindly the majority opinion;
- The importance of respecting everybody irrespective of their status or religion; and
- The importance of not abusing power.

Researches have shown that abusive and neglectful parents do not and can not provide the above stated values and skills and fail to reinforce key interpersonal behaviours among their children. Some have even claimed that abusive parents typically discourage normal social relations among their children (Friedman, 1976; Garbarino, 1977). However, not all children in abusive families can remain without learning some of these good values. As we have discussed earlier, these values can be acquired through other sources such as, the supplemental caregivers, peers, school and mass media etc.

Life skills are usually not taught at school, but learnt through experiencing. Children experience love, trust, hatred and fear, which teach them the values of positive and negative sides. Similarly, traumatic experiences or violence may have long lasting consequences and impact on their adulthood. It is said that, we may not understand love and trust until we have learnt to be without it, and we can not understand living without fear until we have learned to live with it. Thus, sometimes, it is the negative side that teaches us the value of the positive side.

Studies (Clare, 1998; Garbarino, 1982; Stinnett *et. al*, 1979; Lewis *et. al*, 1976) have revealed that the negative and fearful experiences that parents had in their childhood might pass on the message of fear to their children, who in turn may develop inhibitions in taking up challenges. Parents usually know a great deal of what is bad for children, but some do not care much to know about what is good for children. This lack of knowledge prevents them to allow their children to take on challenges in diverse settings. In order to protect them from harm, parents must not deprive them of challenges that induce children to learn social and life saving skills.

Apart from age related experiences during infancy and early school going age, there are several challenging situations that children may have to face in their life. Some of these are more individual and negative events that have impact on their adulthood. Some of the negative events are accident, violence, serious illness of a parent or sibling, loss of a parent and loss of income due to loss of job, destruction of property or natural calamity. Positive events include improvement in family circumstances such as additional income, resolution of a family dispute etc. Studies have also shown that, the capability to handle and cope with negative impact will be more in case of those children who were subjected to the kind of challenges that we have mentioned above in their childhood.

Rutter (1979) revealed that, children and parents would experience the stress building factors as challenges if their primary social and psychological resources are strong. For instance, couples with strong marriage bonds pulled together and produced stronger families when hit with income loss and depressions; and could cope well with the situation. While those with weaker bonds ended up with various forms of psychological crises for family members, especially for the growing children and failed to cope up with the new deteriorating situations. Jones (1965) has shown that individuals who have experienced both positive and negative challenges in their childhood demonstrated signs of greater sensitivity, insight, flexibility and humor in dealing with such events in their adulthood. Thus, a child who experience challenges becomes adept at coping with disadvantages and its vulnerability to stress reduces, as he/she is aware of dealing with such an experience.

Another important area of challenges is mostly faced by the children of disadvantaged families, who are exposed to armed conflict and war related problems such as displacements, deportation and refugee life. Such fearful and traumatic events affect children of different ages in different ways. Much of it is dealt in another relevant chapter in this book. In brief, there are positive and negative ways of dealing with fearful and traumatic situations. The negative way of dealing includes, becoming a victim and retreating from challenges; while the positive way is to face the situation with boldness. Fear can curtail our lives and the more fearful we are the more vulnerable we become; and the more likely that we are attacked either physically or emotionally. However, fear is part of every person's life. Certain amount of fear is essential for our protection, as a warning to care for ourselves.

Hence, children should be allowed to experience fear, anger etc., so that when they grow up they will know the negative effects of such experiences and they do not use it on others. If children are denied difficult situations and experiences in their childhood, they can not test their strength and learn and understand in their own way of dealing with such situations. If children do not have such experiences in their childhood, their ability to cope and handle such situations in their adulthood will be undermined.

By preventing children from being confident in themselves and undermining their ability to cope, you place them at a greater risk in their adult life. If parents expect their children to grow up as emotionally competent adults, they must give them space and freedom to experience on their own; allow them to make mistakes and learn from them; and offer supportive and empathetic feedback.

Disciplining Children

Discipline is something that bothers all parents while their children are growing. There is a need for discipline in every walk of life and at every stage of life. Without discipline, there is no orderliness. Discipline means maintenance of order and obedience; adhering to a system of rules and punishments. The more orderly the children are, the more disciplined they grow up as adults and continue to be orderly in their life. The objective of discipline is to help the child to develop internal discipline—the capacity to make right choices even when there are influences to do otherwise. When parents strive to move in this direction, there is little chance that children reject their values and go astray.

However, disciplining has also negative aspects. Excessive punishments given to children who do not follow certain rules may result in either developing fear or exhibiting rebellious behaviour. What parents think as right may not be right all the time, as values governing behaviour keep changing over time. Children may like to choose which rules they adhere to and why they are doing so, may be justified. Hence, parents should know where to draw a line; when it is reasonable and when it is abusive?

Children who experience physical assault may turn out to develop fear and feel humiliated. They may start blaming their parents and finding fault with them. On the contrary, they may feel that they are wrong and develop a feeling of becoming a bad character deserving all the punishment and hurt themselves. Hence, discipline needs to be considered and applied with great care. Punishments should not turn out to be barriers in preventing the achievement of goals. The physical hurt may be short lived; but the damage that may be done to a child's self-esteem, sense of safety and its right to feel protected can be long lasting.

Children also experience hypocrisy while applying rules and that could have a damaging impact on their lives. It teaches them to do as others say, not as they feel like doing. What is right? Whether what they are instructed to do, or what they are observing? Parents who give a rule that they fail to follow themselves are undermining their own authority. Hence, it is necessary to follow what we want our children to do and not otherwise.

Positive discipline is derived from helping the child to explore and understand what has actually happened. As a parent you may facilitate the child to learn and express the actual feelings and thoughts. If necessary, praise for being honest and open. It allows healing and prevents build up of guilt, shame and fear, which may have negative emotional impact in their adulthood. Be empathetic and tell them that making mistakes and learning from them is welcomed, but not repeating the same mistakes again and again. As parents it is our responsibility to be as sincere and truthful as we can and teach our children to be truthful to themselves (Clare, 1998).

In the end, as Aristotle tells us, "in all things moderation" seems to work as an essential factor in regulating freedom and control. "Both too much and too little control threaten the optimal development of children" (Cited in Garbarino, 1982: 137). However, optimal level depends on the stage of development and varies from child to child. Successful parents are known to avoid extremes of too little control and too much control and accomplish regulation by negotiating with their children (Baumrind, 1980).

Loving and Being Loved by Children

It is not an exaggeration if we say that, "people live for loving and being loved". Love is the highest manifestation of joy. Love is one thing that relieves a person of all the weight and pain in life. Love is a concept, a feeling that can not be physically seen, heard, smelt, tasted, touched or measured. It is described as an ocean surrounded by emotions.

We learn about love by experiencing it. To love is nothing; to be loved is something and to love and be loved is everything. Kindness in words creates confidence; kindness in thinking creates profoundness; while kindness in giving creates love.

Love is the only thing that power can not command and money can not buy. Love will die if held tightly and will fly if held lightly. The purest form of love is described by Clare as, "the complete absence of fear" (1998: 69). Fear of loss of love causes emotional separation among parents and children. Sometimes, disciplining and punishments may give the children a feeling of not being loved and hence, these are contrary to the development of love and success in life.

However, in reality every parent faces situations that are quite tough going. Parents may have hard time when,

- Children behave in ways that attract disapproval from others;
- Children want to extend the boundaries of freedom before their parents feel that they are ready;
- Children reject something that is valued by parents; and
- Children themselves confront parents (Clare, 1998).

Parents should not be fearful of these situations and react with anger or control their decisions. There is a need to explain and negotiate with children and make them responsible for their actions. A child, who has learnt how to make decisions within safe boundaries, is able to participate fully in adult life. Children who are usually restricted and controlled at home may react and exhibit one of the following high-risk behaviours:

- May not participate in family activities;
- May easily be influenced by their peer group members; and
- Will want to make their own decisions with out knowing what they are doing and why they are doing so (Clare, 1998).

Hence, it is the responsibility of parents to enable children to weigh the pros and cons and let them go ahead with what they want to do. As they make mistakes, they learn and be able to use those skills to their advantage. Parents must have patience and sit back and watch their children making mistakes and learning from those mistakes, especially when they reach adolescence. Children must feel that their parents trust them and respect their decisions, as a consequence, they are bound to develop more trust in parents and become more responsible in their actions. This is the greatest way of sharing and enjoying love while parenting.

Self-actualization and Experiencing Emotional Competence

Success in life and what ever we do comes in many forms and shapes. Defining success is difficult as it means different things for different persons. Success may mean the achievement of one's own goals. It can mean complete satisfaction of needs in life. In other words, it is a kind of self-actualization.

The level at which a person functions and the amount of happiness he/ she will derive largely depends on his/her personality. "Personality is the characteristic pattern of behaviour, thought and emotion that determine your adjustment to your environment. These characteristics are significantly stable over a period of time" (Stewart and Martin, 1999: 81).

The amount of self-confidence you will have in going about

your roles depends on this picture of your personality. As a human being one can never be perfect, but some aspects of our personality can be improved at any time of our life. Therefore, it is important to know yourself better and accept those areas that are less than perfect. However, effective living does not require you to be perfect.

Understanding ones own personality leads to self-awareness, which might enable us to make adjustments and improve our relationships with others. Self-awareness is, "becoming aware of our physical, mental, emotional, moral, spiritual and social qualities which, together make you the person you are" (Stewart and Martin, 1999: 62).

There are certain aspects of yourself, which are obvious both to yourself and the people around you, which is known as public self or public zone. Similarly, there are other aspects of yourself, which you know but not the people around you. Some of these you share with your intimate friends and close persons whom you trust. But, still you may keep some things as confidential. This is known as hidden self or semi-public zone. Lastly, there are some aspects, which are not known to either you or people around you. This is called unknown self or private zone.

People who want to keep their public zone larger will become more open, while people who want their public zone smaller may be introverts. The way we relate with our environment depends to a large extent on these. Through counseling, the public zone is made larger, and the semi-private zone is explored to bring out the hidden blocks and feelings that are not useful for your interactions with others. The tensions and stress are thus released to make the person open up and free himself/herself to have better relationship with others.

Here are some of the life needs and goals. It is quite normal that each person's needs and goals may differ. Some of these needs are basic to family life and security, unless those are met, it is difficult to concentrate on other goals. Try to understand which of these goals are important to you and prioritize/rank them so as to know about your priorities in life. These goals could be:

> Health, education, employment, basic life needs, family security, success, self-respect, minimal stress, friendship,

excitement, material wealth, satisfying sex, matured love, spirituality, wisdom, adventure, natural beauty, world peace, etc.

New challenges and experiences can also make you aware of what you never knew you are capable of and bring out your known self. There are standardized tests like interest tests, intelligence tests, and irritability tests, which could be useful to know more about your self. The ultimate objective of knowing about your self is to realize fullness of your potentials and bring about change, in your personality to achieve the set life goals (Reddy, G.N., 2002).

Changes involve shifts in thinking, feelings, behaviour, values, beliefs and attitudes. These are the pillars of your personality. If your thinking has been negative, if you constantly put yourself down, if you always look at the black side of life, counseling can help you to become more positive and this will effect your feelings and bring about positive change in your behaviour. Every part of your personality, character, temperament, behaviour are all delicately connected, so that change in one aspect has its influence on the other aspects as well.

Psychologists, such as Abraham Maslow have conducted several experiments and analyzed levels of achievement in the lives of many so called successful persons like Einstein, Eleanor Roosevelt, Walt Whitman, Abraham Lincon, Thomas Jefferson and so on. They found that no person is perfect in all aspects of life; some were successful in some areas, while others had difficulties and sufferings in some other areas (Maslow, 1970, cited in Clare, 1998).

Psychologists have also identified a set of characteristics and behavioural traits among the successful personalities. Some of these are given below:

- Looking at life objectively;
- Perceiving reality efficiently;
- Accepting uncertainties and unexpected happenings;
- Spontaneity of thoughts and behaviour;
- Sense of humour;
- Creativity and originality;
- Concern for others' well being;

- Problem-centered than self-centered;
- Enjoy privacy and solitude;
- Have strong moral and ethical standards;
- Enthusiastic and welcoming challenges; and
- Honest and responsible (Clare, 1998).

A person's emotional maturity and competence could be judged by these traits. The self-actualisers or successful persons are never shaky and are strong while dealing with a variety of emotions that are classified into two types, fear and joy (Clare, 1998). All other emotions are believed to emerge from these two main ones.

Variations of fear:

- Anger-fear of life not moving as intended;
- Frustration-fear of not getting what you wanted;
- Anxiety-fear of failure, of loss, of future etc.;
- Sadness-fear of loss or change;
- Guilt-fear of being at fault, doing wrong;
- Shame-fear of getting caught;
- Regret-fear of losing something worth keeping;
- Vengefulness-fear of not having upper hand;
- Bitterness-fear of being cheated;
- Jealousy-fear of having less than others;
- Hatred-fear of disliking;
- Possessiveness-fear of losing what is yours;
- Self-pity-fear of taking responsibility for your actions; and
- Loneliness-fear of being unloved/unwanted/alone.

Variations of joy:

- Enthusiasm-joy of getting new opportunities;
- Elation-joy of experiencing achievement;
- Calmness-joy of a sense of well being/contentment and in control of self;
- Peacefulness-joy of fulfillment and happiness;
- Competence-joy of developing skills and using them;
- Confidence-joy of keeping for yourself;
- Self-esteem-joy of being true to yourself; and
- Achievement-joy of positive outcomes as per effort (Clare, 1998).

When we experience emotional feelings associated with joy, we are likely to be contended and successful in life; and when we experience emotions of fear, we are likely to be frustrated and dissatisfied in life. However, emotionally matured persons may not get elated at some achievement or may not get frustrated at loss of something or when they experience non-achievement. They are believed to maintain emotional balance between the feelings of joy and fear. In social life, it is essential to maintain emotional competence for the following reasons:

- To build and maintain relationships which fulfill our emotional needs and enrich our lives;
- To be responsible;
- To reduce stress in our lives;
- To enable expression of needs, thoughts and feelings;
- To achieve one's full potential; and
- To create happier and peaceful society (Clare, 1998).

As parents, we experience a number of uncertainties and unexpected happenings, which may stir our negative feelings-the feelings of fear. Instances are several such as,

- Child suddenly falling sick or meeting with an accident;
- Child not progressing normally;
- School bus does not turn up to pick up the child;
- Child does not reach home in time;
- Child is not able to get up and walk on its own;
- Somebody attacking the child at school; and so on.

It is very critical to maintain calmness and patience during such times when you experience unexpected events, as more tension will worsen the emotional status of a person. It is important to note that the uncertainties and unexpected events are on the increase because of various reasons in the contemporary society and parents better be prepared to face such situations rather than break-down. Parents are also advised to be open to encounter new challenges and experiences and learn new emotional responses as and when they arise.

As parents, who have the responsibility to guide their children, they must recognize and use their own childhood lessons to the fullest advantage of their children. Various positive experiences of childhood could be passed on to children. Similarly, recognize difficult areas and use these as lessons to teach their children how not to do such things. As we know very well, parents are the role models for most children, and parents' behaviour gets copied and mirrored back by children. Childminders, extended family members, schoolteachers, film heroes and adventurous peers, all provide a range of options for children to learn from. Children may adopt behaviours of persons from any of these sources and they may even pick and choose the best they think among the role models.

Thus, parents must be conscious about all these environmental influences, as children show discernment from a very early age. In the contemporary society, though we confront varying opinions as to the efficacy and value of the family system, it continues to play an important part in determining human behaviour, building personality, influencing the course of moral, mental and social evolution and shaping the culture and its institutions. Irrespective of all criticism, and technological advancements and influences of modernization, the family still remain the basic social unit and parents the main actors, who lay the foundation for development of children. After all, childhood shows the way in our life as morning shows the day. More about these aspects of how to improve child-parent relationship has been discussed in the other chapter on "win/win paradigm—a powerful technique for effective parent-child relationship" in this book.

References

1. Baumarind, D., (1980), "New directions in socialization research", *American Psychologist*, 35, 639-652.
2. Bronfenbrenner, U. and Mahoney, M., (1975), "The structure and verification of hypotheses" in Bronfenbrenner, U. and Mahoney, M. (Eds.) *Influences on Human Development*, Hinsdale IL: Dryden Press.
3. Campion, M.J., (1995), *Who is Fit to be a Parent*, Routledge: London and New York.
4. Caplan, G., (1974), *Support Systems and Community Mental Health*, Behavioural Publications: New York.
5. Cherlin, A., (1981), *Marriage, Divorce, Remarriage, Changing Patterns in the Postwar United States*, Cambridge M.A: Harvard University Press.

6. Clare, S., (1998), *Raising the Successful Child,* How to Books: Oxford.
7. Friedman, R., (1976), "Child Abuse: A review of the psychosocial research", in Herner and co. (Eds.), *Four Perspectives on the Status of Child Abuse and Neglect Research,* Washington D.C: National Center on Child Abuse and Neglect.
8. Garbarino, J., (1982), *Children and Families in the Social Environment,* Aldine de Gruyter: New York.
9. Garbarino, J., (1977), "The human ecology of child maltreatment: A conceptual model for research", *Journal of Marriage and the Family,* 39, 721-736.
10. Helfer, R.E., (1980), "Development deficits which limit interpersonal skill, in C.H. Kempe and R. E Helfer (Eds.) *The Battered Child,* University of Chicago Press: Chicago.
11. Jones, M., (1965), "Psychological correlates of somatic development", *Child Development,* 36, 899-911.
12. Kanter, D. and Lehr, W., (1975), *Inside the Family,* San Francisco: Jossey-Bass.
13. Korbin, J., (1977), *Changing Family Roles and Structures: Impact on Child Abuse and Neglect—A Cross Cultural Perspective,* paper presented at the Second Annual National Conference on Child Abuse and Neglect, Houston.
14. Lewis, M., *et. al* (1976), *No Single Thread: Psychological Health in Family Systems,* Brunner/Mazel: New York.
15. Powell, J., (1969), *Why I Am Afraid to Tell You Who I Am?* Chicago: Argus Communications.
16. Reiss, I., (1980), *Family Systems in America,* (3rd ed.), Holt, Rinchart and Winston: New York.
17. Reddy Narayana, G., (2002), *Building Capacities for Sustainable Development,* Kanishka Publishers: New Delhi.
18. Rohner, R. and Nielsen, C., (1978)., *Parental Acceptance and Rejection: A Review of Research and Theory,* CT Human Relations Area Files Press: New Haven.
19. Rutter, M., (1979), "Maternal Deprivation 1972-1978: New findings, new concepts, and new approaches", *Child Development,* 50, 283-305.
20. Spanier, G.B., (1980), "The Family: Alive but not well", *Wilson Quarterly,* Smithsonian Institute: Washington.
21. Stewart, W. and Martin A., (1999), *Going for Counseling,* How to Books Ltd.: London.
22. Stinnett, N. *et al.* (1979), *Building Family Strengths: Blue Print for Action,* University of Nebraska Press: Lincoln NE.
23. Zimmerman, C.C., (1947), *Family and Civilization,* Harper and Row: New York.

3

Children of Disadvantaged and 'Underclass' Families

Introduction

Childhood is associated with nature and biology. Children grow progressively and become visible, as they move towards adulthood. If they are burdened in their childhood and deprived of basic necessities, their physical and mental growth diminishes. Parents must understand this process and structure this gradual 'coming up of age' (Murray, 1989). The disadvantaged families are either ignorant or are not capable to provide for their basic needs and properly structure these processes of childhood due to several disadvantageous factors affecting their livelihood. These include:

- Poverty and deprivation of basic needs such as, food, clothing, housing, water and sanitation, health care and education facilities;
- Nutritional deprivation, resulting in lack of immunity for infections as well as low physical and mental growth;
- Burden of sharing parents' work to sustain families, depriving child's educational development;
- Increased number of children in families, resulting in less attention for children due to heavy burden of meeting survival needs;

- Cultural factors affecting proper parenting of children (control, dependency syndrome, lack of competence, patronage, over protection, etc.).

Changing family environment, deteriorating social values and increasing social and political strife in society have all endangering effect on children. Studies have revealed that, the family bonds and relationships are deteriorating, while materialism is pervading in modern society. Political instability and tensions such as armed conflicts, terrorist activities, separatist movements and wars are increasingly driving children and women to vulnerability and enormous distress. The alleged increase in child abuse, childhood crimes and general disorder in society, reflect on the physical insecurity and moral ambiguity. In short, there seem to be general lack of social, moral and emotional protection for children in the contemporary society.

To add to this phenomenon of disadvantaged families, is new emergence of what is called as the 'under class' culture among many modern families. The families of 'under class' are described by Murray (1989), as 'undeserving poor'; and are culpable in creating a culture of deprivation and crime. Their poverty is based on deviant behaviour and life styles, such as alcoholism, drug abuse, rejection of work, criminal propensities, domestic violence, rejection of marriage, teenage pregnancies, unwed mothers, prostitution, etc. (Murray, 1989; Wyness, 2000). In such families, parents can not and will not exercise "natural" authority over children and their children are prone to be exposed to negative features of adult world, such as, 'youthfulness' of delinquency and committing adult-like crimes. Delinquency, truancy and school aggression are traced back to what parents do or fail to do to their children normally in their childhood.

An attempt is made in this chapter to describe various facets of the disadvantaged families and their children. Apart from the disadvantaged families, a new class of families described by Murray (1989), as the "under class" of families and their characteristics, in reference to child care and behaviour are examined in detail. Behavioural problems that develop among children as a result of deprivations in childhood, changes that have come about in parent-child relationships due to new technological innovations, and the emotional reactions and experiences of children due to family violence and parental separations are analyzed and discussed in this chapter.

Categories of Disadvantaged Families and Their Problems

Disadvantaged families are referred to, "those families lacking the normal or usual advantages of a wholesome family (*Webster's Dictionary,* 1983). To understand the disadvantages of a family, we must first understand the constituents and conditions of a normal family. According to Goode (1982), "a family is a social unit made up of father, mother and children". The other conditions, according to Goode, of a functional family, include the following:

- At least two adult persons of opposite sex residing together;
- Family members engaged in some form of division of labour;
- They will have some kind of economic activity and support, engage in social exchanges and do things for one another;
- Share many things in common such as, food, residence and other goods and social activities;
- Parents take the responsibility to protect and nurture their children and also exercise authority over them; and
- There will be sibling relation among children themselves, with a range of obligations to share, protect and help one another.

On the basis of the above, we may say that those families in which some of these conditions are disrupted, such as absence of father or mother, inability of the family members to meet their needs, and other deprivations, may be considered as disadvantaged families. From a review of literature on disadvantaged families, we can glean at least three categories of disadvantaged families:

(i) displaced, expelled and returnee families;
(ii) families with out a breadwinner, including those families

headed by the aged persons, children and disabled; and

(iii) families living below poverty line, (Agakhan and Talal, 1986). Salient features and enormous problems of these families are explained here.

(i) Displaced, Expelled and Returnee Families

The term displaced refers to those families who are forced to flee from their country of origin to escape persecution because of war or other disasters and seek safety elsewhere. Those families, which flee their country of origin and move to another country are called as refugees, while the internally displaced are those who are forcibly displaced within their own country. The term expelled refers to families, which are sent out or deported from their country of residence or work place to that of their origin. Returnees or repatriates are those families, who have returned home voluntarily from abroad. Asylum seekers and economic migrants also fall under the category of displaced families, since they are also 'uprooted'.

All these are emergency situations, where they face food shortage, hunger and starvation; and they suffer from adverse health conditions such as diarrhea, malaria, as well as traumatic experiences. Emergencies are very common and prevalent in most of the developing countries. A majority of emergencies occur due to wars and internal strife, while a few are due to natural disasters such as drought, famine, floods, cyclones, etc.

These families are characterized by the following conditions:

- Disruption of social and economic fabric, loss of family members and children and displacement of people;
- Fled from their own countries to new places and living in alien and frequently hostile environment;
- Uncertainty of their fate and losing control over lives;
- Experience of violence and threats; and
- Material deprivation and hunger.

(ii) Families without a Breadwinner, Including Those Families Headed by the Aged Persons, Children and Disabled

The families, which are dependent on one of their members for their livelihood, face difficulties when such a person is taken away for national defense or for other reasons missing or separated from the family. This situation creates certain disadvantages in the family. Similarly, when families are displaced, some of the family members get lost or dead and the remaining will be either old or children or disabled persons who can not take care of families, as they themselves are usually dependent on others for survival.

Those who lack social support systems during war, a period of illness, drought or crop failure, for instance, are more vulnerable. Research findings show that there are several groups among the poor considered as more vulnerable. These groups included women headed households, women with irresponsible husbands, orphan children, old people, disabled and the sick (Human Development Report, Tanzania, 1998). Certainly, such families face several disadvantages in social and economic aspects of life and hence they are considered as disadvantaged families.

(iii) Families Living Below Poverty Line

Poverty is so pervasive that there is no country in the world with out some sections of its people being affected by poverty. Poverty denotes a situation where some sections of people can not afford to have minimum basic needs such as food, shelter and clothing. Those who are affected by poverty are the poor. The poor have little money, little food, little power and they are considered as 'little persons'. Exploitation, vulnerability and deprivation always accompany poverty. Poverty does not disappear when a country becomes prosperous, because the rich become richer and the poor are relegated to poverty and dependence in relative terms.

Poverty is usually measured in terms of income, consumption or expenditure. Such measures are comparable between individuals and households. However, such measurement of poverty has been criticized widely because of its nature of causes and effects in society. There is something called the social dimension of poverty, which is not taken into account in the conventional approach and analysis. In the recent analysis on poverty much emphasis is given to the qualitative dimensions of poverty, disadvantage and vulnerability which are poorly represented in the conventional approach

The Human Development Report of the UNDP (1996) has taken in to consideration, the standard of living, educational attainment and the longevity to arrive at the Human Development Index for measuring the country-wise poverty trends. The State of the World Rural Poverty Report of the IFAD (1992) has included several aspects of poverty, such as:

- Material deprivation as measured by inadequate food intake and purchasing power,
- Dependence which depresses the bargaining power of the poor in a world of unequal social relations,
- Lack of decision making power and freedom of choice in production and consumption,
- Isolation as reflected in geographical location-remoteness,
- Alienation because of isolation and exploitative relations,
- Lack of means of production and assets,
- Vulnerability to external shocks and internal social conflicts,
- Insecurity which defines the risk of being subjugated to physical and mental violence (Cited in Niki, 1997).

Due to the reasons mentioned above, those families, which are living below a fixed standard of life or living below poverty line, may be considered as disadvantaged families.

In brief, we may consider 'uprooting' and 'traumatization' to further summarize these experiences of the disadvantaged families. Uprooting refers to the experience of being forced to leave one's familiar surroundings and to settle in a new and unfamiliar environment for an indefinite period that results in stress and prolonged adjustment problems. Traumatization refers to extreme, painful experiences that are so difficult to cope with that they are likely to result in psychological dysfunction both in the short and long term. Uprooting and traumatization are natural consequences of war, refugee situation and natural disasters where family members are separated or displaced, and subjected to abject poverty, and where there is a continuous threat to safety, or displacement.

It has been roughly estimated that 90 per cent of the people in refugee camps are women, elderly and young children. They constitute the most vulnerable groups by their very nature, and their over-representation is an added menace that needs special attention. The other groups that are made acutely vulnerable through these experiences are the orphans and persons with disabilities. But paradoxically, when relief assistance is inadequate, they are the worst hit, and they may not receive adequate food or no food at all. Lack of food itself kills and is a major contributor of death from a number of diseases.

Women and children are especially more vulnerable without social support networks. In case of elderly, very young or ill persons, they face severe survival problems. Women's traditional roles, responsibilities and supportive networks become dramatically altered by deportation, especially when it means separation from husband and children. The family support networks may be completely lost and women become isolated, dependent upon themselves, solely responsible for children in the absence of fathers, they may be subjected to exploitation, emotional and physical/sexual abuse.

In addition, opportunities for self-support are usually very limited. Extended family support from which they drew support may be completely lost. Some engage in day labour if such options exist, others attempt to survive through informal sector activities such as marketing, running food stalls, or brewing traditional beers and liquors. Domestic work among local households is often the only form of permanent employment available, but exploitation is rife, wages are low, working hours are long, and physical abuse is common (Rogge, 1985).

Out of sheer desperation, and because of a total lack of other viable options, many refugee women are forced to prostitution. Women are also crippled by a host of water borne diseases (typhoid, cholera, dysentery and infectious hepatitis) and infections (sleeping sickness, malaria, yellow fever and river blindness) due to their nature of work, anemia, pregnancy related complications due to very poor antenatal care, and infections caused by female genital mutilation (Martin, 1990). Martin (1990) also summarized the three fronts on which refugee women were disadvantaged *viz*.

(1) as principal beneficiaries of the programmes, the inadequacies hit them the worst;

(2) new responsibility to run the family in the milieu of non-access to employment opportunities, training and income-

generation activities, that created dependency on external aid; and

(3) exclusion of women from active participation in the implementation of projects ostensibly designed to assist them.

Children of the uprooted families face greater dangers to their safety and well being than the normal children. Sudden and violent onset of emergencies, disruption of families and community structures as well as acute shortage of resources, with which these children are confronted, deeply affect their physical and psychological well being. Infants and children are the early victims of violence, killer diseases and malnutrition, which accompany population displacements. Some of the conspicuous and observable effects on many young children are: tight food situation that result in very poor diets and malnutrition, lack of educational facilities and opportunities due to huge amount of damage to schools, psychosocial stress caused by the traumatic experiences, and thousands of minors separated from their families (ERREC, 2000).

A considerable number of children develop nightmares, concentration problems, get easily frightened and experience bereavement reactions (Pynoos, R. and K. Nader, 1990); Terr, 1989). Long standing repeated exposures to traumatic events may result in various emotional reactions such as absence of feeling, a sense of rage, or sadness and fear. Fear is the most important underlying emotion. Pynoos and Nader (1990) have also added that their results at school were poor, which points to a disturbance of other cognitive functions. In brief, these children are at development risk, and highly potent in exacerbating the social evils such as 'streetism' of children, beggary, child prostitution, delinquency, drug and alcohol abuse. The mushrooming of child-headed families with enormous potential risk factors is an inevitable outcome.

When large groups of people experience comparable traumatic events, there will be striking differences in the immediate reaction of individuals and families. Many make fair adjustments, while some break down. Veer (1992) has quoted three reaction patterns *viz.* disturbed behaviour, stunning and bewilderment and controlled behaviour. It has been highlighted that the response/reaction depends on the 'protective factors' in their individual life, family environment (availability of competent adults, opportunity for understanding, absence of disrupting conflicts), and other support systems around. The message is that when the protective factors are adequate, the chances of a breakdown are very less, and they tend to make fair adjustment; and vice-versa when the protective factors are absent or inadequate.

Characterization of Families and Children of the 'Under Class'

Charles Murray (1989), in his critique on family life in the western, more prosperous and modern society, has come up with a detailed analysis on the process and pattern of breakdown in family relationships. According to him, certain sections of the population are culpable for creating a culture of deprivation and crime, in an environment of plenty and prosperity. These are called 'under class' families, which have distinct characteristics that are degenerative in nature and their poverty is based on behaviour and life style, rather than on lack of income and unemployment. Children of such families do not have any parental control and are bound to be exposed to negative features of life.

The common characteristics of the 'under class' culture that could be gleaned from the existing literature are described below (Harris, 1980; Murray, 1989; Wyness, 2000; Phillips, 1996; Seabrook, 1998):

- These families are not necessarily poor, but their poverty is based on behaviour and life styles that are not compatible with the normal family life;
- These are families that indulge in alcoholism, drug abuse, rejection of work, have criminal propensities, domestic violence, etc.;
- Moral requirements of sexual life and relationships are not respected, they are prone to indulge in extramarital relationships, rejection of marriage, teenage pregnancies, unwed mothers, prostitution etc.;
- 'Prematurely sexualized children', children with no adult male figure, 'no blame', 'no shame' and 'no pain' society;
- Because of breakdown of relationships within their families, they fail to structure the process of childhood development;

- Children are disordered because they are not acted upon, neglected without love and attention of parents or pampered to buy their love;
- Marriages end in divorces and decay of nuclear families;
- Children get confused with the relationships between "mum's boy friend" or "dad's girl friend", feel terribly anxious and live in a sort of insecurity;
- In some families, children are treated as prospective private assets, disproportionate amount of time, money and emotional energy is invested in the children for want of their love and affection; and
- Children of 'under class' families are prone to become either deviants or indulge in adult-like, more often destructive activities to show off their power and visibility.

Further describing the culture of the 'under class' families, Phillips (1996) has indicated that these families indulge in alleged moral malaise and pass on the same cycle of culture of poverty to the next generation. Such families have minimal contact with their family members, distancing of communication, with the home more or less functioning as a hotel. He described it as perishability of human relationships.

Effects of Technological Changes on Parent-child Relationships

Studies have shown that the technological changes that have come about in society affect child socialization and parent-child relationships negatively (Corsaro, W, 1997; Phillips, 1996; Wyness, 2000). The 'new sociology of childhood' has been described as highly driven by technological innovations, diminishing cultural orientation, bondage to an overdetermined future, addiction to studies, interest in fantasies and fairy tales rather than physical exercises and play with their peer groups.

Children are taught to abandon their childhood and strive for more advanced and subtle ways of thinking. Driven by the 'schooling industry' and aspirations of parents, children spend their greater part of life in trying for success in school. They are over burdened with endless testing and home works. The negative effects of such load of work may result in over strain, anxiety and a sense of failure (Norma Field, cited in Wyness, 1995).

In the contemporary society, child's play is highly restricted and regulated by adults, pushing their children into the competitive world. Due to relative absence of time, space and opportunities for children's play, kids seem to have less time to be kids. Sylva and Ingrid (1988) have described the various learning processes during childhood. The very young child learns and explores routine movements and skills in play. As the child enters a more social world, gradually interacts with more adults and peer-group members, it develops make-believe play and learns about symbols and language. Gradually develops the capacity for logical thought and learns rules of the game. Play becomes increasingly complex as the child grows and his social and emotional experience broadens. They learn to socialize, learn customs and practice them in play.

However, the invent of computer gaming and over protection by parents prevent children from going into playground, rather they stick to indoor activities without much interaction with their peer groups. Since children are highly exposed to mass media, they are also susceptible to the demoralizing influences and are prone to cross moral boundaries. Thus, many positive cultural dimensions of childhood are more or less neglected in the socialization process of the modern society children.

Domestic Violence, Separation of Parents and Child Responses

In the contemporary western society, there had been a ten-fold increase in divorces and cohabitation that one out of three children today are born outside marriage (Smith, 1999). Following separation, a majority of children live with a single parent, preferably mother, depriving the child of love and affection of the other parent. Children naturally want their parents to live with them together. But for many unfortunate ones it is not a reality. Separated children experience feelings such as, sadness, disappointment, anxiety and anger and gradually may develop behavioural problems. Hence, it is necessary to understand the negative effects of stressful events in child's life after separation, in order that parents' responses to domestic violence and separation could be more positive.

Violence as a form of controlling social behaviour of a partner or child is generally regarded as undesirable. Domestic violence takes place due to various reasons of incompatibility among spouses and children. Many studies have shown that seven out of ten men who abuse their spouses also abuse their children and there is bound to be emotional and physical hurt to all family members (Saunders, 1995; Gray, 1998; James, 1994). At the extremity of domestic violence, many children get killed by family members than those who die at the hands of strangers.

In domestic violence, the powerful spouse persecutes the powerless and vulnerable spouse or child. In case of child-abuse, apart from their own parents, stepparents seem to have major role. Normally, domestic violence is not publicized because of various reasons. Domestic violence is considered as a personal matter and hence people distance from intervening. Children also keep quiet because of fear of further abuse. Each party involved is worried about the consequences that may worsen the situation, and every one thinks that he or she is to be blamed for what has happened (Smith, 1999).

Another equally important dimension of child's suffering and stress starts with separation of parents or loss of a parent (Cockett and Tripp, 1994). Separation need not necessarily take place due to domestic violence. But violence can also begin after separation, as children may be directly involved either as a contact person or as a messenger between separated parents. Children are often involved in non-physical abuse, such as, for verbal denigration of the other parent; and as falsifying witness in legal courts, which acts inflict emotional stress on the child.

Children who are brought up in an atmosphere of family violence experience 'emotional abuse', which undermines the self-esteem of the child. Emotional abuse is defined as a "sustained belittling of a child's personality, ability or achievements, whether thoughtless or deliberate (Smith, 1999: xii). Children suffer emotional abuse in many ways. Ignoring, ostracizing, constant teasing and harmful criticism are all ways of emotional abuse, commonly inflicted on children by stepparents. Other forms of abuse include, harsh punishments, disciplining by threats, giving inappropriate work responsibilities (Smith, 1995).

Emotional Reactions of Children to Abuse and Separation of Parents

It is well understood that domestic violence is a common phenomenon in all segments of society, often contributing to stressful childhood for many unfortunate children. Living in a stressful environment does not always result in emotional damage to children. A study undertaken in Canada on children coming from families with domestic violence revealed that, a quarter of such children was within 'normal' limits of functioning (Wolfe, et.al 1985). This was because they either ignored such situations or they were strong enough and genuinely not involved.

In this context, it is interesting to note the observations of some psychologists, who have described two types of personalities among children. The first type are children who are very curious and want to know what adults are doing, what they are talking over phone, where they are going and who is having relationship with whom, etc. The second type of children are more self-contained and able to amuse themselves and be in their own world of imagination and concerns of adults may not be interesting for them. It is also observed that the first type of children get more involved with parents in their struggles than the second category and they are also the ones who are affected most due to domestic violence (Smith, 1999). However, most scholars agree that, irrespective of the type of personality, all children get affected in an environment of domestic violence.

Children often emotionally react due to various reasons such as:

- When their basic needs, especially for stability and security, nurture and care are in jeopardy;
- When there is hostile environment at home or at school;
- When parents are getting separated due to domestic violence or divorce; and
- When inadequate parenting skills exist in a family for a long-time.

Domestic violence seem to be intertwined with most of the above situations and hence, it is considered as one of the dominant factors in accentuating emotional reactions among children.

Emotional reactions among children may take different forms; and may change according to their age and gender. Some of these include:

- Being fearful and withdrawn;
- Being depressed;
- Having poor social skills;
- Demonstrating psychosomatic symptoms;
- Delayed milestones in development;
- Feeling listless and unhappy all the time;
- Poor scholastic performance;
- Exhibiting rebellious and aggressive behaviour involving in fights with peers and teachers;
- In extreme cases, they may become delinquents and may get involved in anti-social activities.

We shall briefly examine the various types of emotional reactions that the disturbed children may experience. While doing so, we shall also discuss their reactions on the basis of age and gender at appropriate contexts.

Fear, Anxiety and Withdrawal Symptoms

Any family involved in domestic violence takes a great deal of emotional energy out of children. Very often children get so much terrified by physical violence that they get tensed and 'frozen' with fear. They even get fever sometimes. A few parents with defective personalities or under the influence of alcohol or drugs may become chaotic and act in a bizarre way; and may even inflict severe physical punishment or subject children to various types of deprivations such as restraint, not giving money or food, social isolation and other forms of emotional abuse. Such children who are deprived of joy and security in their childhood feel being cheated by their parents.

Children keenly watch the moods of parents and their reactions to the other partner or towards children. When there are violent outbursts, children may hide in dark places out of fear. They are also aware that when they interfere to prevent violent acts of parents, they inadvertently become victims. Many instances were reported, when children were physically thrown out or pushed violently, sometimes injuring and causing even death.

In some families, the mother is a victim along with child, while in others, where especially stepmother is involved, mothers may support fathers in abusing the children of the first wife. Such a situation is comparatively harmful for children and in many cases, the children will run away from home. Sometimes one of the parent may lie in order to subject the child for more punishment or even to get rid of him/her. They may subject the children to do hard work for long periods so that they run away from home.

The other concerns of children in violent families are about the day to day maintenance and issues concerned with separation of parents. What if Dad does not pay money to mummy? What about my pocket money, will I get it or not? Will Mummy or Dad get married again? Will the new partner bring children to live with us? How do I get along with them? Will the new members or mummy love me? This kind of anxieties and fear of new family relationships does affect the mental stability of children.

When hostile separations take place, the children may be even afraid of abductions. They get fearful dreams of somebody coming and stabbing mummy or burgling home, witches troubling, etc. Other physical problems include, sleeplessness, withdrawal symptoms, and sometimes giving a feeling that life is not worth living.

Girls will develop other types of fears, become more anxious about their future. Their fears include, how can I manage when I grow up? Do I get a partner who may also abuse me? Should I get married at all? A few may start hating all men irrespective of their nature. Teenagers can feel embarrassed by the obvious sexuality of their parents with new partners, cuddling and kissing openly, it will be disgusting for them. They will lose all confidence and their self-esteem gets plummeted, which may also result in lack of concentration in studies and other normal activities.

Depression

Depression is a result of unexpressed anger combined with a

feeling of isolation, loneliness and keeping away from friends and happy situations. Sometimes, hiding in dark places, locking up in rooms, unable to be reached by anyone. It is a phenomenon that is common both among children and elderly of any age. Children affected with depression always feel sad, which is an expression of lose of the loved parent by separation or bereavement. The child often expresses waves of grief making him/her impossible to think and act normally.

Children of young age may feel why it is happening to them like this? Some studies show that girls often recover more quickly than boys do (Smith, 1999). However, separation from one or both parents makes children feel nothing is going well with them and lose all the enjoyment of life. Some lose their appetite and may not eat for longer periods. This may result in regressing physical development. At home, they feel lonely with nobody to console them and at school, they are miserable with out showing any interest in fun and play, with the result other children ignore them, causing further loneliness. Thus they feel rejected everywhere without knowing that their behaviour is causing such isolation, and become restless having to come to terms with broken promises and lost childhood. They reach to a conclusion that there is no point in carrying about themselves and keeping safe. Many a times, due to their carelessness, accidents may take place endangering their life or making them disabled in life.

Develop Poor Social and Functional Skills

The feelings of insecurity, rejection, failure and being undermined, neglected and often abandoned, are all related and make the children get confused. Since they withdraw from normal activities at home as well as at school, they lose friends, they lose stimulation from parents who may be otherwise busy in their struggles of life. They fail to interact with their peers around, feel ignored by everyone, nobody to share their grief and make them feel happy.

Since they fail to interact with family members and friends around, they will not socialize and fail to learn social skills. They are also prone to regress in mental capacities. If unattended for long, they can gradually develop psychosomatic symptoms and end up with behavioural problems.

However, some studies have also shown positive effects to the sufferings of children due to separation or isolation. Separation can become a catalyst for children to think and up beat in their performance either at school or at home, especially in sports, arts and cultural activities (Smith, 1999). This is a situation, where children can learn to fight low-esteem, utilizing it to a productive end and thereby gain new confidence and satisfaction. More often, it is done to satisfy the living parent when the other parent dies or separates from them. However, such children need facilitation and constant support from the living parent or guardian or teacher to do so.

Neurosis and Psychosomatic Disorders

Typically, children in a situation of secure base and environment to explore, grow up to be self-reliant, to be trusting, cooperative and helpful towards others. In situations where such environment is lacking and due to various reasons specified below, children grow up as anxious, insecure individuals, usually described as over-dependent or immature. Children are more prone to develop neurotic symptoms when they are exposed to one or more of the following situations:

- One or both parents reject the child or be unresponsive to meet his/her needs;
- The child gets separated from one or both parents due to death or divorce etc.;
- Persistent threats from parents, either to desert or to kill the spouse or even suicide; and
- Inducing a child to feel guilty for separation or death of a parent (Bowlby, 1979: 137).

Many studies (Bowlby, 1979; Smith, 1979 and 1999; Wyness, 2000) have revealed that the experiences which they had during their childhood and adolescence will have implications in explaining many forms of emotional distress and personality disturbances that continue into their adulthood. Many adult cases referred to psychiatric clinics with neurotic symptoms, depression or phobia, were found to have been exposed to certain typical patterns of pathogenic parenting and emotional detachment, to which unwilling separation give rise.

Studies have also revealed that many forms of psychiatric disturbances can be attributed to deviations in development of attachment behaviour or, more rarely, to failure of its development (Bowlby, 1979; Sylva and Ingrid, 1982). According to the advocates of the 'attachment theory', human infants develop attachment behaviour during the first nine months of life, which may prolong. Whoever is principally mothering the child becomes its principal attachment figure. In healthy development, it becomes gradually less after three years of age. Later on, it is more likely that the child attaches to the person who has more social interaction with the child.

The function of attachment is more or less protection and security. Thus, most of the time child has an attachment figure, often a spouse, a parent or a sibling. Usually when the child's attachment figure is around and there is no threat of any sort, the child is willing to socialize with others; ceases to show attachment, and instead, explores his environment with peers. Separation from such attachment figure result in depressive behaviour among children, unless compensated with other alternative arrangements. The child feels rootless and lonely; and anxiety over separation from such figure can even turn out to be neurotic (Bowlby, 1979).

Very young children, when they experience any threat of separation from their attachment figure, may start excessive clinging to mothers, suck finger, chew paper or mud and bite nails. Little elderly may indulge in breaking things, tear paper, clothes, pull out hair, punch and hit others, kick and stamp at things. They may avoid going to school saying they had stomach pain, teeth pain etc. At nights they may do bed-wetting, get nightmares and dreams such as crocodiles biting them and snakes running around etc.

The other dimension to this kind of neurotic behaviour is the experiencing of discrimination and deprivation among siblings and other peer group members. In some instances, parents may not or do not treat all of their children alike. They may provide excellent conditions for some and adverse ones for the others, especially in case of girls and children of stepparents. Children always compare their situation with other siblings and even with their peers. They get a feeling that they are not treated in the same way as other children of their age and feel inferior with their self-esteem plummeted. They develop some sort of complex and start feeling angry at everything, especially at their parents, for being treated harshly or differently from other siblings.

Anti-social Activities

Children who are exposed to conditions described above may, over a period of time, develop tremendous mental strain and when there is no positive outlet, they may indulge in bullying and attacking other weaker children. Some become noisy and over active at school. They can not concentrate on studies and fail to cope with academic expectations. Some may even over-eat and develop physical ailments too. When father is not around and nobody to control, they feel free to do anything. Girls may respond in quieter ways than boys, for safety reasons.

Studies have revealed that a larger proportion of adolescents is showing signs of delinquency currently than in the past and there is an absolute increase in antisocial behaviour among youngsters (Marynia, 1962; Bolton, 1980; Garbarino, 1982). Studies also support that contemporary juvenile delinquency has assumed proportions too intolerable, and has become too dangerous to too many people, to be dealt with. No other teen-age development causes greater concern for parents than adolescent delinquency. Surely, not all adolescents are delinquents, but the defiant nature is, however, most common among all adolescents.

Delinquency is of many kinds, starting from lesser forms, such as, petty crimes, minor offenses, truancy, to that of major offenses such as, murders, suicides by pregnant girls, gangs involved in violence, marauding, armed robberies, drug offenses, etc. Naturally we must be aware of the causes for such turbulent life of a person in such young age, before attempting to correct such antisocial behaviour among delinquents.

Adolescents may often run away from home, may indulge in adult-like crimes and may join armed groups to take revenge and to show off their power. Some boys who are angry with their fathers may even think of revenging, especially hurting or even killing their parent's new partners. Those who are introverts may indulge in self-destructive behaviour such as cutting skin, nailing, breaking limbs etc., and become depressed all the time.

Recent evidences reveal that, the problems of adolescents, such as adolescent unwanted pregnancies, abortions and related complications, infections such as STD/HIV/AIDS, drug abuse, child prostitution, orphan status due to civil strife etc., are growing at an alarming phase needing attention of one and all. The young out side marriage group are likely to change sexual partners and risk greater exposure to infections; millions of adolescents live and work in streets, many turn to selling sex for a living; and some are forced into sex. On the other hand, the young are reluctant to seek help and counseling services. The impact of HIV/AIDS infections is said to be heavier on young girls than boys, because of pregnancy-related complications, sepsis, abortions, premature and still births and congenital infections.

When parents encounter any of these problems among their children, it is wise to act upon the assumption that expert help is needed. Waiting and hoping for improvement may prove disastrous at a later stage. These symptoms should be tackled as soon as detected, especially in the age group of eleven to fifteen. Failure to do so may have adverse consequences in adult maladjustment. This is an area where parents have to take primary responsibility and play key role; if they don't, and if the children are allowed to develop anti-social and destructive attitudes, the whole society at large has to suffer. Much more discussion on these aspects of tackling adolescent problems will follow in another chapter in the book.

References

1. Agakhan, S. & Talal, H.B., (1986), *Refugees: The Dynamics of Displacement*, Zed Books Ltd., London.
2. Ager, A., Ager, W. and Long, L.D., (1991), *A Case study of Refugee women in Malawi, A Report for the UNHCR*, Center for Social Research, Zambia, Malawi.
3. Bolton, F.G., Jr. (1980), *The Pregnant Adolescent: Problems of Premature Parenthood*, Beverley Hills, CA: Sage Publications.
4. Bowlby, J., (1997), *The Making and Breaking of the Affectional Bonds*, Tavistock/Routledge: London.
5. Cockett, M. and Tripp, J., (1994), *The Exeter Family Study: Family Breakdown and Its Impact on Children*, Exeter: University of Exeter Press: London.
6. Corsaro, W., (1997), *The Sociology of Childhood, California*, Pine Forge.

7. ERREC, (2000), "Humanitarian Update," *ERREC News Letter*, Vol. 5, Issue 2.
8. Frederic C. Cuny, Barry N. Stein and Pat Réed, (1992), *Repatriation During Conflict in Africa and Asia*, Center for the study of standards in Crisis, Texas.
9. Garbarino, J., (1982), *Children and Families in the Social Environment*, Aldine de Gruyter: New York.
9. Goode, W.J., (1982), *The Family*, (2nd edition), Prentice Hall Inc., New Jersy.
10. Gray, B., (1998), "Intake and Criminal Record Checks", *Family Mediation*, 8(2), 5.
11. Harris, C., (1980), "The changing relationships between family and societal form in western society", in M. Anderson (ed), *Sociology of Family*, Harmondsworth: Penguin, pp. 396-413.
12. IFAD, (1992), *The State of the World Rural Poverty*, IFAD: Rome.
13. James, G., (1994), "Discussion Report for the Area Child Protection Committee Conference: Study of Working Together Part-8 Reports", *Department of Health ACPO Series*, Report No. 1: London.
14. Martin, B.I., (1990), *War and the Psychosocial Trauma of Salvadoran Children*, American Psychosocial Association: Boston.
15. Marynia, F.F., (1962), *The Adolescent*, Collier Books: New York.
16. Murray, C., (1989), "The under class", *Sunday Times Magazine*, 26 Nov., pp. 26-45.
17. Niki, H., (1997), *CIRDAP Approach to Rural Development*, CIRDAP: Dhaka.
18. Phillips, M., (1996), *All Must Have Prizes*, Little, Brown and Company: London.
19. Pynoos, R. and Nader K., (1990), "Children's exposure to violence and traumatic death", *Psychiatric Annals*, 20, 6, 334-344.
20. Rogge, J.R., (1994), *Too Many, Too Long, Sudan's Twenty Year Refugee Dilemma*, Row man and Allenheld, NJ.
21. Saunders, A., (1995), "It Hurts Me Too: Children's Experiences of Domestic Violence and Refuge Life", *Women's Aid Federation, England*, National Institute of Social Work, Child Line.
22. Seabrook, J., (1998), "Children of the Market", *Race and Class*, 39, 4, pp. 37-48.
23. Smith, H., (1999), *Children, Feelings and Divorce*, Free Association Books: London.
24. Smith, H., (1995), *Unhappy Children: Reasons and Reminders*, Free Association Books: London.
25. Sylva, K. and Ingrid, L., (1982), *Child Development: A First Course*, Basil Blackwell Ltd.: Oxford.
26. Terr, L.C., (1989), 'Treating Psychic trauma in Children: a preliminary discussion', *Journal of Traumatic Stress* 2, 3-20

27. UNDP, (1996), *Poor People's Perspectives: UNDP Report on Human Development in Bangladesh*, UNDP: Dhaka.
28. Veer, G., (1992), Counseling and Therapy with Refugees, John Wiley & Sons, England.
29. Webster's Encyclopedia, (1983), *Unabridged Dictionary of the English Languages,* Portland House, NY.
30. Wolfe, D.A., *et.al*, (1985), "Children of Battered women; the relation of child behaviour to family violence and maternal stress", *Journal of Consulting and Clinical Psychology,* 53, 657-65.
31. Wyness, M.G., (2000), *Contesting Childhood,* London: Falmer Press.

4

Child Rights and Children in Need of Special Protection Measures

Introduction

Providing an environment, which fosters democracy and stimulates emotional, psychological, social and cognitive growth of children is a universal requirement, for all the countries, which have ratified the Convention on the Rights of Children. Full realization of goals of the CRC and empowerment of children, parents, communities and nations is a responsibility that the international community has assumed and striving to achieve.

However, due to various reasons, such as, lack of resources, lack of political commitment and convenience of using children as soldiers and as child labourers, there has been no significant reduction in tackling the problems of the exploited children. This amounts to blatant violation of child rights at every level.

Political strife leads to armed conflicts. Africa, Afghanistan, Cambodia, South America, Palestine, Yugoslavia and Bosnia are some of the regions, which are worst affected by armed conflicts and warring feuds. In these countries there are about 40 to 45 per cent of child population and there is every possibility that most of them are at-risk along with their mothers.

Further, many parents who join armed conflicts or the army may die leaving single parent families. Such single-family mothers are economically unable to provide for the basic needs of their children. Discipline of children in single-parent families is often not effective. Thus many children live in vulnerable environment paving opportunities for their exploitation.

Ill-treatment or abuse of children takes many forms such as, physical and emotional abuse, sexual abuse, nutritional abuse and neglect and abandonment. A child may suffer with one form or a combination of any of these forms of abuse. All neglected children may not be subjected to physical abuse. If the child is unwanted, she may be rebuked frequently and tortured mentally debilitating the child's growth and development.

There are several cases, where girl children were abandoned in streets, forest bushes and even dumped in garbage and latrine pits. All abused children experience varying grades and intensity of trauma. Various studies have revealed that those children who were subjected to abuse in their childhood were more likely to abuse others when they become adults (Smith, 1999).

Historically and culturally viewed, children are generally excluded as a unit of reference, because they are not expected to have a stake in the social, economic and political arrangements. They do not have vote, can not claim income and do not have any formalized role in school or at home. There is a notion that children are, in moral and social terms out of position (Wyness, 2000). Hence, parents, institutions and policy makers by and large are still expected to decide on behalf of children, assuming to know what is in the 'best interest' of children.

However, the child rights activists have reputed such ideas and have mobilized support to include the right of the child for 'self determination' in the CRC, thus rendering children visible within the public sphere. The social focus on children has been on the increase then on. In this chapter, we shall analyze the various social and structural problems that the children are facing in our society and examine the remedial measures taken at various levels, that is, parents, community, national and international levels to provide for meeting the children's needs, safeguarding their interests, protecting them from exploitation and sexual abuse and facilitating harmonious development of every child in our society.

Categories of Children in Need of Special Protection Measures (CNSPM)

Children in Need of Special Protection Measures (CNSPM) are those children whose basic needs such as food, shelter, medical care, educational opportunities, security and psychological well being are not met (Bwibo, 1995). These basic needs are not met because of increasing social, economic and political problems. As far as African countries are concerned, the single most important cause for this situation has been the political strife and armed conflicts leading to displaced families and refugees. Poverty, malnurishment, famines, girl child neglect and commercial exploitation are some of the other causes for the increasing number of CNSPM.

Apart from economic reasons, there are other social and cultural causes for increase in number of the CNSPM, which include, joint families transforming in to nuclear families, lack of earning male member at home, incapacity to provide for basic needs because of large number of children, growing indiscipline among children and care free atmosphere among parents. The CNSPM may be categorized into five groups, *viz.* abused and traumatized children, orphans, street and working children, child prostitutes and children with disabilities. These categories are described in the proceeding pages.

(a) Abused and traumatized children

Child abuse and neglect by parents or guardians has been on the increase because of adverse social and family circumstances. Neglected children suffer from psychological and emotional stress. The 'life events' approach reveals that those children who were subjected to abuse in their childhood were more likely to abuse others when they became adults, what is known as 'intergenerational transmission of abuse' (Smith, 1999).

The factors responsible for child abuse operate at two levels, with the child and with the parents. Those factors that operate at the child level are:

- The child may be born out of unwanted pregnancy or

illegitimate relationship;

- It may be a stepchild;
- Disabled child;
- HIV infected child; and
- Difficult economic and social circumstance in the family.

Characteristics of the neglecting parents include:

- Step parent:
- Single parent;
- Easily angered;
- Alcoholics;
- Ill with psychiatric disorder;
- Marital discord;
- Unemployment and loss of earning capacity; and
- Poverty situation.

Ill-treatment or abuse of children takes many forms such as, physical and emotional abuse, sexual abuse, nutritional abuse and neglect and abandonment. A child may suffer with one form or a combination of any of these forms of abuse. All abused children experience varying grades and intensity of trauma.

The most commonly recognized abuse is physical abuse, which is also considered as "battered baby syndrome". Child abuse occurs when the parent or a caretaker of the child misuses the privileged position over the child to commit acts that are contrary to social norms. Such acts are detrimental to the health and normal development of the child.

Sexual abuse is another form, which inflicts severe emotional distress, especially among girls. An adult family member, such as a relative or a parent, having pathological characteristics may subject a child to sexual act, which can usually take place at home. A friend or a stranger could commit it by befriending or kidnapping the child. Factors that are identified for sexual abuse of child are relative closeness, degree of autonomy and opportunities available. Abusers were found to have inappropriate lifestyles, propensity to crimes and mostly targeted on children of lone parents and those on low-income groups (Smith, 1999).

In response to the problem of child abuse, social and political demands have been rising for a more protective child-care framework all over the world. Three areas of concern were identified for the new initiatives: (1) a need to prevent child abuse, (2) a need to identify child abusers and bring them to book and (3) a need to educate children and public about the child abuse and its prevention (Wyness, 2000). The overriding concern is to ensure that children are safe and under adequate protection. Children themselves are being empowered to be more active in identifying and preventing child abuse by providing knowledge, skills and resources, through school-based and mass media programmes.

(b) Children abused as soldiers

It is deplorable that children as young as eight years were reportedly used in war to fight, carry ammunition to soldiers, supply water and fuel wood, and work as messengers and spies. These children were usually forced, abducted and kidnapped to fight as soldiers. There also instances where the children themselves come forward to offer their services to take revenge on those killers of their near and dear persons in war.

Several reports have highlighted that exposure to stressful events increases a child's risk to develop health and psychological problems. Lack of essential food, vitamins etc., in early childhood will cause lasting bodily malformations in later years (Freud and Burlingham, 1943).

Similarly, break-up of family life, repeated displacements and constant physical threats deprive children of their natural background for their emotional and mental development. Traumatic stress disorders and symptoms are usually caused by loss of one or both parents, constant threats from aerial bombardment, continued displacements, torture inflicted on self or loved ones and witnessing of murders (Tesfay Aradom, 1991). It is well known that almost every conflict separates children from their families (Ressler, Boothy and Steinbock, 1988).

There are several studies, which portray that tens of thousands of children's bodies and minds were injured by violence. One survey of the children directly affected by war revealed the following staggering results: 77% had witnessed murder, 88% had witnessed physical abuse, 51% had been physically abused themselves, 63% had witnessed rape or sexual abuse, 64% had been abducted from their families and 28% were trained for combat (Swartz and Ann Levett, 1989; cited in Tesfay Aradom, 1991).

For children, who are displaced, deported and those who are temporarily sheltered at the Internally Displaced Persons (IDP) camps, years of lost schooling and vocational training take equivalent number of years to replace. This loss is a major set back to development of the country, as well as the individuals, who become unemployed after the demobilization takes place. They will not have education or employable skills to get jobs and do not have sufficient capital to start their own small business and thus become wasteful resources of the country.

Population movements, family breakdown, rape, sexual violence and the erosion of traditional values dramatically increase the potential for STDs, HIV/AIDS infections, especially among girls, who are sexually abused during armed conflicts. In the course of military duty child soldiers may get injured, maimed or killed. Besides this, they are severely traumatized psychologically and emotionally. They are tortured while extracting information and even sexually abused by the soldiers. In prolonged war situations these children witness violence and torture and lose hope for normal life including schooling. They have the fear of being separated from parents and may have no hope of being reunited. When war ends they need counseling and proper rehabilitation, otherwise they may turn out to be anti-socials.

The national and international responses to this problem of children used as soldiers and those involved in armed groups has been dealt at length in the next chapter and hence we are not narrating the same here.

(c) Orphan children

An orphan may be defined as a child under the age of 18 years, who has lost both or one parent, as well as a child who has living parents but they are not in a position to take care of the child because of their physical and mental incapacity (MLHW, 1992). Studies have shown that, young children who have lost both parents, who have been traumatized by war and displaced from their family surroundings were at greater risk for psychiatric disorders, antisocial behaviour and delayed cognitive and physical development. There were also evidences indicating that the long-time pathogenic effects of adversity in early childhood could be ameliorated or prevented through appropriate and timely measures taken to provide supportive social and family environment for the affected children.

Orphans without either parent are especially unlikely to get adequate emotional and psychological support, even if their material needs were met. Particularly in countries with high level of poverty, orphans may 'fall through the cracks' and be left to their own devices. They may drift on to the streets, may join gangs indulging in crimes, and may end up as drug addicts (UNICEF, 1994). Thus orphans are the most helpless and most needy among the CNSPM.

Characteristics of Orphans

A study of 90,000 orphans, conducted by the Ministry of Labour and Human Welfare, Asmara (1992) revealed the following: There were 52 per cent of male and the rest were female. Forty one per cent of them were below the age of six. Thirty eight per cent of those, who were above seven years of age were illiterate. Regarding the status of parents, 60 per cent were paternal orphans, 31 per cent were maternal orphans and nine per cent were total orphans, where both parents did not exist. About one per cent of them were disabled, while two per cent of them were reported to have been experiencing traumatic disorders. Studies have shown similar state of affairs in other affected countries too.

Strategies concerned with recovery, reintegration and rehabilitation of orphans include the following:

- *Advocacy* to implement the U N Convention on the Rights of the Child (CRC), which underlies all efforts to rehabilitate and protect children needing special protection measures.
- *Reunification of orphans with blood relatives and host-families:* This strategy will build on the local tradition whereby extended families and communities assume responsibility

for the children's welfare and development. In so doing, the host families could be supported with income generating assets to enhance their income so that they will be able to take care of the children in a sustainable manner.

- *Strengthening institutional capacities:* This includes strengthening of the governmental and non-governmental infrastructure and capabilities of the staff to cope with the emerging demands for improved childcare and protection. This may include inter-sectoral coordination, provision of social and rehabilitation services such as, adoption arrangements, education, training, job placement and counseling services.
- *Involving children themselves as their own advocates,* in order to create positive attitude towards children, who should be viewed as active partners in their own development.

(d) Street children

Street children include those who work and live on the street full time fending for themselves. There are also those who work on the streets during day time and get back to home at night with their street earnings to support their families. A street child has been defined as "a girl or a boy for whom the street has become his or her abode and or source of livelihood: and who is inadequately protected, supervised or directed by responsible adults" (Belsey, 1996:12). One estimate reveals that, anywhere between 15 and 30 million children spend their time surviving on the streets of major cities of the World. The phenomenon of 'streetism' has been traced to abject poverty, the need to earn income, severe overcrowding in available accommodation/housing, family breakdown, intra-family violence, abusing and absentee parents.

Street children earn their living by begging, doing petty jobs like parking boys, carrying shopping bags, shoe polishing, moving in trains and cleaning bogies etc. Some studies have shown that a minority of these children indulges in illegitimate activities such as, theft, pickpocketing, snatching chains, running away with goods and prostitution. However, such children were found to have the support of organized criminal gangs (Whaites, 1996:4).

They feed on waste and unhygienic food and are malnourished most of the time. Street children who solicit from beaches, parks tourist bars and hotels were found to be attractive to tourists. It was reported in one study (ILO, 1998: 185) that, the street children readily accepted to provide full access to their persons, and performed acts that the westerners get exited with, such as kissing, cuddling, massaging, washing hair and legs and sleeping along with the tourists.

Since, most of them sleep on the pavements they are exposed to cold and rain. The elder ones and gangsters sexually assault most of these children and they are at risk of contracting STD/ HIV infections. The adolescent girls are often raped and become pregnant not knowing what to do. The street children have no hope of schooling and their future is grim. Many a times, they get involved in anti-social activities such as, trafficking, drug smuggling, sniffing and smoking and may grow up as criminals unless rehabilitated. The number of such children in towns and cities is rapidly increasing and is worrying the policy makers and parents of almost every country.

Characteristics of Street Children

'Streetism' among children correlates to a large extent with socio-economic factors such as poverty, civil strife, unemployment, non-enrollment in schools, etc. Studies have revealed that, a majority of street children are boys, but the numbers of girls seem to increase of late. Most of them share poor social and economic cultures, while a few run away children belong to higher socio-economic categories. Although a majority loses contact with their families, studies have shown that, some kept in touch with their families. Many of them were on the street at the behest of their parents; to work and help their families in difficult circumstances. However, a minority of them was found to live on the streets, often together in gangs under one or more gang leaders. This group of children is the most needy among the street children.

The following are some general characteristics of street children:

- They live for greater part of their time in streets;
- Their family ties are either non-existent or are very weak;

- They value their liberty and freedom and have their own set of values;
- Their life is disorganized and often impoverished from day to day;
- They may indulge in illegal activities and may be harassed by police and sent to remand homes;
- They form their own groups and gangs to protect and promote their rights; and
- They can be very creative in getting what they want.

(e) Child labour

Childhood is a time for playing, enjoying and learning about nature. But there are millions of children who have to work more than 12 hours a day in order to survive. They have no time for play, for education, for family affection. Among the rights of the children is protection from hazardous employment, which is likely to affect their health or interfere with their education and development. However, there are many loopholes in the legal mechanism to enforce this right. Hence, many children are exploited, by persons who employ them in urban homes as domestic servants or 'ayahs', teashops, restaurants, mechanical shops and in small industries as manual labour; and in farms to pick tealeaves, cotton, etc. Since, the children do not know their rights, they end up being exploited by receiving low wages and working for long hours.

According to some estimates, there is anywhere between 300 to 500 million child workers in the World. The World Vision International has reported that there were about 250 million children working as prostitutes, drug traffickers and indentured labourers (WVI, 2000:102). India has the largest number of child labourers, between 50 to 100 million, while most of the child labourers were found engaged in the agricultural sector and urban and rural unorganized sectors. They were mostly found working in family-based and self-employment activities, rather than in large factories and establishments. They also work as rag-pickers, domestic servants, vendors, shoe-shine boys, assistants to tailors, carpenters and other artisans, helpers in tea shops, auto garages, petrol pumps and in transport vehicles (*The Hindu*, Nov. 14th 1995).

Many of the processes and occupations that children were

engaged in seem to be hazardous. In India, children were found to work in match and fireworks, gem polishing, carpet and glass making, slate making, brass and lock making industries. Many studies have shown that these industries were the most hazardous to the health of children. The following were some revelations:

- Children mixing chemicals in the boiler room get lungful of toxic fumes, suffer high degrees of intense heat and run the risk of being badly injured in fire accidents.
- In the carpet industry children inhale large quantities of woolen particles causing asthma and chest ailments. Their eye sight and spinal cord problems start at an early age because of fixed postures and continuous work.
- Children working in glass industry were exposed to silica, which cause chronic ailments such as silicosis among children.
- In fire works, and beedi making industries, piece-rate system of payment drove children to work for long hours, in addition to the commuting time, which together came to nearly 12 to 14 hours (Mani, 1995).

The above instances describe the amount of torture the children undergo at their young age, risking their health, mental and physical growth. More than anything, there is a danger of remaining in employment with depressed skills. As adult workers they continue to be employed in low paid, unskilled jobs thereby perpetuating poverty. Millions of these children continue to be illiterates, which is highly detrimental to the human resource position of any country.

The demand for child labour has several causative factors. Firstly, children are considered as a valuable asset to some of these industries due to their nimble fingers enabling them to do certain jobs that elders can not perform at the same speed (like making knots in the weaving of carpets). They are also obedient, less aggressive and easily manageable work force. Children are paid less and are not entitled for social security benefits that adults are entitled for. More than any of the above factors the need to supplement family income among resource poor families is quite high in the developing countries. Hence, parents encourage them to work at younger age. Some of the other causes for perpetuating child labour are:

- Poverty;
- Lack of supporting member in the family;
- Poor scholastic performance;
- School drop-outs;
- Lack of legal protection; and
- Lack of awareness about legal provisions and exploitation by the middlemen.

The prevalent cultural, social and economic system also contributes to dropout of children from schools. Once, dropout, the child is engaged in some form of labour. These are compounded by the bureaucratic system of schooling requiring several certificates for benefiting from schooling and other welfare schemes such as scholarships. Lack of access to school and reading materials, especially among children of the poor families also contributed to the lack of interest in schooling among the poor.

The female child worker is especially disadvantaged, as she is exposed to responsibilities beyond her level of development. Sexual harassment by male members of the employers is reported to be very common and as a result these girls are also exposed to unwanted pregnancy and infection with HIV. Some of them may thus end up as child prostitutes.

Normal development of the working child is curtailed, by being forced to work at younger age, the child forgoes the opportunity for education, time to play, to be protected and loved. As a result, many of them get depressed and exhibit psychopathic tendencies at a very young age. Although several conventions were held and rights were accorded to protect and develop children, there has been little sustained effort to save children from exploitation, from being denied the right to childhood, education and better skills and enable them to play a positive role in the development of a nation.

The major international effort made towards elimination of child labour and child exploitation was undertaken by the International Labour Organization, which in 1979 had organized an international conference on child labour, calling for social and legislative action for the progressive elimination of child labour. The ILO had also come up with the International Programme on the Elimination of Child Labour (IPEC) in 1992, under which technical and financial support was provided to all countries tackling the problem of child labour.

The IPEC had recognized education of the affected children as the critical factor in the reintegration process of the child labourers. Under its educational initiatives many NGOs have started programmes such as platform schools, non-form education centers, intensive camp approach especially to enroll girl school dropouts to formal education stream, etc. These have been fairly successful in weaning away child labourers and bringing them back to educational institutions (Joseph, 1995).

The other major protective and welfare measures to recover and reintegrate street children and child labour to the mainstream of development include:

- *Advocacy, implementation and enforcement of CRC,* which is clearly against the economic exploitation and abuse of children. The Campaign Against Child Labour (CACL) is an important strategy aimed at taking the issue to the public consideration and seeking their support in elimination of child labour. The CACL could influence the governmental machinery to be more active and supportive to the cause and also request for making necessary changes in the legislation inorder to strengthen the fight against child labour.
- *Prevention and reintegration:* This needs special consideration on the part of the national governments to provide opportunities for the vulnerable families to earn minimum income to support their families through credit programmes or income generating assets. The government should also make sure that minimum services such as education, health care, cheap housing are available, accessible and affordable to all citizens, especially the poor. This also includes provisions for education, skill training, job placement services for the needy children.

- *Public awareness generation:* It is very important that adults and children together make efforts to create an environment where child labour is no longer tolerated. Unscrupulous people who want to employ children for exploitation, should be prevented from doing so not just by the law and the government action but by public disapproval and action. Media and information campaigns must be made use of to a greater extent to bring about a change in value system to avoid child exploitation in any form.

(f) Children with disabilities

A disabled person is one who is affected by some form of physical or mental deformity and as a result he/she suffers with functional limitations and activity restrictions. Most disabilities are caused by a health condition, such as a disease, a congenital malformation, a trauma, or due to malnurishment. There are many types of disability, such as the physical impairment, hearing impairment, visual impairment, mental or learning disability and behavioural impairment.

All forms of disabilities are stigmatizing. They often prevent people from learning, from finding worthwhile work, from being happy and contributing to the society. Two commonly used words by persons who work with the disabled are 'rehabilitation' and 'therapy'. Rehabilitation means returning of ability, or helping a disabled person to manage better at home, work place and in the community. Rehabilitation includes all measures aimed at reducing the impact of disability for an individual, enabling him or her to achieve independence, social integration, a better quality of life and self-actualization (Helander, 1989).

Therapy means treatment. Physiotherapy is the art of improving position, movement, strength, balance, and control of the body. Occupational therapy is the art of helping a disabled person learn to do useful or enjoyable activities (Werner, 1987). Creation of supportive environment for the Children with Disability (CWD) is one of the important areas of improving the status of CNSPM. Measures initiated in regard to dealing with CWD and rehabilitation programmes for them are discussed in detail in a separate chapter in the book.

(g) Child prostitutes

Child prostitutes are those persons below the age of 18 years, offering sexual favours in return for cash or other material gains. Child prostitution and child pornography has been defined as " the act of obtaining, procuring or offering the services of a child or inducing a child to perform sexual acts for any form of compensation or reward (or any acts that are linked to that offense) even with the consent of the child" (UNESCO, 1996: 27). Child prostitution is one of the two main aspects of sexual exploitation, the other being child pornography. Child pornography refers to the acts of visual, written or audio depiction of a child for the sexual gratification of the user (ILO, 1998). Young girls are not only victims of commercial sexual exploitation; there has been a notable increase in the number of young boys being drawn in to the sex tourism.

Studies have shown that there were many prostitutes (about 20 %) below the age of 18 years, indicating that the child prostitution has been growing. Moreover, it was also observed that many of them were drawn into this profession when they were very young children *i.e.* during 12-15 years and remained trapped into adulthood. As many as 50 per cent of the prostitutes were separated from their parents during their very young age of 9-18 years.

Child prostitution, unlike adults, "constitutes a form of coercion and violence against children, and amounts to forced labour and a contemporary form of slavery" (World Congress against Commercial Sexual Exploitation of Children, 1996). Involving children in commercial sex work is a serious crime, and it is detrimental to their development, both physical and emotional. It is, therefore, regarded as one of the most alienating forms of labour and a violation of human rights.

Although it is a global phenomenon, child prostitution is reported to be most serious in Asia and Pacific region, Africa and Central and South America, while increases have been noticed in all other parts of the world (ILO, 1998). Studies have shown that the extent of child prostitution ranges between ten per cent to 30 per cent of the total participants in prostitution. Studies conducted in Malaysia, Philippines and Thailand have revealed that the extent of children involved in different forms of prostitution in bars, restaurants, massage parlours and houses of prostitution has even reached 50 per cent of the total number involved in the profession (Bruce, 1996; Srisang, 1990; ILO, 1998). There have also been many media reports of sex rings recruiting teenage schoolgirls to persuade their classmates to enter the profession.

Many types of child prostitution have been identified, such as street prostitution, sex tourism, prostitution with the use of pimps, brothel prostitution and prostitution with parents as contractors (Srisang, 1990; ILO, 1998). About ten per cent of those in the profession were found to be young boys. The trafficking of young girls has been reported to be on the increase in recent years in countries such as Myanmar, China, Combodia, Laos, Vietnam and Thailand. There have been reports that hundreds of girl children from Nepal, Bangladesh and Pakistan were smuggled every month to India for involving in child prostitution (Shamin, 1997).

The overriding reasons were to get a job, early marriage and conflicts with parents. Young girls usually entered into prostitution in a desperate attempt to escape poverty. Various studies have revealed that, poverty was a major cause in as many as 42 per cent of the cases, while unemployment (12%) and peer influence (8%) as other causes. Unfortunately, prostitution rarely leads people out of poverty (UNICEF, 1994). Prostitution is also stigmatizing, often nurtures feelings of shame which is a debilitating factor. The risk of acquiring STDs and HIV/AIDS is highest among young girls, as they tend to neglect safe practices to sex and their immunity is relatively low.

The demand factor is another important dimension of the child prostitution. Many adults and old men have a belief that they would get rejuvenated if they have sex with virgins and young children. There is also a strong notion that the young girls are safe as far as contracting of STDs, HIV/AIDS was concerned. Hence, the demand for the young girls has been growing. The money offered by the old persons was higher than that offered by youngsters and hence the girls also went behind old persons.

However, vulnerability of children has been one of the crucial factors distinguishing child prostitution from that of adults. Children do not voluntarily enter into prostitution. Adults seeking advantage from children, persuade or deceive, threaten, exploit and commit other acts of violence such as, confining them and forcing them to entertain customers. Children are commonly sold, trafficked, tricked or lured, and forced to enter the profession. Thus, prostitution exploited the immaturity and helplessness of children. Unlike adults, who have the bargaining power, children do not have the ability to negotiate the terms of their labour. The degree of victimization was greater when the child involved was younger.

Studies have also shown that infertility due to infections on the one hand, and high risk of pregnancies on the other, was a common feature among child prostitutes. In case of infections, they have less access to medical advice and treatment. In case of pregnancies, their babies tend to be born premature, exhibit postnatal growth deficiency and developmental delays and face a high risk of perinatal mortality. As mothers, they could not also be role models for their children, as a result, the 'chain effect' of negative behavioural abuse and consequences continued to perpetuate (ILO, 1998).

The need for counseling services and guidance to young persons for problem solving, stress release and informed decision- making is immense. Even in countries where prostitution has been legalized and their working conditions were greatly improved, child prostitution can not be condoned. Children lack mental, emotional or social maturity to deal with their circumstances and hence they should not be held responsible or stigmatized.

At the first place they should learn about the dangers of unprotected sex, and secondly, they should pursue schooling or vocational training so that they may be able to lead more dignified and productive lives when such option is available for them. Unfortunately, many of the young girls involved in prostitution are illiterates and rehabilitation of such persons through vocational training becomes very difficult. Parents should also be supported with economic assets, guidance and counseling to provide for the psychosocial needs of these young girls and in creating a congenial home environment.

At the international level, there were several conventions passed that sought to protect children from sexual exploitation and related problems such as trafficking and slavery. The first such effort was made through the UN Convention on the Rights of the Child passed in 1989. The CRC had the necessary Articles: 19, 32, 34, 35, 39, in which the State was made responsible to safeguard, prevent, protect and rehabilitate the sexually exploited children.

Apart from the CRC, ILO had several conventions such as, Forced Labour Convention, 1930 and the Abolition of Forced Labour Convention, 1957, which directly dealt with the forced forms of child labour. The major step in this direction was taken in 1996, in the International Labour Conference, where a resolution concerning Elimination of Child Labour was passed. The resolution called upon all States, employees and worker's organizations "to develop formal policies and set priorities so as to immediately proceed to put an end to child labour and commercial sexual exploitation of children" (ILO, 1998: 189).

Consequently, all the signatory nations have come up with their own policies and legislation, which spelled out detailed actions in terms of:

(a) total prevention and elimination of children of both sexes below 18 years in the commercial sex industry;
(b) prohibition of luring, threats, exploitation and acts of violence in the sex business; and
(c) imposition of punishments on all persons with a part in inducing children into the commercial sex industry, and punishment of officials negligent in, or choosing to ignore, their duty to enforce compliance with relevant policies, laws, rules and regulations (ILO, 1998).

Recovery and reintegration measures included:

- Provision of full-scale assistance services such as, lodging, education, skill training, job-placement and counseling;
- Provision of income generating assets and training in relevant trades; and
- In the case of foreign children, sending them to their own countries and liaisoning with relevant agencies to ensure their rehabilitation and adjustment to a normal life.

In fulfilling the above, several strategies were adopted by

the government as well as NGOs, such as opening drop-in centers, shelters and hostels for the sexually abused children, administered by professional social workers, where the affected persons received residential care, education and learnt alternative ways to support themselves and their families. Some centers have facilities for training-cum-production in handicrafts and other useful trades.

The other common programmes included on-site services through outreach activities to meet the children's needs for food, clothing and recreation. The outreach workers also provided counseling and made arrangements for their temporary stay and arranged referrals to other service providing institutions. Reunification with their families was also attempted through the outreach programme. Support therapists encouraged child victims to release their feelings of anger, hostility, pain and frustration. However, it must be recognized that, commitment of all stakeholders and political and social will were crucial factors in addressing both the root causes and consequences of child prostitution.

Convention on the Rights of Children (CRC)

Many international organizations, national agencies, voluntary groups and committed individuals work towards safeguarding and protecting children from various crimes inflicted on them. To mention a few, UNICEF, Save the Children, International Coalition to Stop the use of Child Soldiers, International Labour Organization and many national level children's groups work to implement the Convention on the Rights of Children (CRC) and facilitate country level monitoring of the CRC. There are many provisions made in the CRC to protect, care and develop children all over the World and most of the countries have ratified these conventions. At the country level several legal and welfare measures are introduced to safeguard child rights and protect children who are in need of support. Let us first examine some of the important provisions made in the CRC and then proceed with a discussion on other arrangements made at country level and community levels.

The child rights movement can be traced back to 1920s, when certain voluntary groups such as Save the Children, advocated for certain "rights for children and labourers for their universal recognition". Then in 1924, The League of Nations adopted certain rights to protect children from war situations. Later, in 1948 the UN General Assembly approved the adoption of a Universal Declaration of Human Rights, implicitly including children's rights. However, the major breakthrough came in 1989, when the UN General Assembly adopted the separate Convention on the Rights of the Child (CRC). The CRC provided for survival rights, protection rights, development rights and participation rights to children. Some of the salient features of these are described below (Radda Barnen, 1996).

(i) Survival rights

The essence of this provision is given in Article-6, which states that, every State which is a signatory, recognizes that every child has the inherent right to life and the State party shall ensure to the maximum extent possible the survival and development of all children. The other Articles related to this provision are 7,8,9,19, 20 to 35 and 38.

(ii) Protection rights

The rationale for introducing these rights, is that, all children, because of their age and development characteristics, need special protection which must be made available regardless of their sex, nationality, culture, and so on. Therefore, the State institutions, individuals and children themselves all have the responsibility to exercise and respect these rights. The various protection rights are categorized into three groups, *viz.*, protection against discrimination (Articles: 2, 7, 23 and 30) protection against exploitation (Articles: 10, 11, 16, 19, 20, 21, 25, 32 to 37, 39 and 40) and protection in crises and emergency situations (Articles: 10, 22, 25, 38 and 39).

(iii) Development rights

Development rights include all kinds of education (formal and non-formal) and the right to a standard of living adequate for the child's physical, mental, spiritual, moral and social development. The concerned Articles in the CRC include, information and education (Articles: 17, 28 and 29); play recreation and cultural participation (Article: 31); personality development and freedom of thought and conscience (Articles:

5, 6, 13, 14 and 15); identity, nationality and name (Articles 6 and 7); family identity (Articles: 10 and 11); health (Article: 24); and the right to be heard (Articles 12 and 13).

(iv) Participation rights

The rationale for introducing specific articles promoting child participation is based on some of the following assumptions:

- We recognize that the child is a developing individual with feelings and opinions of its own;
- We believe that children are best placed to articulate their own needs and that given proper support respect they will make sensible and responsible suggestions and decisions concerned with development;
- We also know that children are honest, caring and imaginative.

The Articles that concerns participation are, accessibility to children of all information and education materials (Article 17) and parent's joint responsibility for the upbringing and development of child (Article 18). Through these Articles it is intended to safeguard the best interests of the child.

General Measures for Implementation of the CRC (Art. 4, 42 and 44) at the State Level for Monitoring Purpose

It was made mandatory for every State to submit a progress report every five years once, in order for the UN agency to monitor the implementation of CRC and the problems faced during the process of implementation. The report that is submitted to the UN General Council every five years must include the following information concerning the survival rights, protection rights, developmental rights and participation rights of children:

- Measures, plans and programmes initiated to guarantee the child's right to life and to ensure their physical, social, psychological, mental, spiritual and moral growth with human dignity;

- Measures taken for registration of births and deaths, investigations in case of suicides, suspicious deaths or child abuse cases and risks that children are subjected to;
- Provide statistics on all above categories and mention provisions to prevent such incidents;
- Provision of special health care facilities for treatment and rehabilitation of children;
- Information on all health indicators such as, infant mortality, child morbidity (diseases/illnesses), service coverage, immunization, etc.;
- Provide data on child and infant mortality and morbidity including gender, age, region and residence;
- Measures and programmes initiated to contain infant mortality and child morbidity;
- Budget allocation for child health care services;
- Involvement of NGOs in child health care;
- Changes that have come about during the reporting period in the health aspects;
- Efforts made to combat malnourishment among children and provisions made for nutritious food and clean drinking water;
- Statistics on growth monitoring among children;
- Statistics on pregnant women who have access to pre-natal and post-natal health services and immunization;
- Awareness campaigns on breast feeding, disability management, hygiene, preventive health measures and guidance for parents and public;
- Prevalence of HIV/AIDS among children and special measures taken for their rehabilitation;
- Measures to rehabilitate AIDS orphans;
- Measures adopted to abolish all forms of traditional harmful practices prejudicial to the health of children, such as, genital mutilation, child marriages, forced marriages etc.;
- Measures taken to improve girls' education, societal attitudes regarding girls education, school's "girl-friendly" environment, presence of female teachers;
- Involvement of UN agencies and international cooperation in tackling these problems;
- Policy measures taken to universalize education;

- Budget allocated to various levels of children's education;
- Measures taken to teach the children in local languages;
- Mechanisms developed to ensure access to quality education for all children, including girls, children with learning disabilities and children in especially difficult circumstances with out any discrimination;
- Measures adopted to provide educational infrastructure and qualified teachers to ensure quality of education and accessibility to children;
- Data on the rate of enrollment by age, sex and residence and rate of illiteracy among children below 18 years of age;
- Any systems of non-formal education available to continue education for school drop-outs;
- Development of different forms of education including vocational education;
- Changes that have come about in educational status during the period of reporting along with relevant data;
- Monitoring mechanisms introduced including research;
- Measures taken to prohibit violence, corporal punishment etc., in disciplining children in schools;
- Mechanisms for reporting and receiving complaints from children and their parents;
- UN and international cooperation in respect to educational programmes for children;
- Policy measures initiated to include CRC and human rights in the school curriculum;
- Difficulties, obstacles and problems encountered in fulfilling the child rights concerning educational development;
- Legal measures provided for children to express freely with out fear of repression, including family life, school life, administrative or juvenile justice, institutional and other forms of care, and asylum seeking;
- Participation of children in schools and public bodies;
- Portions on CRC included in training courses of professionals such as, Teachers training course, Nursing schools, Social work schools, Psychology departments, Sociology departments, Medical schools and Law schools;

- Consideration of children's views in formulating policies, laws and judiciary decisions;
- Information on the children's right to freedom of thought, conscience and religion by children;
- Protection of minority religious rights and teachings of children; and
- Measures taken to protect the right to freedom of association and the children associations in existence along with their role in protection of child rights.

The periodic reports must also include information on the steps taken for implementation of the CRC and the problems faced, if any in the process. Each nation is expected to ratify and make the following arrangements:

- All legal aspects brought forth in relation to the CRC;
- The Committees and administrative structures setup to implement and monitor CRC;
- Measures that have been initiated to disseminate and publicize widely, the CRC principles and provisions, to the public including children in their local languages;
- Measures taken for educating and training officials concerned such as, professionals, social workers, teachers, law enforcement officers including police, lawyers, judiciary, immigration officers, defense forces, doctors and health workers;
- Measures taken to include CRC in school curriculum and training programmes;
- Awareness and advocacy campaigns conducted during the reporting period;
- Participation of children in the activities for promotion of CRC;
- Broadcasting of CRC aspects in Radio, TV and media coverage;
- Actions initiated on the concluding observations adopted by the Committee in relation to the previous report;
- Follow up action taken on the suggestions and recommendations made by the Committee upon the previous report;
- Actions taken should reflect legislation, policy, creation

of new institutions, administrative structures and mechanisms and allocation of resources;

- It should contain the changes on the status of children brought about during the period of reporting along with quantitative data;
- Remedies available to redress public grievances on child rights;
- National Strategy/ National Plan of Action on children's rights;
- Steps taken to gather data/ statistics on relevant indicators and conduct research for policy formulation on child rights;
- Steps taken to monitor and evaluate the implementation of the CRC at all levels (Central, Regional and Sub-Regional levels);
- Steps taken for reporting to the Parliament on CRC;
- Steps taken to involve NGOs in the implementation of CRC;
- Agreements reached with international agencies to foster implementation of the CRC; and
- Difficulties, constraints and problems encountered in the process of implementation and monitoring of CRC.

The Debate on 'Welfare Oriented Rights' Versus the 'Right to Self-determination' of the Child

The contemporary thinking that, "children must be treated as active participants in shaping their social identities at an early age, rather than viewing them as passive subjects of social structures", is gaining importance in most of the western countries. The child rights activists and NGOs working for implementation of CRC are actively promoting such ideas. They have a firm conviction and believe that, children are capable of making sense of their social environment and that it is no longer appropriate to confine them to paternalistic and oppressive culture in society (Wyness, 2000).

Some ethnographers (James, A. and Prout, A. 1997; Opies, 1969) have documented that, children perform more effectively as social agents when they are separated from parental control and separation is viewed as a virtue in that, left to their own devices, children are able to perform complex social tasks. Hence, the view that children need to be accepted as social actors on the same terms as adults is getting strengthened.

Children in modern society are no more the preserves of adults; they seem to be contesting their subordinate role within the family; and they are viewed as key agents in the contemporary changes that are taking place in families and adult-child relationships (Wyness, 2000). However, there is a strong view expressed by most parents that, children can not be expected to accept unconditional authority of parents, if they are encouraged to believe that they have similar political and social standings as those of their parents and teachers (*The Times*, 30 December 1993). Thus, the dichotomy between protectionism and liberation does continue to exist with two opposing view points—should the children have same rights as adults or not.

There appears to be a conflict going on between the 'welfare oriented rights' to care and education (provision and protection) and the 'right to self determination' (Franklin, A. and B. Franklin, 1996). There seems to be no opposition for the former opinion, which strengthens the hold and authority of parents and state authorities over children; while the later seem to be more controversial, in the sense that the right to self-determination is expected to take away certain responsibilities and powers from parents and those in authority. This kind of rights given to children can threaten the protective and paternalistic roles of adults and disturb family relationships.

However, a majority seems to feel that it is neither desirable nor feasible to liberate children. Nevertheless, parents and schools need to consider this emerging need for more democratic functioning or citizen-based ethos in dealing with their children. There is also a greater felt need among the concerned that, efforts should be made in the direction of giving more and more educative and training programmes aimed at a more active and informed parent-child-teacher population in society.

Child Rights Movements to Protect and Monitor Child Rights

Although there are a variety of policy tools available to the international community to respond to the plight of different categories of children and adolescents in need of special protection measures, there are gaps between such policies and concrete action carried out on children's behalf. The progress report called " We the Children" issued by the UN Secretary General, containing information about 135 national level reviews, vividly depicts the current state of gloomy picture of the global child. According to this report, which was prepared for the Special UN General Assembly on Children-2002:

- More than 10 million children die each year from preventable causes;
- Over 150 million still suffer from malnutrition;
- The resources that were promised in the World Summit on Children 1990 are still to be realized and there has been inadequate investment in social services;
- Among an estimated 31 million refugees and displaced persons worldwide, the majority are children and women;
- According to an ILO estimate, some 250 million children work in developing countries, of whom nearly 50 millions work in hazardous circumstances; and
- More than 2 million children were reported to have been killed and 6 million reportedly disabled because of armed conflicts; and
- More than 4.3 million children under the age of 15 have been victims of AIDS.

On the positive side, there have been many tangible results for children:

- Currently, three million fewer children die than a decade ago;
- Polio has been brought under control, almost near total eradication in many countries;
- Over 100 countries have brought down infant mortality by one-fifth;
- Universal Childhood Immunization has been routinized saving millions of children; and
- Net school enrollment has been considerably increased.

However, the report noted that, "the World has fallen short of the goals of the World Summit on Children, not because they were too ambitious or were technically beyond reach, but it has fallen short because of insufficient investment" (UNICEF, 2001). It was also recognized that, for any effort made at the international or national levels, people's support is crucial. Hence, the Global Movement for Children (GMC), has taken up the task of bringing about a positive change, involving each and every one of the individuals and institutions at every level.

The GMC is a massive international effort for protecting child rights and promoting their development by involving all nations, leaders, intelligentsia, youth, adolescents and children, in brief every citizen of every nation. The main goal of GMC is to stimulate and motivate World leaders and leaders of all nations to regard children's physical, emotional and intellectual well being as their responsibility and ensure every child's right to dignity, security and self-fulfillment. The GMC sought to influence the World leaders to be accountable for the agreements they were expected to reach at the UN Special Session on Children (2002).

"Say Yes for Children" a campaign, as one of the programmes of GMC, was aimed at reaching out to children and enabling them to participate and initiate debates among all stakeholders about actions and responsibilities. All those rallying behind the children's cause shall also be urged to join the GMC by making commitment to take action at local, national and global levels to promote and protect children's rights. The results of the Pledge were to be presented at the UN General Assembly Special Session on Children (UNGASSC), which was held in May 2002 at New York.

The UNGASSC aimed at three outcomes reflecting what all parents and citizens sought for their children:

- A good start in life, in a nurturing and safe environment that enables children to survive and be physically healthy, mentally alert, emotionally secure, socially competent and be able to learn;
- Completion of a basic education of good quality; and
- The opportunity for adolescents to develop their individual capacities to the fullest, in safe and enabling environments that empower them to participate in, and contribute to, their societies (UNICEF, 2001).

References

1. Belsey, M., (1996), "Commercial Sexual Exploitation of Children: The Health and Psychosocial Dimensions", *WHO Paper, World Congress Against Commercial Sexual Exploitation of Children*, Stockholm, Sweden, 27-31 August.
2. Bruce, F., (1996), *Children and Prostitution: Don't give up on me* Geneva, International Catholic Bureau.
3. Bwibo, N.O., (1995), "Children in Especially Difficult Circumstances" in *Primary Health Care: A Manual*, (Eds.) Mukelabai, K., *et. al.* Nairobi: UNICEF.
4. Franklin, A. and Franklin B., (1996), "Growing pains: the developing children's rights movements in U.K", in J. Pilcher and S. Wagg (eds.) *Thatcher's Children*, London: Falmer Press.
5. Freud, A. and Burlingham, D.T., (1943), *War and Children*, Medical War Books.
6. Helander, E., (1989), *Prejudice and Dignity: An Introduction to Community Based Rehabilitation*, UNDP: New York.
7. The Hindu 1995, "Children's Day: Another Working Day? *The HINDU*, November 14, 1995.
8. James, A. and Prout A. (Eds.), (1997), *Constructing and Reconstructing Childhood*, London: Falmer Press.
9. Joseph, M.P., (1995), *IPEC in India 1992-95: Some Lessons Learnt*, unpublished note.
10. ILO, (1996), *Child Labour: Targeting the Intolerable*, Geneva: ILO.
11. ILO, (1998), *The Sex Sector* (Ed.) by Lin Lean Lim, ILO: Geneva.
12. Mani, T.R.S., (1995), "AITUC for the Elimination of Child Labour in India" (unpublished note).
13. MLHW and UNICEF, (2000), *The Situation of Separated Children in IDP Camps in Eritrea*, MLHW and UNICEF: Asmara.
14. MLHW, (1992), *Orphan Children in Eritrea*, MLHW: Asmara.
15. Opie, I. and Opie P., (1969), *Children's Games*, Oxford: Oxford University Press.
16. Radda Barnen, (1996), *Social Work and Administration: Methods and Techniques*, Swedish Save the Children, Stockholm, Sweden.
17. Ressler, E.M., *et. al.*(1989), *Unaccompanied Children: Care and Protection in Wars, Natural Disasters and Refugee Movements*, New York: Oxford University Press.
18. Shamin, I., (1997), "Trafficking in Children and Child Prostitution", *Paper Presented in the National workshop on Child Labour Organized by ILO/IPEC*, Dhaka, 5-7 January.
19. Smith, H., (1999), *Children, Feelings and Divorce*, Free Association Books, London.
20. Srisang, I. (Ed.) (1990), "Caught in Modern Slavery: Tourism

and Child Prostitution in Asia", *Report and Proceedings of the Chiang Mai Consultation of the International Campaign to End Child Prostitution in Asian Tourism,* Chiang Mai: Thailand, 1-9 May.

21. Tesfay Aradom, (1991), *Children, War and State Sponsored Violence,* (unpublished report), Boston College.
22. United Nations Economic and Social Council, (1996), Rights of the Child: Question of a Draft Optional Protocol to the Convention on the Rights of the Child, on the sale of Children, Child Prostitution and Child Pornography as well as basic measures needed for their Eradication: *Report of the Working Group on its Second Session, Doc. E/CN. 4/1996/101,* New York: UN.
23. UNICEF, (1994), *Children and Women in Eritrea,* Asmara: UNICEF.
24. UNICEF, (1994), *Children of War Wandering Alone in Southern Sudan,* UNICEF: New York.
25. UNICEF, (2000), *Children and Armed Conflict,* (unpublished note), UNICEF, Asmara.
26. UNICEF and MLHW, (2000), *The Situation of Separated Children in IDP Camps in Eritrea,* MLHW and UNICEF: Asmara.
27. UNICEF, (2001), "Global Movement for Children- Progress Report, May 14, 2001, (unpublished note).
28. Werner, D., (1987), *Disabled Village Children,* The Hesperian Foundation: USA.
29. Whaites, A., (1996), "The Path to Prostitution among Street Children", *Together: A Journal of World Vision International,* No. 52, October-December, Monrovia: California.
30. World Congress against Commercial Sexual Exploitation of Children, (1996), *Draft Declaration and Agenda for Action,* Stockholm, Sweden, 27-31 August.
31. World Vision International, (2000), The Right to Peace: Children in Armed Conflict, *Working Paper* No. 2, March 2000, WVI: Geneva.
32. Wyness, M.G., (2000), *Contesting Childhood,* London: Falmer Press.

5

Children and Adolescents Affected by Armed Conflicts and Other Social Problems

Introduction

Due to decline of moral and ethical values among human beings and increased propensity to violence as a means for resolving political and social problems, there is a significant increase in conflicts and wars subjecting innocent people, especially children and youth to unnecessary and unwarranted suffering. The so-called human rights continue to be violated despite many international conventions and commitments.

War destroys the economy, the infrastructure, manufacturing units, school buildings and hospitals in the country. When soldiers invade towns and villages, they destroy houses and loot their belongings. Villagers loose livestock and stop cultivation due to the danger of land mines planted in their agricultural fields and passages. State-run welfare programmes vanish. But in every conflict situation, children who have been separated from their parents are the most sufferers. Break-up of family life, repeated displacements and constant physical threats deprive children of their natural background for their emotional and mental development.

In view of the above, this chapter is written with the following objectives:

(1) increasing awareness among public regarding the problems and plight of child soldiers and those affected by war;

(2) examining problems of refugees and those who are temporarily sheltered in internally displaced persons (IDP) camps;

(3) analyzing the psycho-social impact of armed conflicts on children, especially in the African Continent;

(4) reviewing other social problems that the adolescents face in society apart from war related ones; and

(5) providing some workable solutions to tackle these problems.

Prevalence of the Problem

Child abuses and victimization is not adequately reflected in most reports, as it is a very sensitive issue. However, based on the existing reports and estimations made by the concerned organizations, the following details could be gleaned. Reports of UNICEF and Coalition to Stop the Use of Child Soldiers reveal that there are around 300, 000 children under 18 years of age involved in armed conflicts around the world. About 120, 000 of them are in Africa.

Over the last decade:

- More than 2 million children have died as a result of wars;
- More than 6 million children have been injured or disabled;
- More than 1 million children have been orphaned or separated;
- More than 20 million were either displaced or became refugees;
- More than 12 millions have become homeless;
- Between 8, 000 to 10, 000 children were killed or maimed by landmines every year (UNICEF, 2000);
- More than 250 million children work as prostitutes, drug traffickers and indenture labourers (Melanie Gow et. al, 2000);
- Most refugees and Internally Displaced Persons (IDPs) are in Africa and Asia. The following countries have some of the large IDPs: Sudan (4 million), Afghanistan (more than two million), Angola (2 million), Colombia (1.8 million), Burma (1 million), Iraq (900,000), Burundi (800, 000) and Srilanka (500, 000); and in general half of the

refugees and Internally Displaced Persons (IDPs) were children.

Activities of Children in Armed Conflict Situations

Children under 15 were involved in many armed conflicts and some of them were found to be as young as 8 years. They were involved in a variety of activities such as, soldiers, porters of food and other materials, messengers, spies, robbers and as sex slaves/comforting girls. Case studies from El Salvador, Ethiopia and Uganda reported that a third of child soldiers were girls; while their number was high in armed opposition groups mainly involved in prostitution and as comfort girls.

> Consider the following narration of 'Kadogos': In some cases as young as nine- start out as runners or bodyguards for officers. Some work as porters helping troops to ferry water and ammunition, others as spies. "They are very good at getting information. You can send them across enemy lines and nobody suspects them because they are so young". But as soon as they learn to use arms, child soldiers are used for fighting. Some fight as soldiers and some as rebels. "They make good fighters because they are young and want to show off. They think it's all a game, so they are fearless," said Colonel Songolo (Kibumba, P.T, 1999).

Motivation to Recruit or Join in Armed Conflicts

Motivations differ for recruitment of children in armed conflicts for the governments, armed private groups and children volunteering themselves.

(a) For the governments, the factors to use children include:

- A culture of impunity for war criminals,
- Lack of birth registration records allowing adolescents to be forced as conscripts,
- Need to augment armed forces,
- Need for providing services to soldiers in war,
- Proliferation of light weapons that children can easily manage, and
- Effectiveness of using children in front activities.

(b) For private armies, the factors include:

- Easy to abduct,
- Easy to intimidate,
- Chief labour, and
- Multiple uses of children, such as for planting bombs and carrying out surprise attacks, apart from sex slavery.

(c) For children volunteers, the factors include:

- Lack of educational and employment opportunities,
- Collapse of social services and governance,
- Collapse of law and order providing a feeling of insecurity to children,
- Ideological/ political affiliations,
- Urge to take arms as a game to show off their capacity/ experience the power of a gun, and
- To take revenge on the perpetrators of violence on their near and dear ones.

War Affected Refugees, Displaced and Unaccompanied Children

War destroys the economy and infrastructure such as roads, bridges, manufacturing units, school buildings and hospitals. All state-run welfare programmes vanish. But in every conflict situation, no other group of people suffer more than the children who get separated from their parents and forced to fend for themselves. The reasons and causes for their separation are many. Some get separated accidentally in the confusion of fighting. Many children are deliberately separated from their parents, as they send the children to towns and camps situated outside their home area to find safety, food, work and particularly schooling. People believe that life in the IDP camps, however controlled, was secure and comfortable during the situation of war. The IDP camps become a magnetic force for children, as they could get food, cloths, medicines and schooling free of charge.

One rapid appraisal study conducted by the UNICEF and MLHW in IDP camps of Eritrea revealed the following. "Although many were unintentional separations, the parents of the children reluctantly told them to flee to safety. In areas still under the Ethiopian occupation, children took dangerous journeys over mountains and cliffs to reach the IDP camps due to worsening of the situation. The children have witnessed raping of girls and women and experienced beatings/harassment by the soldiers prior to their flight. They have also seen dead bodies of children and women killed by heavy artillery" (UNICEF, 2000: 4). However, they have reported that they could come in contact with their parents soon after reaching IDP camps through the authorities.

The study also reported gender differences among the separated children. Among the separated children below the age of 14 years, the number of boys and girls was almost equal; where as in the age group of 15-18 years, the boys were 610 (68%) and girls were only 287 (32%). Traditionally girls were not allowed to travel alone out side their homes. However, due to reasons of safety and security girls are also being sent to IDP camps albeit reluctantly. In occupied territories several rape and molestation cases were reported. These women and young girls have a high probability of exposure to infections, such as STDs, HIV/AIDS. They also had to undergo trauma subsequently (UNICEF and MLHW, 2000).

Cultural factors do play a significant role in this process. The children in African countries have a high degree of mobility built in to their lives at a fairly younger age. In traditional pastoral communities, boys would leave their home and move from one place to another with the cattle for several months. Secondary schools have always involved boarding; and children had to stay away for years to get higher education in boarding institutions. In some cases, boys get together and leave their home for extended periods fending for themselves, as they find nothing worthwhile at their home place. In this process, they may be abducted/drawn to private armies or may end up finding petty jobs in towns and cities. But, it is reported that they eventually return to their home with bride money and other bounty to settle down in their hometowns.

However, when the war breaks out, the situation is totally different. People along with their children flea especially in the nights and trek miles to reach safer places, especially the refugee and IDP camps. When aircraft drop bombs around them, some die and others get injured. For unaccompanied children it is especially hard to trek and many may not survive the week-long journey. Everybody enroute exploit them and they soon become hungry and weak and can not move along. The weaker get left out to fend for themselves.

These memories continue to disturb even when they are outside the war zone. The traumatic after-images of the horrors continue to affect their lives for longer periods. These were events, which were sudden, intense and extraordinary to normal human experience and beyond imagination to the younger ones. The unaccompanied children and orphans in the camps lived a tense and fragile peace and suffered silently.

Children in Refugee and IDP Camps

Refugees are those people who flee their country of origin and move to another country; while the displaced are those who are forcibly displaced within their own country. Both are emergency situations, where they face food shortage, hunger and starvation and adverse health conditions such as diarrhea, malaria as well as traumatic experiences.

The refugees are characterized by the following factors:

- Lost homes, relatives, children, parents etc.;
- Uncertainty of their fate and losing control over lives;
- Fled from their own countries to new places;
- Experience of violence and or threats;
- Material deprivation and hunger.

Since the Second World War, there have been many wars in the African countries, which have been reportedly resulted in about 2.5 million refugees and 10 million people internally displaced. Over 60 per cent of these persons were women and children who were highly vulnerably according to the OAU summit report (Mukelabai, Bwibo and Onyango (eds.), 1995). In the Eritrean and Ethiopian war of the years 1998 to 2000, about 50, 000 people became refugees and nearly one million persons were reportedly internally displaced. Emergencies are very common and prevalent in African countries. A majority of emergencies occur due to wars and internal strife, while a few are due to natural disasters such as drought, famine, floods, cyclones, etc.

Due to armed conflicts, children experience many unnatural and abnormal incidents that debilitate their psychosocial development. Their experiences include the following:

- Seen combatants shooting and killing people indiscriminately;
- Seen people and animals burning and dyeing in bombardments;
- Seen people fleeing with fear to escape shelling and bombing;
- Been chased from home by armed men;
- Been imprisoned with parents; and
- Been separated from parents forcefully.

Such experiences leave children in a state of helplessness and powerlessness. Nightmares, flashbacks, fear and other psychosomatic symptoms are commonly observed among such children. However, when they manage to reach the IDP camps or the refugee camps, arrangements are made to meet their needs to reduce their problems gradually, if not immediately. The "protective factor research" team (Vanistendael, 1996, cited in UNICEF report, 1999) has put forth a standard list of characteristics which demonstrates the coping mechanisms of community and assisting children and families in acquiring strength and normalizing life situation. These factors included the following:

- Stable, ongoing, emotional relationships with at least one parent or other closely related adult;
- Social support from inside and outside of the family;
- An emotionally positive, open, guiding and norm oriented educational climate;
- Social models that encourage constructive coping;
- Balance of social responsibilities and achievement demands;
- Experiences of self-efficacy, self-confidence and positive self-concept; and
- Experience of sense, structure and meaning in one's own development (Vanistendeal, 1996).

An assessment study of the IDP camps in Eritrea conducted by the UNICEF and MLHW (1999) has revealed that there were some of these arrangements put in place, although many of these were disrupted due to sudden and unpredictable conditions prevalent during war time. The report further stated that," while the solid foundation that children experienced in the past has ensured that life in the camps is free of crime and social violence, serious strains have been placed on the community coping mechanisms" (UNICEF, 1999: 40). In these camps, school experiences, games and cultural activities have been interrupted, leaving children lonely with worries and fears, without mediating effects of productive and normal activities. Outside the camps, the host families and communities were overstretched both emotionally and financially in their attempt to care for the expelled and deported persons. These groups themselves were in desperate need of external help.

Responses to Emergency Situation

The immediate response to the emergency situation should be to save lives and protect them from further vulnerability. The following are the requirements in such situations:

- Provision of shelter, makeshift dwellings, tents, huts etc.;
- Provision of food, household necessities, cloths and blankets etc.;
- Provision of clean water and sanitary facility;
- Registration of all persons including the displaced and the missing; and
- Setting up communication system for tracing lost persons and reuniting families.

The international organization responsible for relief and rehabilitation is the UNHCR (United Nations High Commissioner for Relief) established in 1951. Other UN agencies include:

- United Nations Children Fund (UNICEF),
- World Food Programme (WFP),
- United Nations Development Programme (UNDP),
- World Health Organization (WHO) and
- United Nations Human Rights Organization (UNHRO).

Several NGOs also support in the relief work, such as:

- Red Cross and Red Crescent;
- Oxfam;
- Save the Children;
- Cooperation for American Relief Everywhere (CARE); and
- African Medical and Research Foundation (AMREF).

International Regulations in Emergency Situations

There are established international regulations to safeguard the refugees particularly the children and women. Some of these regulations are that, all parties involved in a conflict should,

- Guarantee peace zones to enable relief and rehabilitation work; and
- Provide periods of tranquillity-mutually agreed periods of cease-fire, during that time, relief supplies may be delivered, immunization and health teams may operate under safe conditions, basic water supply and other equipment be provided to the refugees and the displaced.
- Similarly the Convention on the Rights of the Child states that, " all feasible measures be taken to ensure protection and care of children who are affected by armed conflict" (Bwibo, 1995).

However, many countries in conflict rarely practice these international regulations and have flagrantly been violating. For instance, in Somalia and Yugoslavia, it was reported that, even the relief workers were killed in wartime.

Psychosocial Impact on War affected Children

(a) Violations of the convention on rights of children

Providing an environment, which fosters democracy and stimulates emotional, psychological, social and cognitive growth of children is a universal requirement, for all those countries, which have ratified the CRC. The full realization of the goals of CRC and empowerment of parents, communities and nations is a responsibility that the international community has assumed and striving to achieve.

However, due to various reasons, such as, lack of resources, lack of political commitment and convenience of using children as soldiers, there has been no significant reduction in tackling the problems of children in armed conflicts. This amounts to blatant violation of child rights at every level.

(b) Physical and mental growth disorders among children

Several reports have highlighted that exposure to stressful events increases a child's risk to develop health and psychological problems. Lack of essential food, vitamins etc., in early childhood will cause lasting bodily malformations in later years (Freud and Burlingham, 1943).

There are several studies, which portray that tens of thousands of children's bodies and minds were injured by violence. One survey of the children directly affected by war revealed the following staggering results: 77% had witnessed murder, 88% had witnessed physical abuse, 51% had been physically abused themselves, 63% had witnessed rape or sexual abuse, 64% had been abducted from their families and 28% were trained for combat (Swartz and Ann Levett, 1989; cited in Tesfay Aradom, 1991). To this grim figures should be added thousands of children who have experienced deaths in their own families at the hands of authorities or the rebel groups.

This kind of extreme stresses caused by war and exacerbated by starvation lead to a number of mental changes that eventually result in character problems at a later stage, such as, psychotic thinking, considerable violence, much dissociation, extremes of passivity, self-mutilative episodes and a variety of anxiety disturbances (Terr, 1991; cited in Tesfay Aradom, 1991). The study also showed that 20- 30% of the sample exhibited social isolation, uncontrolled aggressive behaviour, communication impairment, sleep disturbances and eating disorders. Another study on war affected children showed that many children exhibited psychosomatic disorders such as head aches, stomach disorders, anorexia, loss of weight and encopresis (Carli, 1987).

Infants and toddlers separated from parents had visible manifestations of deeper emotional and mental struggles such as, intense crying, reluctance to accept substitute care givers, food refusals, digestive and sleep disorders. Thumb sucking, bedwetting, nightmares, fear of objects such as ghosts and withdrawal syndrome was also very commonly found among the displaced and orphans. Such traumatic stress disorders and symptoms are usually caused by loss of one or both parents, constant threats from aerial bombardment, continued displacements, torture inflicted on self or loved ones and witnessing of murders (Tesfay Aradom, 1991).

(c) Ethical and moral consequences

During wars and conflicts children experience a feeling of betrayal. Children get a feeling that the authority figures, and role models such as parents, teachers, and others, whom they have trusted, all have repeatedly breached the expected moral standards of behaviour. As a result of identifying with aggressors and violence, children's sense of right and wrong may become blurred. They will gradually accept looting, stealing as legitimate; that killing enemies in front or for political reasons is different from murdering. Children get convinced that certain violent acts are morally permissible and violence is the most important response for solving the problems of existence (Macksoud, 1991).

(d) Loss of education and employable skills

The most far-reaching effects of war on education are the loss of human resources and the breakdown of infrastructure and community networks. For instance UNICEF has reported that:

- In East Timor, 95% of schools and other educational institutions were destroyed in the 1999 conflict.
- During the Rwanda crisis over two-thirds of the teachers were killed or fled the country.
- In Iraq the whole education system has been devastated due to the prolonged conflict (UNICEF, 2000).
- Afghanistan is one of the worst affected countries where girl's education was in jeopardy both before the war and afterwards due to the Taliban.

For children, who are displaced, deported and become refugees, years of lost schooling and vocational training take equivalent number of years to replace. Their loss is a major set back to development of the country, as well as individuals, who become unemployed after the demobilization takes place. They will not have education or employable skills to get jobs and do not have sufficient capital to start their own small business and thus become wasteful resources of the country.

(e) Exposure to drugs, alcohol and HIV/AIDS infections

Children get used to cigarettes, marijuana and alcohol during the armed struggles and there is every possibility of getting addicted. In some cases, children were forced to take drugs and alcohol to commit atrocities on civilians. Population movements, family breakdown, rape, sexual violence and the erosion of traditional values dramatically increase the potential for STDs, HIV/AIDS infections, especially among girls, who were sexually abused during armed conflicts.

(f) Damage to family life

The destruction of houses, crops, agriculture infrastructure, disintegration and displacement of families and communities, destruction of social services and other facilities damage the family life beyond regeneration, taking a heavy toll on children. The families are left with no means of productivity, either in agriculture (because of land mines and loss of cattle) or in service sector. Girls are at particular risk, because of rape, unwanted pregnancies and humiliation in society. All these rupture the family life compounded by unemployment and housing problems.

Distinct Social Problems Associated with Adolescents

The problems associated with adolescents needing special recognition are a recent phenomenon and there has been little focus on the impact of conflicts on adolescents. The World Health Organization has defined an adolescent as a person aged between 10 to 20 years. By the year 2000, adolescents comprise 20 per cent or 1.2 billion persons (UNICEF, cited in WCRWC, 2000). Adolescents are characterized by strong and demanding opinions, hard to deal with and craving for recognition at home, school and at work places and possess adult-like behaviour.

Adolescents have distinct experiences, distinct needs and distinct capacities to generate a livelihood for themselves and their families, and take on leadership roles. The health of the social fabric in a society largely depends on how well the energies of adolescents are constructively channeled for nation building activities. The study by the Women's Commission for Refugee Women and Children (2000), has highlighted up on the distinct problems and needs of the war affected adolescents. According to this report,

- Adolescents are more likely to be recruited to military service and armed groups. Such an experience at that age may result in severe psychological effects such as desensitization to sufferings of people and may develop in to social deviants.
- Adolescents attend school in far fewer numbers and girls are more likely to miss out their education due to security concerns and vulnerability.
- Adolescents are more vulnerable to economic exploitation and may be subjected to unsafe working conditions, discriminatory payment of wages and forced labour.
- Adolescent girls are more likely than children to be sexually abused and abducted to be used as sex slaves.
- Sexually abused adolescents are at a higher risk of contracting HIV/AIDS.
- Lacking opportunities for employment and meaningful role in society, adolescents are more vulnerable to be used by anti-social elements and armed groups engaged in conflicts, drug smuggling and prostitution, etc. (WCRWC, 2000).

Recent evidences reveal that, the problems of adolescents, such as adolescent unwanted pregnancies, abortions and related complications, infections such as STD/HIV/AIDS, drug abuse, child prostitution, orphan status due to civil strife etc., are growing at an alarming phase needing attention of one and all.

Problems of adolescents are multiple, the young out side marriage group are likely to change sexual partners and risk greater exposure to infections; millions of adolescents live and work in streets, many turn to selling sex for a living; and some are forced into sex. On the other hand, the young are reluctant to seek help and counseling services. The impact of HIV/AIDS infections is said to be heavier on young women than men, because of pregnancy related complications, sepsis, abortions, premature and still births and congenital infections.

The major reasons for such state of affairs are many and these could be:

- Deteriorating social and economic conditions and exploitative environment;
- Increasing civil strife and wars leading to orphans and displaced families;
- Early maturation of girls leading to early sexual activity;
- Deterioration of cultural values and social control of parents and elders in families;
- Lack of work, employment and recreation facilities;
- Negative influences of peer groups and mass media; and
- An urge to experiment and risky behaviour patterns among the adolescents.

Adolescent Sexual Activity and Unwanted Pregnancy

Many studies have revealed that in African countries, more than 80 per cent of the girls were exposed to sexual activity before attaining the age of 18 years (Kinoti, 1995). Many factors such as early attainment of puberty, breakdown of traditional norms and values, western influence through Television, economic hardship, urbanization have led to more liberal attitudes and practices by adolescents. Lack of control by elders and increased freedom of the adolescents always lead to early sexual experiences, most of which were unprotected resulting in unwanted pregnancy and risk of acquiring infections.

Teenage pregnancies contribute to one third of all pregnancies in Africa. It is well known that teenage pregnancies have a higher incidence of complications and maternal mortality. Unplanned pregnancies lead to high school dropouts causing severe psychological and social consequences and loss of carrier opportunities. Studies have also shown that the contraceptive use among adolescents is as low as five per cent (Kinoti, 1995). It is mainly because of lack of awareness and the negative perception that contraceptive use is associated with promiscuity and increased sexual activity.

It is reported that over 20 per cent of maternal mortality are among the teenagers. Unsafe abortions are very common among these teenagers, as these are mostly the result of illegitimate sexual contacts and most of them will end up with complications and hospitalization. Frequent, unprotected sex can end up with repeated abortions leading to blood loss, anemia, and various forms of injuries to the birth canal and even death. Unsafe abortion is therefore a major problem among adolescents.

STD, HIV and AIDS Among Adolescents

Unprotected sex as is the practice in the case of adolescents is associated with high incidence of STDs. Due to incomplete physical development, they are also prone to acquire infections. An estimated 36 per cent of the teenagers were reported to have had STD in the developing countries. Frequent changing of sexual partner and unprotected sex ultimately exposes them to acquire HIV/AIDS, which is rising at an alarming rate in the African countries. Early detection and treatment of STD is expected to reduce the incidence of acquiring HIV/AIDS.

Drugs and Substance Abuse

Addiction to drugs is often the end of the road for education and carrier development. Although drug addiction is not a serious problem in many countries, drug and substance abuse among the adolescents has reached alarming proportions in the underdeveloped countries, especially among students and street children. Drug abuse ranged from alcohol, tobacco and various other stimulants. Those who could afford were addicted to drugs such as the cannabis, sativa, ashish etc. Most of them were reported to have become criminals committing petty crimes and stealing money for buying drugs, ultimately ending up as anti-social elements in the society.

Delinquency

Studies have revealed that a larger proportion of adolescents is showing signs of delinquency currently than in the past and there is an absolute increase in antisocial behaviour among youngsters (Marynia, 1962; Bolton, 1980; Garbarino, 1982). Adolescence is the most exciting and trying period of life, providing enough intrinsic challenges. Studies also support that contemporary juvenile delinquency has assumed proportions too intolerable, and has become too dangerous to too many people, to be dealt with. No other teen-age development causes greater concern for parents than adolescent delinquency. Surely, not all adolescents are delinquents, but the defiant nature is, however, most common among all adolescents.

Delinquency is of many kinds, starting from lesser forms, such as, petty crimes, minor offenses, truancy, to that of major offenses such as, murders, suicides by pregnant girls, gangs involved in violence, marauding, armed robberies, drug offenses, etc. Naturally we must be aware of the causes for such turbulent life of a person in such young age, before attempting to correct such antisocial behaviour among delinquents.

It may be gleaned from several studies (Marynia, 1962; Bolton, 1980; Garbarino, 1982), that there are several factors, in variety of combinations that are responsible for such disturbances among adolescents. These include:

- Hereditary factors, natural indwelling criminality, what is commonly known as "bad blood";
- Poverty and an environment of deprivation;
- Factors connected with the type of child rearing, emotional qualities and family relationships;
- Personality traits of the child, unresolved inner conflicts, repressed emotions, etc.;
- Deteriorating moral values and disorders in society, for instance raising corruption, as a result, parents and elders loosing moral authority over adolescents;
- Competitiveness for achievement among children in school and among parents in their professional life, urging them to earn more and become more powerful; as a result lacking time and control over children; and most importantly,

- The urge among adolescents for self-assertion, proving bravado of his masculinity; for instance, gangsters and armed robberies, etc.

Delinquency in modern world has become a public responsibility and there are many individuals, institutions and organizations to deal with the problem effectively. These include Juvenile Courts, Remand homes, Certified schools, child guidance clinics and counseling services given by religious priests, psychiatrists and social workers. Nevertheless, these are only rehabilitative efforts, while the problem warrants preventive measures too. Hence there is a need for multi-pronged approach at family, neibourhood and community levels.

It is well said that, "patience is a virtue for adolescents, as much as for the parents and others who care for them" (Garbarino, 1982: 113). Then it will be the individual family and parents who have to take primary responsibility. Parents will have to learn to understand the personalities of their young children better; they will have to teach their children responsibility; and they will have to exercise greater authority by supplying more strength when necessary (Marynia, 1962).

Then comes the role of neighbourhood groups/associations, teacher-parent associations, community recreation centers, creation of public facilities such as playground, library, parks etc. Through these out-lets parents and elders can get involved in an active way in caring for their youngsters, as well as, their children could also be positively engaged. School services, such as counseling and recreation facilities could play a major role apart from family, as the youngsters spend more time in school, with their peers and learn many valuable lessons that are useful in life at the school. As adults, our task is to encourage a socially enlightened environment that allows adolescents opportunity to safely take advantage of it.

Female Genital Mutilation (FGM)

Another culturally approved harmful practice affecting adolescent girls and women in Africa and Middle Eastern countries is the Female Genital Mutilation (FGM). The Demographic and Health Survey (1995) showed that, female circumcision is almost universal, with 95 % of women having been circumcised in Africa. There are three generally recognized types of circumcision: clitoridectomy, excision and infibulation. Infibulation is the most severe form of female circumcision involving removal of external genitalia, followed by joining together of the two sides of the labia majora using threads, thorns to narrow the vaginal opening (WHO, 1996). Almost one third of the women circumcised were reported to have undergone infibulation (EDHS, 1995: 165).

Several reasons are reported for undergoing the circumcision, the main ones being, custom, religious demand and a good tradition. The other reasons reported are cleanliness, preservation of virginity and better marriage prospects for girls. Female circumcision is reported to be more prevalent in rural and backward areas compared to urban areas. A large majority of women (72 %) have indicated in the EDHS survey that, they were against the practice of circumcision. They consider that it is a bad practice, a painful personal experience, creates several medical complications, prevents sexual satisfaction and more than any thing, it is against the dignity of women (EDHS, 1995: 177).

One of the major reasons for pleading against FGM, are the medical complications associated with it. In most cases, the traditional birth attendants and elderly women who do not have any medical training perform FGM. Bleeding is unavoidable since damage to the blood vessels is inevitable. Shock from loss of blood and pain due to absence of anesthesia are experienced. Infection due to unhygienic conditions, tetanus and septicemia (blood poisoning) also occur and these can lead to long term morbidity and even mortality (Rushwan, 1990). Apart from these, the hardening of the scar tissue could cause pain during sexual intercourse as well as at the time of delivery.

In addition to health related complications, girls also lose education and opportunities for skilled jobs. For the above reasons, of late, most of the knowledgeable and urban women are against the practice of FGM.

Remedial Measures

Prevention and Protection of Children Affected by War Groups

The Convention on the Rights of Children (CRC), the Optional

Protocol raising the age of recruitment to armed forces from 15 to 18 years, the Machel's study on the Impact of Armed Conflict on Children provide an important framework for mobilizing the international community towards fulfillment of children's rights and developmental needs.

Practically everyone working for the children affected by war is committed to first reunite them with their families. One major problem of reunification is the large population displaced and fled to refugee camps far away from their homeland; as a result it is increasingly difficult to trace the children's families.

The next step is to explore and trace their relatives and reunite children with the host families. Restoring traditional coping mechanisms is an important area of work, which has been highlighted recently by the international experiences. For instance, in Eritrea, the community net-work is so intact, despite hardships, the affected children are taken care of by every family and they feel secure, safe and welcome in to their families, though not related (UNICEF, 1999). Great sense of responsibility and support were shown by all the community members, especially for child-care.

Once reunited, the Government and NGOs must make efforts to reconstruct the economy of the host families by providing income-generating assets. Agricultural implements and livestock that were lost should be given and land mines removed to restart the cultivation. There is a need to rehabilitate the basic educational and health services in the areas affected by war.

The UNICEF and other NGOs working for rehabilitation of the children affected by war have the following strategies to tackle this issue:

- Guaranteeing the rights of children as enshrined in the Convention of Rights of the Child;
- Protecting the children from military conscription and other forms of abuse;
- Providing physical security, food and nutrition, educational and health facilities; and
- Returning the children to their parents or guardians at the shortest time possible (UNICEF, 1994: 49).

However, the dilemma of most governments is the lack of means, which is reflected in the following statement:

> In October 1998, the Executive Director of UNICEF sought assurances from the government, "to demobilize child combatants, not to recruit new child combatants, and to provide amnesty for those children who had been fighting on the side of the rebel movement". The reply from the Deputy Defense Minister was that, "he wished with all his heart to disarm all children," but explained that, "he lacked the means for now" (cited in Coalition to Stop the Use of Child Soldiers, 1999: 95).

Hence there is a pressing need to:

- Set-up separate fund for tackling the problems of children affected by armed conflict;
- The operational guidelines should be different for disbursement of such funds in emergency situations, relaxing the regular procedures of fund disbursement followed in usual times;
- Strengthen early warning systems and establish peace zones, child focused humanitarian cease-fires etc., even during the conflict; and
- Make increased efforts in sharing information across national authorities, communities and civil society organizations to promote coordinated and effective response to all problems of children affected by the armed conflicts.

Prevention and Management of Adolescent Problems

Experiences have shown that it takes a longer time for behavioural change to occur among the affected persons. Adults must therefore be good role models to provide positive influence to teenage behaviour. Determinants of behavioural change include education and awareness, knowledge, moral values and norms, and perception of consequences and negative aspects of problems. A powerful tool to improve the awareness and knowledge about these problems is the peer group education, to involve adolescents in a participatory manner to identify their problems and search for solutions through the help of a facilitator. An action research study undertaken to involve adolescents through Information Education and Communication (IEC) based interventions showed that, it was very effective and useful to involve teenagers to analyze their problems, spread messages of negative consequences of STDs and unwanted pregnancy. They had improved their knowledge, over a period of two years, on sexuality, use of contraception and safe methods when required, and made consistent efforts to mobilize community support for the programme (Kinoti, 1995). Apart from the above the preventive measures may include the following:

- Improving knowledge on reproductive biology among adolescents;
- Identification of risky behaviour and counseling to change such behaviour;
- Recreation facilities as a viable alternative;
- Education on the magnitude and consequences of the major problems that the adolescents are facing;
- Formal and informal education on the mechanism of transmission of STDs and HIV infections and ways and means of protecting one self;
- National policy on illicit drug trafficking and use with provisions for severe penalties for the recalcitrance; and
- Public education awareness campaigns on the dangers of drug abuse, AIDS and other social problems.

The curative measures include the following:

- Providing special care for the pregnant adolescent to avoid further complications;
- Post-abortion counseling and contraception for adolescents to prevent repeated unwanted pregnancies and abortions;
- Services for the diagnosis and treatment of STDs should be decentralized to the health center level and made accessible to the majority of the population;
- Development of treatment, counseling facilities and support systems for the drug addicts; and
- Active involvement of adolescents and youth in the IEC programmes to tackle social problems.

Discussion on adolescent health may include clear understanding of the milestones in human development, puberty, adventurous and risky behaviour of the adolescents and the need for responsibility on the part of parents and adolescents for appropriate behaviour and practices. Health and sex education issues must include the following:

- Reproductive biology and human development;
- Milestones in social responsibility;
- Risky behaviour patterns and their consequences;
- Recreation as an alternative;
- The preventive and curative services and their location of availability;
- Methods for prevention of STD and AIDS infections; and
- Methods for prevention of drug abuse.

Continuing Education and Counseling Services to Minimizing Social Deviance

The impact of HIV/AIDS infections is said to be heavier on young women than men, because of pregnancy related complications, sepsis, abortions, premature and still births and congenital infections. Drug abuse is also reported to be on the increase. It is necessary to strengthen counseling services at the community level to cater to the needs of the affected youth. Counseling units must be established and provided with professional counselors and social workers to deal with various social and psychological problems of the youth.

There is also urgency for public awareness building and practical preventive approaches to social problems by involving the youth in implementation of programmes. Early detection and treatment of STD is expected to reduce the incidence of acquiring HIV/AIDS. Increasing access to contraceptives and reproductive health care and providing post abortion counseling services could be other important strategies in this direction.

The traditional harmful practices, such as the Female Genital Mutilation (FGM), are also being continued due to lack of proper education and knowledge about what is being done to the women in general and girls in particular. In most cases, it is being done at an younger age where they have no knowledge about it or they do not understand the consequences of it. They are not involved in decision making about their own bodies. As such, it is undemocratic and violates human rights in general and rights of the girl child in specific. Hence, public should be educated about the harmful effects of the FGM.

Continuing education and refresher courses need to be supported for updating their knowledge. There is also a need to improve awareness on various social and psychological problems that the youth of modern days are facing at all levels, right from the community to the level of village administrators and committee members, whose role as duty bearers and their collaboration in the programme can greatly improve delivery system and prevent the emergence of similar problems. Hence capacity development activities need greater attention as well.

References

1. Bolton, F.G., Jr. (1980), *The Pregnant Adolescent: Problems of Premature Parenthood*, Beverly Hills CA: Sage Publications.
2. Carli, A., (1987), "Psychological Consequences of Political Persecution: The Effects on Children of the Imprisonment or Disappearance of their parents", *Tids Krift for Norsk Psykologforening* 24, 82-93.
3. Coalition to Stop the Use of Child Soldiers, (1999), *The Use of Children as Soldiers in Africa: A Country Analysis*, CSUCS, Switzerland.
4. Freud, A. and Burlingham, D.T., (1943), *War and Children*, Medical War Books.
5. Garbarino, J., (1982), *Children and Families in the Social Environment*, Aldine de Gruyter: New York.
6. Gow, Melanie *et. al.* (2000), *The Right to Peace: Children and Armed Conflict*, World Vision International.
7. Kibumba, T. Pitman, (1999), "Child Soldiers Fight War in Eastern Congo", *Reuters*, 9 Feb.
8. Machel Graca, (1996), *Report on The Impact of Armed Conflict on Children*, submitted to UN General Assembly.
9. Macksoud, M., (1991), *How to Help Children Affected by War: A Manual for Parents and Teachers*, Center for the Study of Human Rights: Columbia University.
10. Marynia, F.F., (1962), *The Adolescent*, Collier Books: New York.
11. Ressler, E.M., *et. al.* (1989), *Unaccompanied Children: Care and Protection in Wars, Natural Disasters and Refugee Movements*, New York: Oxford University Press.

12. Tesfay Aradom, (1991), *Children, War and State Sponsored Violence*, (unpublished report), Boston College.
13. UNICEF, (1994), *Children of War Wandering Alone in Southern Sudan*, UNICEF: New York.
14. UNICEF, (2000), *Children and Armed Conflict*, (unpublished note), UNICEF, Asmara.
15. UNICEF and MLHW, (2000), *The Situation of Separated Children in IDP Camps in Eritrea*, MLHW and UNICEF: Asmara.
16. UNICEF and MLHW, (1999), *Children in Eritrea Affected by the Border Conflict: A Psychosocial Needs Assessment*, MLHW and Unicef, Asmara.
17. Vanistendael, S., (1996), *Growth in the Muddle of Life Resilience: Building on People's Strengths*, International Catholic Child Bureau: Geneva 2nd edition.

6

Children with Disabilities: Family Members Meeting the Challenges

" The challenge of coping with children with disabilities is not so much for the child to adjust with the family than for the family to adjust and accommodate the challenging needs and abilities of their children with disabilities".

Introduction

This chapter is geared to understand and explore those factors that influence the family's adaptation to having a child with a handicap (CWD), that will serve as a base for intervention plans that are suggested in the next chapter on optimizing child's abilities through parents' participation. The basic premise set here is that the CWD is not just a child but, part of a complex family network and we can never fully understand it unless we try to understand him/her as a member of the family system he/she is engulfed in. Till recently, only the child's behavior and development has been studied. The need to explore the environment that surrounds the child is of recent origin starting with Bristol and Gallangher (1982). There are intergenerational factors that influence parental attitude and behaviour and these aspects also can never be ignored, more so in societies like India. There are also larger cultural groups like extended family, church, relatives, friends, community, political systems etc., which influence the family system either directly or through the other social systems.

Some of the factors that are of profound consequence are the meaning of disability to the parents and family members, their problem solving capacities and resources, the characteristics of the child, roles and relationships within family. Some factors affect the CWD directly while other factors show their impact on family members in varying degrees. We will be trying to examine only some of the factors that have direct implication for intervention as it is beyond the scope of the present chapter to probe in to all the factors mentioned above. Based on this extensive exercise coupled with the author's own experience, a desired paradigm is recommended. The areas discussed include:

- The families of children with disabilities (CWDs);
- Attitudes and responses of family members;
- The phases of accepting disability by the family;
- The impact of disability on significant family members;
- Critical factors influencing family's response to disability; and
- The desired family paradigm.

The Families of Children with Disabilities (CWD)

Basically, the family serves as the first significant training and nurturing ground for the newborn infant. The key to growth process depends on opportunities that the family affords the child as a safe place to find him/her and others in this world. The child finds this ground as a real mesh inhabited by family members. Given in Fig. 6.1 is a schematic representation of the family mesh, a CWD is born in to and brought up. The main actors of the above mesh are the immediate family members viz. the mother and father, brothers and sisters and then the other extended family members. These persons have their strengths, weaknesses, fears, attachments, needs, desires and dreams. But there are other actors too *viz.* the professionals or teachers the child may come in to contact with, neighbours, peers and the community around. All these persons exert some kind of influence on the CWD directly or indirectly, though it begins its first relationship with the mother.

And for a young child what matters most are the parents and siblings who live in the same family and in some cases the grand parents or extended family members. As we can see in Fig. 6.1, the family is an interacting unit, between father and mother, between children and parents, between children among themselves, between father and children, between mother and children and so on. What forms the base of these interactions is a set of attitudes and responses that create the healthy or non-healthy climate for the CWD to live and grow in. These attitudes and responses have a lot to do with the adaptation, adjustment, acceptances of CWDs by the family members, and in turn successful integration of CWDs within the community. It is partly through these feelings and responses that the child will sense who he/she is.

Most often we can observe an interdependence of these attitudes and responses. When the attitudes and responses are positive among parents it would evoke similar feelings among siblings and other family members. This positive attitude and response is on the other hand controlled by the quality of relationship maintained by parents among themselves, which may be the resultant of their own past upbringing, experiences, available social support and so on. Each family member has grown in to an assigned role in the family, but each, according to unique experiences and an essential personality, has also developed in to a different person. Each has strengths and weaknesses, each has fears, attachments, needs, desires and dreams that will provide the arena with multitude of possibilities for the personality development of the child.

It is therefore, obvious that, the complex interrelationships among all members, and subgroups, which form within the family, and any modifications therein, will work their influence upon each member individually and on the group as a whole. The birth of a child with a disability (CWD) is known to create 'ripples' in to a family atmosphere and relationships. It arouses problems, which will require role re-definitions and changes from each family member, initially towards accepting the disability in the new member. Even after the initial acceptance, exceptional demands will constantly be encountered.

Demands for time, for family restructures, for changing attitudes and values, and for new life styles will be made. Families will not only have to deal with these internal pressures but also with pressures exerted by outside social forces. Relatives, well-meaning friends and casual acquaintances often create additional problems by expressing their negative attitudes and false beliefs, which the family cannot avoid. Therefore, the family mesh remains a highly complicated net work and CWDs have to be seen as an integral part of this complex and intriguing family mesh. The single factor that has considerable influence on CWDs is the family climate that has been created and shaped by the attitudes and responses of parents followed by siblings and others.

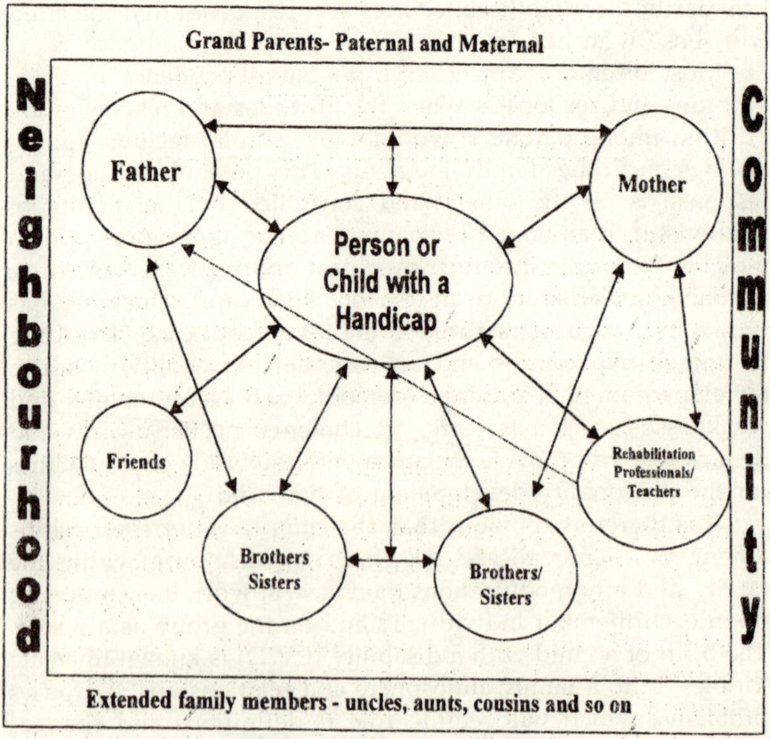

Fig. 6.1: The Family Mesh

Family, Attitudes and Responses

It is partly through the disguised attitudes, along with more expressed feelings, that the child will sense who he/she is. His self-concept will be born out of this. If the family members as a group will respond positively to him, he/she is likely to see himself/herself in a positive light. He/she may learn that he/she is beautiful, capable, alert, and that he/she has great hope for the future awaiting outside the family. On the other hand, if their responses are negative, he/she may learn that he/she is limited, unattractive, embarrassing, dull, and that his/her future is dim.

Numerous studies have been undertaken in studying the attitudes and responses of parents of CWDs during the last three decades. The most consistent finding is that attitudes and responses of parents vary widely and it is interdependent on a few critical issues that are discussed in this chapter. In general, it has been observed that the parents tend to adapt to their CWD over a period of time and possess more or less healthy attitudes and responses, though they are definitely being stressed by the birth of a CWD. The extent to which they are disturbed and their role accommodations will be determined by their previous experiences, learning, and personalities of those involved. The healthy person will make the healthy adjustment.

Those who are functioning at the brink of despair will usually find that any such catastrophic event will push them over into neurosis and possibly bring forth hitherto successfully repressed feelings, anxieties and fears. This results in expression of negative feelings towards the child. But, extreme negative responses such as hatred, rejection and positive responses such as over-indulgence are found only among small proportion of parents and it is this group of parents whose attitudes and responses can be of potent harm to the development and the very lives of CWDs. The various responses of parents can be put in a continuum as below. We may also note that there is no particular or permanent position when it comes to attitudes and feelings, and they are transitory. The same parent can oscillate from one end of the continuum to the other, based on interventions and other supportive or non-supportive factors. Fig. 6.2 represents this continuum. What is desired is a balanced as well as consistent positive attitude towards CWDs.

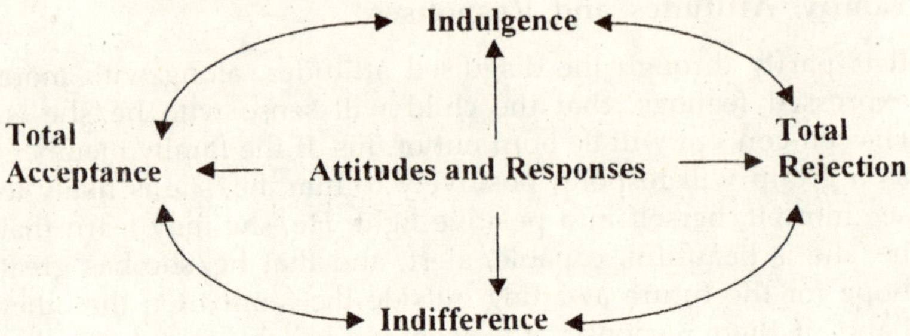

Fig. 6.2: Continuum of feelings

Some of the most common reactions and responses of parents and family members are presented in Fig. 6.3. The basket indicates that the responses can be positive, negative or neutral. The presence of a CWD strengthens some families, and it breaks some others, while the majority of the families remain without being unduly disturbed or shaken up. It has been observed that, most healthy families will meet the problem in a realistic and productive manner, making the family a closer and more meaningful unit (Buscaglia, 1985).

It is questionable and improbable that any single crisis such as the birth of CWD will cause it any great devastation. But the overriding response or reaction is more negative than positive. In general, it has found to wreck or disturb families than build families. However, some recent studies have clearly pointed out that it is not the mere presence of the CWD that create negative or positive climate in the families, and build or break families but other predisposing family factors. These factors are probed in the latter sections.

Given below is a compilation of feelings expressed by parents in clinical settings. These are manifestations of positive and negative responses. Clinical research and experience has repeatedly shown that, the greatest influence upon whether the child is either rejected or accepted in the family depends on the attitude of the mother If she is able to deal with the occurrence with reasonable acceptance and assurance, in an integrated manner, the family will also do so. If the mother is despondent, tearful, disappointed, awkward, and wanting, so too, will be her husband and other children (Buscaglia, 1985). What we as professionals aim at is to encourage more and more positive responses so that the negative ones get extinguished or over-powered and incapacitated.

Fig. 6.3: Basket of common feelings and reactions

Phases in Accepting Disability by the Family

The first bits of clinical evidence regarding the initial impact of a handicapped child on the family came mainly through personal testimonies and clinical case studies that reported a range of potential emotions from anger, despair, guilt and often courage (Turnbill and Turnbill, 1985). These initial reports, by implication, indicated the range of reactions that such an event may create. Farber (1959) was one of the first investigators to separate different kinds of stress that were created by the discovery of a handicapped child in the family. One common pattern seems to be grief reaction that stems from the symbolic death of the 'normal child' that had been expected. This is also known as the 'deviancy crisis' or 'novelty shock' (Wolfensberger, 1983). It is not uncommon for prospective parents to look forward eagerly for the chiid who is 'normal and responsive' in every respect, and to think about the stages that the child will go through on its way to adulthood.

Buscaglia (1985) found that it was the usual care-giving demand that seems to represent the dominant source of problems or stress in the family, in other words the 'chronic stress crisis'. However, it has been reported by most of the authors that it is the initial reaction that is very crucial and once the parents are assisted through it, they will be able to cope rather effectively with the rest of the process. The very commonly observed initial reaction of parents especially the mother to a handicapped child passes mainly through four phases (also see Fig. 6.4):

Shock-denial → Reaction phase → Adaptation→ Acceptance and action

The corresponding feelings of parents are presented below in Fig. 6.4. These phases in other words known as the 'stage theories' was popular among many professionals in the 1980's and 1990's. Often the first stage is shock and the last stage is acceptance or adjustment. What comes in between these two can vary tremendously from positive to negative attitudinal and behavioural changes.

Frequent Oscillation of Phases

Parent is told ↓ Psychic/crisis	Manifestations		Interventions Required
1. Shock-denial ↓	Emotional trauma, confusions, at a loss feelings; disbelief, agitation as to why this should happen to me, a sense of " mourning".	Can last from two minutes to several days	⇒ Empathy ⇒ Emotional support ⇒ Catharsis.
2. Reaction Phase ↓	Expression of : sorrow, grief disappointment,, anxiety, aggression, denial, guilt, failure,	Process oi reintegration through defense mechanisms	⇒ Listening to parent ⇒ Family study and guidance ⇒ Relaxation techniques ⇒ Counseling in neurotic depressive feelings.
3. Adaptation and understanding → ↓	Coming to terms that it is natural a child with handicap ... search for cause, cure, training and rehabilitation →		⇒ Parent training in individual and groups ⇒ Involving parents, siblings, family member ⇒ Co-therapists ⇒ Self-help groups ⇒ Individualized special training, surgery support.
4. Acceptance on action →	Parents begin to organize, seek help and information, plan for meaningful participation.		⇒ Self-help groups ⇒ Self-advocacy groups
	CRISIS RESOLUTION		

Fig. 6.4: Phases of parental reactions

This four-phase theory would paint an archetype of the perspective that parents would unavoidably undergo emotional change/catastrophe as a result of the disabled child (Ferguson and Ferguson, 1989). This tendency to convey that the child handicaps parents, causing a secondary psychosocial condition, overlooks the psychosocial context in which the parent-child relationship works. Emotions do arise in various forms and degrees in parents; but what parents feel is the product of myriad influences, not any single factor. The parental stress/reaction is "reality stress", the product of an inadequate support/service system and not due to any neurotic distortions (Wolfensberger, 1983). For example, a lack of support services and constant 'nagging of the mother' by family members for the birth of a disabled child may leave her with little assistance or respite in coping with the unavoidable needs of the disabled child. Such a parent may begin to feel tense, frustrated, angry, guilty, impatient, depressed, and the inevitable wish that 'the child were not born/dead'.

The fact remains that, though many parents do not necessarily develop neurotic reactions, most parents do pass through a stage of initial anxiety, which can be put off in the beginning itself or fanned to flame. For those with adverse emotional reactions, initial professional intervention and support can facilitate quicker and lasting adjustment. The absence of required support and intervention would delay the transition phases considerably. As a result, the parents can go on mourning the birth of a handicapped child for months or years together without providing the requisite care for the child. This is dangerous and therefore, it is recommended that the earlier we intervene with professional support the better will be the chances of good positive response from parents as well as children with disabilities.

Therefore, early support and counseling is highly essential. More recently, attention has turned from 'deviancy crisis'/initial reaction to the 'chronic stress crisis' that is, the difficulties and day-to-day life-long pulls and stress of having had to live with and care for the growing disabled child. However, very little empirical work has been done in this area.

General Impact on Family

In contrast to the normal family's progressive evolution, where the child is first an infant requiring constant care, then a pre-schooler, then in elementary school, then secondary school, then out of the home at work, then with his/her own children, the presence of a family with a moderate or severely handicapped child markedly delays or fixates the family, taking it out of the normal sequence. This creates a kind of 'disjunction' in the family evolution process (Faber, 1975), where by, family development is slowed and family roles are thrown out of synchronization or family development sequence. This disjunction does not allow easy communication between families with a handicapped child and families without a handicapped child. As a result, many families feel socially restricted and isolated.

This loss of synchrony may be particularly evident at certain points in time across the life span of the family. Mac Keith (1975) identified four major crisis periods in the maturing family development patterns in families with disabled children. The first crisis occurs when the family becomes aware that their child is handicapped; the second when the child begins receiving services; the third crisis is identified when the child leaves home and school; and the fourth when the aging parent can no longer care for the handicapped offspring.

Moreover, these disabled children pose certain increased needs that call upon modified behaviour on the part of family members. Five areas/problems that weaken the family's solidarity and that require special attention from the researcher and the service provider (Gallagher, 1983) are that:

- The child has lessened ability to form reciprocal and mutual reinforcing transactions with parents;
- The handicapped child's greater dependency needs force the caretakers within the family to spend more time and effort coping with the child's needs;
- There is the danger of a mutually reinforcing social interactions with other adults and children within the extended family, friends and neighbours;
- Families must cope with the symbolic death of their hopes and aspirations-acceptance and realistic expectations; and

- Many varied family structures must cope with these problems.

Parents of disabled children were generally portrayed as ridden by 'guilt', 'shame', 'anxiety', 'hostility', 'unfortunate feelings' etc., and this notion was disproved by Narayan (1993) in her study, which exposed that, quite many parents are not ridden by any of these feelings. These stereotypic images of parents should go. Therefore, we need to be cautious not to be hasty in ascribing guilt to the parents or in invoking it to explain their behaviour, just based on reports, in the absence of studies that made use of objective assessment instruments. Similarly, Wolfensberger (1967) takes a novel approach to the idea of guilt, suggesting that it may be beneficial, as a little guilt go a long way in motivating a parent to provide the extra attention, effort and even love that the disabled child would rightly require, and in averting feelings of parental neglect and rejection and even preventing institutionalization.

Specific Impact

It is a well-established fact that no two parents will respond in a similar fashion at the birth of a disabled child, so too family as a unit and family members. Their responses vary from 'normal' to very positive and very 'negative', and may also oscillate between two extremes. The disabled child has to face these multiple responses. Given below is an attempt made to present the impact of disabled children on significant family members *viz.* mother, father, siblings and grandparents and marital relationships of parents, as well as their common responses. But it may be noted that most of the existing research studies have concentrated on families of children with mental retardation, and very few studies dealt with families of young children with other types of disabilities. This is partly due to the fact that the social stigma and caring and training needs of children with mental retardation are more challenging than other disabilities.

Effect on Marital Relationship

Sound marital relationship is fundamental to happy and well-adjusted families. Studies both from India and western countries have substantiated the belief that satisfactory marital relationship and family cohesiveness would help parents to successfully cope up with any kind of stress, and even ward off external negative influences. Effect of disability among children on the marital relationship of their parents has been a subject of considerable research during the last two decades. The overriding conclusion is that there is no predictable trend, and the responses of the couples vary widely. In some cases, it brought parents together, in some cases it made no differences at all, while in a few other cases, it led to marital breakdown.

Several studies have examined the effect of a handicapped child on the relationship between parents. Tizard and Grad (cited in Hornebee, 2000,p.116), found a higher proportion of families with a child at home to have good relationships compared with the institution sample (62% as against 42%); and fewer to be disturbed (3% as against 13 %). The conclusion is that there is no evidence to show that keeping a disabled child at home had an adverse effect on family life, but that, on the contrary, the better-adjusted families seemed better able to cope with the problems of an abnormal child. Nihira et al. (1980) found that, where there are already families with marital disharmony, they were more likely to report feelings affected by the handicapped child, but, which was cause and which was effect could not be determined. Darling and Darling (1982) based on an extensive review of marital dissolution among parents of young children with disability and without, concluded that in general, among American population the marital dissolution rate for the handicapped group was approximately 50% higher than that of other families. In any case if intervention has to make a difference, it has to be early as most of the marital dissolution occurred before the child was 6 years.

However, marital dissolution was not observed as a direct result of the birth of a disabled child but along with many other accompanying factors. Marital dissolution was more likely to appear in families which were experiencing personal or financial difficulties before the birth of the child (Darling et al., 1982); in cases where the child was conceived premaritally (Tew et al., 1974); in families in which the care of a defective child is not a shared value (Bristol, 1984), or in families where the demands of the child outstrip the available resources of the family and the services found in the community (Hornby, 1995a; 2000).

An important and consistent finding is that, a stable and satisfying marriage does lessen the stress experienced by parents in managing children with handicap (Hornby, 2000, p.114). The point is that, factors such as social support, family support, and financial security have as much to do with family harmony and behaviour as does the disabled child. It is certainly not inherent in the family structure that a disabled child drives parents and children apart from each other (Narayan, 1993). However, some of the potential marital difficulties experienced by parents of children with disabilities that we need to consider are:

- Additional demands of caring for a CWD;
- The strain involved in having had to meet various professionals;
- Non-availability of father for treatment and the necessity for the mother to re-interpret everything to the father;
- Difficulties in sexual relationship caused by lack of privacy, fatigue, sense of isolation and fear of producing another CWD;
- Wife-blaming tendency for the birth of the child with a disability;
- Nagging parents-in-law; and
- Working status of the mother that creates additional stress.

Mother and Disability

Most of the demands towards care of the CWD fall on mother. Perhaps, at first, the child will require constant nursing, special medications, unique treatments and special diets. As a sole nurse in most cases, the mother will often has to give inordinate amounts of attention to the child and has less opportunity for relaxation and personal interaction with the other members of the family (Buscaglia, 1985). There has been a plethora of studies dealing with the adjustment and coping patterns of mothers with their children with disability.

Mothers carry out the bulk of house care and childcare in most of the families and childcare is mainly conceived as mother-care. Mothers tend to be the ones who take children to professionals and have more contact with them. They therefore, have more opportunities to discuss about their child's disability with them than fathers. Mothers tend to have more contacts with other sources of support also, such as, other mothers of children with similar disabilities, friends and family members. These factors are likely to help mothers move through the adaptation process smoothly and quickly, while the fathers struggle to come to terms with their children's disability.

Father and Disability

The role of father and the effect of having a child with a disability has generated much mythology and assumptions but very little research. It is often assumed that the 'tough unemotional male' is less likely to be affected by the disability of the child. Available information reveals that the discovery of handicap will be disturbing equally to father and mother (Mc Conachie, 1982). But, it is observed that the fathers would find less difficult to cope up with their children as they grow up with more visible signs of handicap (Lillie, 1995). There is also some evidence that the fathers are less likely to accept the existence and extent of mental handicap among sons.

Wing (1975) has observed that fathers of handicapped children are less likely to develop psychological problems (20% fathers to 57% mothers), that is more than 1:2 ratio expected in the general population. The great majority of the mothers attributed the symptoms to 'concern' over their handicapped child, whereas, few of the fathers did so. It can possibly be that those fathers are not as affected by the concerns of the care of the handicapped child as the mothers. But when compared to fathers of children without disabilities or chronically ill children, there are studies which found (Cummings 1976) that fathers of children with mental retardation were more depressed and had lower self-esteem. Houser and Seligman (1991) reported that fathers of severely retarded children were more vulnerable to social stigma and extra-familial influences.

It is also evident that the fathers are reported to experience a higher level of depression, personality difficulties, and marital relationship problems than fathers of non-handicapped children (Meyer, 1986). But, Hornby (1995 b) found no significant difference between fathers of children with Down's syndrome and other fathers on variables *viz.* stress, depression, personality factors, and marital relationships. This divergent observation may be borne out of the different disabilities addressed and therefore, no conclusive inference can be made though we no longer can claim that the fathers are unaffected by the handicap of the child and that they too do experience problems in varying degrees.

To a certain extent the problem was encouraged by the way the professionals deliver their service to the family. Fathers are not often invited. The majority of the contact is with the mother. Cummings (1976) opined that when fathers are not involved they may continue in unduly pessimistic or optimistic beliefs concerning their child's future, feel diminished competence in handling their child and have little chance in meeting and sharing experiences with other fathers of handicapped children. Clearly involvement of fathers is essential and services should be accommodating and flexible to allow this.

Siblings and Disability

Just as professionals were slow in recognizing the interactive factors in which the handicapped child impacted upon the parents, so are we limited in our appreciation of the roles played by the siblings. A literature review by Vadasy, Fewell, Meyer, and Schell (1984) revealed increased vulnerability of the siblings to stress and other problems. They found that the type of handicap has little to do with sibling reaction, but the younger and closer age-spaced siblings seem to have difficulty adjusting.

It appears that siblings play different roles depending upon the age and gender. Farber (1975) found that daughters who interacted frequently with their retarded siblings were higher in role tension. Vadsey *et al.* (1984) found that sisters in general were more prone to stress than brothers. But it has been argued that the position that siblings are inevitably affected by the presence of a handicapped sibling is totally incorrect. They found that all siblings did not respond negatively, and positive responses and relationships were also available. They found that the attitude of parents have a direct correlation with the attitudes of siblings towards children with disabilities.

Hornby *et al.* (2000) have identified a few factors that are principally responsible in arousing positive and negative impact among siblings. Factors that contribute to sibling maladjustment are:

- Excessive care-taking responsibilities;
- The need to overachieve to compensate for the sibling with a disability;
- Worry about future care-taking responsibilities;
- Worry about 'catching disabilities' or future possibilities of producing CWDs;
- Difficulty to share with the affected sibling;
- 'Cut-off' feeling from the community and friends as they are embarrassed that it will affect their friendship net-work;
- Less attention from parents which may be real or imagined as the child with disabilities demands more of parental care;
- Avoiding to discuss concerns with parents; and
- Guilt for their neglect and resentments.

However, siblings have also demonstrated positive qualities (Ferrari, 1984; Crnic and Leconte, 1986). They include:

- Choosing careers in the helping profession such as social work, teaching and so on;
- More insightful and tolerant of other's difficulties;
- More certain of their goals in life;
- Greater social competence; and
- Developing maturity beyond their years.

The Critical Influencing Family Factors

We have seen that all parents are not unduly disturbed or placed under stress, although they are more stressed than the normal population. However, there are individual differences in their reactions, with the vast majority of the parents coping with great difficulty, some coping very well and some failing to cope at all. There are various factors that account for these variations in 'coping'. To understand this, we need to know as to how stress works on people.

Recent research has acknowledged this complex and interacting nature of stress and coping, and has utilized Hill's (1959) ABCX model of family stress to explain this phenomena. Mac Cubbin and Patterson (1982) have further developed this model. Hill's original scheme begins with the identification of four components of the family's experience of stress. They are:

A—the characteristics of the stress event-interacting with;
B—the family's crisis meeting resources-interacting with;
C—the perception and definition of events-producing; and
X—the crisis reaction (as in Figs. 6.3 and 6.4).

A—The stress event

This is the problem situation that presents itself to the family for solution. For example, financial burden, sudden loss of job of the breadwinner, meeting with an accident, death, and in the present case the birth of a child with a disability. There are few studies that found the following factors as definitely contributing factors while a few others have not observed them as contributing. Based on the author's clinical experience and studies reviewed, the following may be stated as factors that contribute to the stressful events:

(i) The type of handicap: It has been reported that mental retardation and autism create more stress for parents than other types of disabilities (Bristol and Schopler, 1984; Meyer, 1986 and Gopal, 1994). So too, in the case of children with behavioral difficulties and multiple handicap.

(ii) Severity of handicap: The prevailing assumption based on clinical evidences is that, there is a positive relationship between the severity of handicap and the severity of stress experienced by parents (Bristol and Schopler, 1984 and Patterson, 1982).

(iii) Child's age and birth order: Parents of younger children are less stressed than parents of older children as they are still more hopeful of progress and improvement in the child (Gallagher and Bristol, 1989, p.302). In our clinical population, it was generally observed that the parents of first-born children are more stressed than the second -born and so on. This is because parents will have high expectation for a normal first child. Once they have a normal child, and then get a CWD, the frustration level is considered to be comparatively lesser.

(iv) Child's gender: It is believed that disability among boys is generally tolerated than among girls. Also, parents would have higher career expectation on the male child than the female child and would therefore, get unduly disturbed when a male child is disabled, and run from pillar to post in search of best available care (Bristol and Schopler, 1984 and Gallagher and Bristol, 1989). Therefore, the birth of a male disabled child gives rise to more stress than a female child. It is also widely believed that finding a marriage partner is difficult or almost impossible in case of a handicapped female than a male. However, this dichotomy is more prevalent in the case of lower middle or families of lower socioeconomic status.

(v) Co-morbid symptoms: These include associated problems such as challenging behaviours, chronic illnesses, and other problems such as fits that contribute towards the severity of the problem and delayed or poor 'response' to interventions.

(vi) Unwanted child: A child born out of an unwanted or unplanned pregnancy can be an added reason for rejecting a child with a disability (Tew *et al.* 1977).

(vii) Number of children affected: Clinical evidences clearly point out that parents with more than one disabled child are more stressed than those with only one disabled child.

(viii) Timing of the stress: The birth of the child with a disability can be more traumatic if it was immediately followed by other sorrowful events in the family such as loss of a parent, loss of job, or terminal illness among a family member and so on, than otherwise. In some cases a prior stress event prepares the family with better coping and problem-solving skills (Buscaglia, 1985). It can be a severe 'blow' to a family when the child with a disability is born to parents after years of waiting than a child born otherwise.

(ix) Working status of the mother: Working mothers reported more problems than non-working mothers in a study conducted by Narayan (1993).

B—The family's resources

McCubbin and Patterson (1982) defined resources for family adaptation as, "the psychological, social, interpersonal, and material characteristics of individual members, the family unit, and the community that may be brought in to play in reducing tension, managing conflicts, and, in general, meeting demands and needs". Limited research has been done in the area of coping factors with regard to families of handicapped children. The family resources can be internal and external as given below:

Internal resources—

- The parenting ability (adequate education, sound and financial position, good health, self-confidence, emotional maturity and mental health);
- Home-management skills (adequate support);
- Family cohesiveness especially, support of spouse and happy marital relationship;
- Friendships (enough friends to share the stress, confide and seek guidance, and feel valued and cared for);
- Social support (adequacy of support from children, maternal and paternal relatives, friends and other parents of disabled children;
- Problem-solving capacities; and
- Coping strategies such as,
  - *(a)* believing that the child's intervention program had their family's best interest at heart,
  - *(b)* learning how to help their children improve,
  - *(c)* believing in God,
  - *(d)* believing that their children will get better, and
  - *(e)* positive attitude to life and things in general.

Among all these, the predominant influence came from the spouse's support. Mothers of children who reported adequate support from their spouses reported fewer depressive symptoms, happier marriages, and received higher scores from ratings on acceptance of the disabled child and quality of parenting (Bristol and Schopler, 1984). Such resources might be added, strengthened, developed or depleted in response to the situation. These resources will also mediate with the adverse effects of demands made.

External resources

Ferguson *et al.* (1989) have cited studies that found marked difference in the stress level of parents *viz.*, the parents who were availing day care and other services reportedly had much lower level of stress and higher levels of marital integration than those who were not availing such services. Availability of affordable 'formal services' like early intervention services, home-based management, inclusive education, vocational training, therapeutic services etc., can offer palliative support resource for the affected family. Other aspects that count are the availability of right professionals, counseling services, access to services, concessions and scholarship for children with disabilities and so on. Parents who are also helped with some knowledge and insight in to themselves and their exceptional child will be able to deal with and solve their problems in their own way (Buscaglia, 1985).

X—Crisis reaction (as in Figs. 6.2 and 6.3)

This depends on how the above discussed three factors *viz.*, the characteristics of the 'stress' event, the family's crisis in meeting resources and the perception and definition of disability. This model rejects the causal-link between a given problem (A) and reaction (X). It brings in the intervening or mediating factors viz. resources (B) and subjective meaning of the problem (C). The model has been found to be effective in understanding as well as predicting factors that account for healthy adaptation in families of children with disabilities. It is an ecological model that recognizes the social and contextual nature of adaptation over a period of time and provides indicators that can facilitate healthy adaptation of families to children with disabilities. It can also serve as a base for assessment of family adaptation and for planning appropriate support for strengthening its capacities towards successful adaptation.

The Desired Family Paradigm

Family is the basic social unit, in which a child disabled or otherwise is born, nurtured and grows up. It is the first significant training ground for a newborn infant. Best understood from a socio-psychological perspective, the family of disabled children is one at par with any other family, in which there are continual reciprocal effects, family-child, family-community-child, family-resources-internal and external, each upon the other. Any crisis/ stress in any one family member affects each in turn depending upon the emotional climate and crisis meeting resources of the family.

What a child with a disability becomes is shaped by the multitude of responses of these family members *viz.*, father, mother, sisters, brothers, grandparents, and others. The disabling condition at times makes the child more 'vulnerable' to family influences whether positive or negative. The presence of a child with a disability coupled with family's resources and interpretation of 'disability' can render the family atmosphere negative and growth stifling. A child with a disability is also at the mercy of the family in meeting its special needs for development, which the family can opt to ignore.

Given our concern as the optimum normal development of the child with a disability—we need to ensure that the feelings and attitudes of family members are positive, the family climate is one of acceptance, and the family is committed to enabling the child with a disability to grow and function as near normal as possible. The discussions clearly indicate that factors such as acceptance and adaptation to the disability condition of the child, adequacy of psychological and social resources, family's subjective perception of disability are inter-dependent and intertwined with the healthy adjustment of the child. When the above factors are absent or deficient in quantity and quality, it leads to maladjustment of children with disabilities.

Our concern is to see that these elements are present in adequate measures so that the family climate promotes the optimum development of children with disabilities, resulting in even children with severe disabilities experiencing better quality of life in terms of self-image, confidence, feelings of security and functional competence to face the outside world.

It is also loud and clear that, it is the strong and healthy families that make good adjustments with children with disabilities; while, weak families may break down or fall apart. The factors mentioned above can be 'predictors' of healthy and at-risk families *viz.* attitudes and responses of the mother, father, siblings and other significant members, the characteristics of stress, adequacy of family's coping resources, and proper perception of the problem. Inadequacies are 'warning signals' for professional interventions.

Fig. 6.5 presents the desired family paradigm that is implied by the above discussion making use of 'Johari-window'. The challenge of professionals is to guide and aid families towards this healthy paradigm of functioning so that children with disabilities find a stable and secure family to grow, to love and contribute. Negative attitudes, low levels of family health and cohesion, fewer resources and low degree of acceptance of the child with a disability accompany poor development of the child. While, positive attitudes and high levels of family health and cohesion, adequate resources and high degree of acceptance of the child with a disability accompany optimum development of the child.

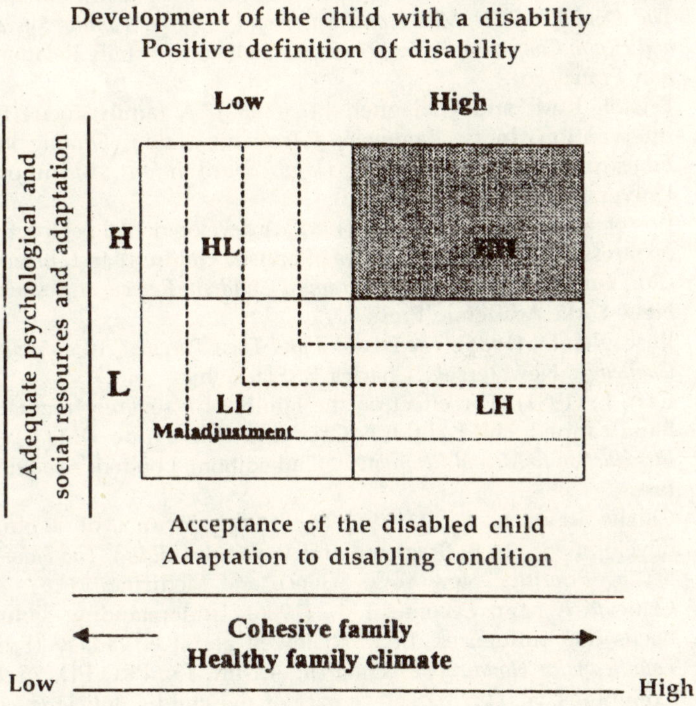

Fig. 6.5: Desired family paradigm

This however, is the 'ideal'. We generally come across situations where one aspect is very low and another one high, for example, coping resources are very low when the positive attitude is very high. Such situations need not necessarily lead to optimum development of the child with a disability though the parents and family may manage without many problems. Nevertheless, this is the reality we need to work with. We may concentrate on strengthening the strong positive areas so that it can to some extent compensate for the weak areas in the initial stages. Our aim is to increase the positive influences in order to nullify the negative repercussions, and also as to approximate the family influences to the desired positive level.

References

1. Bristol, M.M., (1984), *Families of Developmentally Disabled Children: The Double ABCX Model and Successful Coping, Family System and Health Conference Report,* National Council on Family Relations, San Francisco.
2. Bristol, K.M. and Gallagher, J.J., (1982), A family focus for intervention. In C. Ramey & P.Trohanis (Eds.), *Finding and Educating the High-risk and Handicapped Infant,* Baltimore: University Park Press.
3. Bristol, M.M. and Schopler, E., (1984), A developmental perspective on stress and coping in families of antistic children. In I. Blacher (Ed.) *Families of Severely Handicapped Children: Review of Research,* New York: Academic Press.
4. Buscaglia, L., (1985), *The Disabled and Their Parents: A Counseling Challenge,* New Jersey: Charles B. Slack, Inc.
5. Carr, J., (1981), The effect on the family of a severely mentally handicapped child. In E.F Carr and T.E. Appe (Eds.), *An Introduction to Mental Retardation,* (2nd edition), London: Academic Press.
6. Clarke-Stewark, K., (1979), The family drama of a child development. In B. Brazleton and V. Vaughn (Eds.), *The Family: Setting Priorities,* New York: Science and Medicine.
7. Crnic, K.A., and Leconte, J.M., (1986), Understanding sibling needs and influences. In R. R. Jewell and P.F. Vadasy (Eds.) *Families with Handicapped Children:* Austin, TX: PRO-ED, 75-98.
8. Commings, S., (1978), The impact of the child's deficiency on the father: A study of fathers of mentally retarded and of chronically ill children, *American Journal of Orthopsychiatry,* 46, 246-255.
9. Darling, R.B., and Darling, J., (1982), *Children Who are Different: Meetings the Challenges of Birth Defects in Society,* St. Lovis: C.V. Mosby.
10. Farber, B., (1975), Family adaptation to severely mentally retarded children. In M. Begab and S. Richardson (Eds.), *The Mentally*

Retarded and Society: A Social Science Perspective, Baltimore: University Park Press.

11. Ferguson, M.P. and Ferguson, D.L., (1989), Parents and Professionals, In P.knoblock (Ed.), *Understanding Exceptional Children and Youth,* Boston: Little, Brown and Co.
12. Ferrari, M., (1984), Chronic illness: psychosocial effects on siblings-1 *Journal of Child Psychology and Psychiatry,* 25, 459-76.
13. Freidrick, W., (1979), Predictors of the coping behaviour of mothers of handicapped children. *Journal of Consulting and Clinical Psychology,* 47(6), 1140-1141.
14. Gallagher, J.J., (1983), The Carolina Institute for Research: Early identification of the handicapped, *Journal of the Division of Early Childhood,* 7, 18-24.
15. Gallagher. J.J. and Bristol, M., (1989), Families of Young Handicapped Children. In M.C. Wang, M.C. Reynolds and H.J. Welberg (Eds.) *Handbook of Special Education Research and Practice,* 3, 295-317.
16. Gopal, R., (1994), Impact of mentally retarded on the family, *Indian Journal of Psychology,* 3, 31-37.
17. Hill, R., (1958), *Social Stresses on the Family Social Casework,* 39, 139-50.
18. Hornby, G., (1995a), *Working with Parents of Children with Special Needs,* London: Cassell.
19. Hornby, G., (1995b), Effects on fathers of children with Down syndrome. *Journal of Child and Family Studies,* 4(2), 239-55.
20. Lillie, T., (1993), "A harder thing than triumph: Roles of Fathers of Children with disabilities," *Mental Retardation,* 31(6), 438-443.
21. Mc Conachie, H., (1986), *Parents and Young Mentally Handicapped Children: A Review of Researches Issues,* London : Croom Helm.
22. Mc Cubbin, H.I. and Patterson, J.M., (1982), *Family Stress, Coping and Social Support* (pp.26-47), Springfield IL: Charles. E. Thomas.
23. Mackeith, R., (1973), The feelings and behavior of parents of handicapped children. *Developmental Medicine and Child Neurology,* 15, 524-527.
24. Meyer, D.J., (1986), Father of handicapped children. In R. R. Fewell and P.F Vadasy (Eds.), *Families of Handicapped Children,* Austin, Tx: PRO-ED, 35-73.
25. Narayan, S., (1993), Knowledge, Altitude and Perception of Parents of Mentally Handicapped Children, *Indian Journal of Social Work,* Vol. LIV, No.3, 437-447.
26. Neuhans, M., (1975), Parental Attitudes and the emotional adjustment of deaf children, In Dessinger, J.K. and Arnold, C.R, Studies in the *Psychological Foundations of Exceptionality,* California.
27. Perdersen, F., (1976), Does research on children raised in father-

absent families yield information a father influence? *The Family Coordinator,* 4, 459-463.

28. Revathy, T., (1994), Role of Grandparents in the rehabilitation of handicapped children, paper presented at *the ix World Congress on Mental Retardation* at New Delhi, India.
29. Tew, B.J., Payne, E.H. and Lawrence, K.M., (1974), Must a family with a handicapped child be a handicapped family? *Developmental Medicine and Child Neurology,* 16, 95-98.
30. Turnbill, H.R. and Turnbill, A.P., (Ed.) (1985), *Parents Speak Out Then and Now* (2nd ed.). Columbus, OH: Charles E. Merrill.
31. Vadasy, P., Fewell, R., Meyer, D. and Shell, G., (1984), Siblings of handicapped children: A developmental perspective on family interactions. *Family Relations,* 33, 155-167.
32. Wing, L., (1976), The principles of remedial education for autistic children in L.Wing (Ed.), *Early Childhood Autism* (2nd ed.) Oxford: Pergamon Press.
33. Wolfensbenner, M., (1967), Cited in Ferguson *et al. Ibid,* pp.

7

Optimizing Child's Abilities Through Parents' Participation

> ***"Unless the family is empowered, factors impeding the child's development remain or multiply. When parents are enabled through interventions in individual or group situations or both, much can be done to mitigate the negative effects and help the child to develop to his full potential".***

Introduction

This chapter is devoted for a thorough discussion on how parents could be the most potent resource in promoting development of children. After working with parents as a professional social worker and as researcher, the author has come to believe that collaborative working relationship between professionals and parents is a key factor in providing the optimum benefits for children in general and children with disabilities in particular. The author has mainly drawn on her experiences and research findings in order to provide information, which will help professionals, develop the attitudes, knowledge and skills considered essential for working effectively with parents.

Parents' participation is very often overlooked and taken for granted by professionals to realize that they end up paying heavy price for that. Parents can play a range of roles in educational set-ups *viz.*, as parents co-therapists, first-hand information providers, resource persons, advocates, assistants, decision-makers, catalysts and as partners. While executing these roles, they can be a 'buffer' or 'trigger', diminish or intensify disability, promote or impede development, and can play supplementary or complementary roles. Factors that promote or hinder their positive role-play are dealt with. Variables that influence levels of participation and typical ways in which they are involved in schools and rehabilitation set-ups are also discussed.

Various strategies for working with parents are considered, and a model for family and parent intervention is suggested. Indications for family interventions are looked in to. Different forms of parental participation in children's rehabilitation are considered. These include assessments, setting of education or training goals, follow-up at home, review of progress and so on. Skills for improving parent participation and skills for working with challenging and difficult parents are also considered. These skills can also be generalized into any other set-ups concerned with parents.

Rationale for Involving Parents

First and foremost, it is considered that parents are children's natural teachers since they teach self-help and language skills in the early years. Parents are privileged to spend most of the time with their children, and they have more time than anybody else does for their children. Involving parents would have long-term gains for their children since parents would have learned skills they can use throughout childhood. Studies on early intervention have also shown that PP resulted in faster, better and durable impact.

Training parents to work with children is more cost-effective in terms of professional's time, and more so in the context of acute shortage of adequate number of them. Most importantly, the whole process of rehabilitation of children with disabilities (CWDs) has to do with 'interpersonal' relationships—human interactions, be it speech therapy, physiotherapy, behaviour therapy and nerve-stimulation. If a therapist handles a child with a smile in his/her eyes, affection in the heart, and genuine concern, the response of the child would be many folds better, than if someone handled the child with frown and anger. Nobody is more blessed with this 'humane touch' than the child's own mother and father. There are other benefits too as shown in Box 7.1. Having said so, we shall now turn to the roles of parents (Fig. 7.1).

Box 7.1: Benefits of PPP

- Improved communication between parents and children;
- Higher level of performance/progress in the children;
- High school attendance and less destructive behaviour;
- Increased likelihood of completing the entire program (schooling/therapeutic interventions);
- More positive parental attitudes and behaviour;
- More likelihood of adequate follow-up support by parents;
- Increased self-confidence and a sense of accomplishments among parents;
- Increased parental satisfaction with the center/schools;
- Improved professional and educator morale;
- Higher parental expectations of children;
- Improved school/center climate;
- Increased likelihood of parental participation at higher levels-policy;
- Parents typically are powerful reinforcing agents; and
- Parents know their children better than others and generally spend more time with their children than do professionals.

Roles Envisaged and Performed by Parents

The origins of professionals involving parents can be traced to the early intervention programmes, such as Project High/Scope and the Portage Projects implemented in UK in the sixties, which rose in popularity throughout the world. The importance of PP subsequently began to grow resulting even in legislation making it mandatory to involve parents in education programs (Federal Legislation PL 94-142 passed in 1975). Subsequently, many other areas for involving parents such as 'early intervention projects', 'reading', behaviour training, were explored and made use of. Recently, involving parents in assessments, review of their progress both in ordinary schools and special schools has become very common. Parents emerging as partners in service delivery is a revolutionary concept contemplated by many but practiced by a very few.

In this journey through PP, we have discovered that there are numerous roles that parents can take on and they are based on our approaches or understanding of parents. There are various approaches to parent-professional relationships, based on different set of assumptions, goals and strategies. These approaches range from those, which attempt to minimize parental involvement to others that actively promote it. Parents play various roles; such as, informants, facilitators, volunteers/ helpers, co-therapists, decision-makers, advocates, resource persons/experts, partners and so on. Among these, the latest and most preferred but practiced less is the partnership model. The most important roles are explained below.

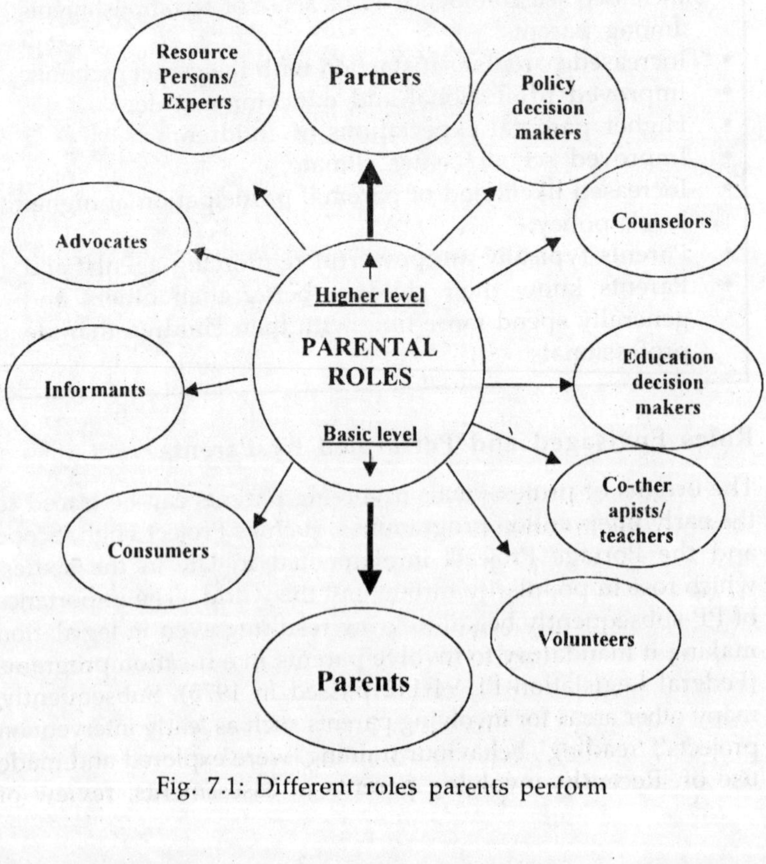

Fig. 7.1: Different roles parents perform

Parents as parents: Diamond (1981), a physically handicapped psychologist has shared her insightful experience as a trainer: "Something happens in a child while relating to a disabled child; he/she forgets that they are kids first. I used to think about that a lot when I was a kid. I would be off in a euphoric state, drawing or coloring r cutting out paper dolls, and as often as the activity would be turned into an occupational therapy session. "You are holding the scissors right", "sit up straight so that your curvature doesn't get worse". "That era was ended when I finally let lose a long and exhaustive tirade". "I am just a kid! You cannot therapize me all the time! I do not think about my handicap all the time like you do."

Children with disabilities need time to be children—to play, to be 'unprogrammed', to make mistakes, to be clumsy, to enjoy. Sometimes parents need help in learning to be parents, and treat their children as children first, and then as children with disabilities. Parents also need help in not giving 'too much' (indulgence) and not 'too less' (neglect) but proper care to CWDs just like they would do to any other children. Raising a CWD demands the best a parent can give.

Informants: It is a fact that nobody else knows better about a child than his/her own parents. Professionals till recently have tended to undervalue the knowledge parents possess of their children. This has resulted in many parents feeling frustrated at the 'deaf ear syndrome' of professionals, who tended to talk at rather than listening to what parents have to say. Parents can share useful information such as the child's adaptive behaviour, self-help skills, peer interaction in the neighborhoods, medication schedule, language development, development history, previous diagnostic reports and any special concerns that should be concerned while assessing the child.

Helpers/volunteers: Many parents are involved in assisting teacher/professionals, as helpers or volunteers. They fulfill a wide range of helping roles including such activities as preparing classroom materials, minding the class for the special teacher on a regular basis or when the teacher is busy with some other activities of the institution, take charge of recreational activities, helps in attending to the needs of children with severe disabilities and so on.

Co-therapists: Here the professionals consider themselves as main sources of expertise on CWDs, but recognize the benefits of using parents as a resource. They consider that some of the resources can be transmitted from them to parents so that the parents can carry out some form of intervention with their children. For example, in the case of children requiring physiotherapy every day, it is not possible for the physiotherapist to provide therapy every day, and the family members are taught the techniques that can be practiced at home for a stipulated period of time. The therapist however, remains in control and decides on the intervention to be used. It has been found that mothers were very effective in carrying out the behavior therapy, physiotherapy, speech therapy and other therapeutic interventions based on the instructions and guidance given by the professionals. In addition to child outcomes, these parent programs have been found to be promoting family adjustments, and functioning.

The evaluation of the utility of training of mothers to work with their own children with autism was shown to be superior to direct instruction by trained staff (cited in Gallagher and Bristol, 1989, p.308). A broad-based family intervention was found to have reduced the rate of institutionalization from one-fifth to one-tenth. Based on an extensive review of various experimental studies, Baker (1984.p.344) has conclude that: "there is compelling evidence that parents who have participated in the training increase their knowledge of teaching principles and their skills in applying these with their child".

Decision-makers: In the IEP (Individualized Education Program), parents could insist on certain services which they feel are very essential to their child. For example, parents must have noticed the child's special liking for music, and insist for more exposure in that area, while setting the IEP. So too in case of other therapeutic interventions. The parent is given a say in the decision making process, while the professional's role is to provide them with relevant information and a range of options from which to choose. Professional would also guide them to choosea from the alternatives available. In this way, parents are much more likely to be satisfied with the services that they receive, to feel more competent about their parenting, and also less likely to be dependent on the professionals.

Resource persons/experts: It is based on the assumption that parents have important expertise to contribute and that the interaction between parents and teachers around the management of the CWD will enhance the intervention program as well as the objectives of the rehabilitation center or school. For example, two parents with sports background were involved in designing curriculum and training in the area of physical education. This was a novel way of involving parents in children's training, which increased the resources available at the center and provided opportunities for parents and professionals to learn from each other. But, this involves a great degree of openness and maturity in the professionals to let parents know what is being done and how it is being done, which can be threat to many professionals.

Facilitators: While the training and management is the task of the professionals, the parents duty is to see that the child reaches to the school/center on time, with required materials or equipment and if possible, following up the home-tasks judiciously.

Advocates: This term is used here to mean securing the rights and interests of a client, and in this case the rights of children. Advocacy can take different directions but is mainly directed at state agencies, local policies of NGOs, government service agencies, or potential employers.

Parents as counselors: Counseling of one segment of the population with troubles by another segment with similar troubles has greater positive impact; as it is wide spread it is achieving a qualitative change and even assuming a quasi-professional aspect by getting organized with recognizable objectives. One of the most valuable contributions that parents have made has been in the area of counseling and supporting each other with noble and successful daring examples in making a new and better life for their children.

Parents as group members: Most parents mature quite rapidly under the stimulus of the group. Self-pity fades when they find that they are not alone. Soon they will be seeking to learn from and emulate the parents who have met their problems successfully. And before they know it, they are experiencing the healing that goes with helping another family. They can slip back at any stage.

Parent as partners: The most appropriate model for effective working relationship between professionals and parents is the partnership model, in which professionals are viewed as experts in their profession (social work, occupational therapy, physiotherapy, education and so on), and parents as experts on their children. In this case, the relationship can be a partnership, which involves the sharing of expertise and control in order to provide the optimum training for all children. Both can play complementary and supplementary roles, thereby increasing the potency of the relationship.

For example, the parent will share her skills in speech and language stimulation, and music, and the professionals with guide regarding the specific therapeutic aspects of speech therapy—how of stimulation and why. An essential aspect of the partnership envisaged is that it must be based on mutual respect. For example, it requires professionals and parents to listen to each other and give due consideration to each other's views. It involves a long-term commitment to a wide range of activities. It must encompass a sharing of planning and decision-making responsibilities. The four key elements of such a partnership are *two-way communication, mutual support, resource sharing and collaboration, joint decision making and enhancement of learning at home and institution.* For example, a fundraising program of the school, parents may help with the best contacts, and involve in that activity only and not beyond that. Still it serves the purpose. Parent-professional participation (PPP)—involves time, to grow and mature.

Graduation from Recipients to Partnership

Fig. 7.1 indicates a subtle line that divides the roles of parents in to higher and basic levels. The lower level marks the basic roles of parents, while the upper side denotes the 'higher' level functions. It is not possible for all parents to jump into higher level role-parents in the beginning itself, when they are struggling to cope with the reality crisis. At the same time, it is a fact that each and every parent can graduate themselves to perform the higher level functions over a period of time with the required support and guidance from professionals. It may be noted that the parents self-help groups that sprung up in the eighties had very little support from the professionals.

However, professional support if delivered in the way it

should be, is intended to make these 'moves' more effective and rewarding. Parents who are able to be effective in discharging higher level functions may not necessarily be effective in carrying out the basic functions. For example, there is a parent who is a scientist who is excellent at advocacy levels and in preparing policy documents, but is very poor when it comes to following up the child's home programs. In reality, most parents become effective in performing the basic functions and get stuck at that level. As professionals, we should not be dissatisfied with this. Only few parents may be able to rise to higher levels. Many factors account for this such as availability of time, personality traits, professional background, personal commitment, rich experience, support received and so on.

Another paradox here is, very often we professionals are comfortable with parents as long as they are good at carrying out their basic functions. We do get disturbed when they start questioning our faulty systems such as institutionalization (as a policy and not as a necessity) or raising their legitimate demands for more guidance from teachers, or flexibility in school policies, idea of inclusion of parents in the school committees and so on. We are happy as long as they stay at the comfort zones of reinforcing the existing system. But we try to suppress them when they challenge us or stir us from these zones. There are institutions that even called of parent associations when they started questioning issues such as:

- Making use of their disabled child for impressing upon the visitors without permission from parents;
- Over-training the child in dance for the interest of the institution to the neglect of the child's vocational skill development;
- Exorbitant charge for services that cannot be reasoned out;
- Professionals using CWDs for their career development;
- Professionals not sticking to their commitment; and
- Professionals fixing up meetings to suit their convenience.

Issues are numerous that drive professionals to suppress

parents from being assertive to advocacy levels. It happens when professionals view these issues as 'threats' rather than opportunities for growth promotion. The reason for the functioning of many parent organizations as separate entities is borne out of this professional suppression. Its implication is loud and clear. It is very often professionals who control the 'empowering' process of parents from being good parents to partners in seeking equal opportunities for their children with disabilities. By saying so we do not overlook the very few professionals who have grown to accept parents as partners. There is also no undermining of the incidences where the parental efforts did end up causing more harm than good in the successful implementation of services, owing to their vested interests. But, the positive impacts undoubtedly override such stray incidences of negative repercussions. No doubt, partnership with parents is one of the formidable challenges that most professionals have to face.

Parents Involvement Process

We will be able to race out a process to positive, productive, substantive PP. It is neither easy, nor short nor does solve every problem, but it is highly potent and it works. The author (Narayan, 1993), has observed in her study that a combination of factors are responsible in facilitating adequate PPP, such as knowledge, attitude, perception of the problem and expectation of parents. She observed three types of parents with adequate disposition, parents with near adequate disposition and parents with inadequate disposition. The first group of parents possessed all the above characteristics in adequate measures, whereas, it was deficient in other groups. The implication is that, increase these positive qualities to derive optimum results in terms of PPP.

The process begins with the first interaction of professionals with parents as described earlier. The process will more or less follow a developmental sequence but, as with any other process, can respond flexibly to the needs and characteristics of any particular parent or group of parents. They are briefly sketched out below:

Chart 7.1: Parents Involvement Process

Step-1

- — Parents and professional begin to communicate on a regular basis, based on individualized strategies
- — Efforts towards personal relationships continue
- — Child's strengths are emphasized, optimistic and positive attitude to weaknesses.

Step-2

- — Parents come to center to accompany children/class room visitors
- — Needs for information about the child and knowledge are met/addressed

Step-3

- — Parents participate in the therapeutic programs/wider variety of classroom activities
- — Broader perspectives, more global understanding of disability, and management
- — Opportunity to meet and interact with other parents
- — Involvement of parents in areas of skill and interest

Step-4

- — Parent-to-parent support
- — Still broader concerns
- — May initiate involvement beyond classroom/therapeutic sessions
- — Embryonic stage of parent group

Step-5

- — Parents get organized as a group
- — Informal meetings and get-togethers take place
- — Discussion on common issues/problems
- — Discover endless possibilities for PP
- — Birth of projects/programs

Step-6

- — Involvement in policy making and program development
- — Powerful agents of change

Parents need to change their nature of involvement. For example, it is much less appropriate for parents of teenagers to visit and spend time working in their children's classrooms. Yet, clearly, one important component of parent-professional interaction is consistent communication such as the 'phone hours'—a time set to call up and talk without feeling that they are violating privacy. Whatever their specific strategies are, professionals must build structures for continued involvement with parents. Professionals- teachers, social workers, therapists must work together to create better methods of empowering parents.

Having discussed about the roles and process, we may conclude that families should have a choice about their type and level of involvement. Along with greater services, there must be greater options. Not every parent can become a good teacher, or co-therapist, nor every father can become a surrogate mother. The great diversity of family needs and resources calls for a program that will make available a menu of services to meet those differing requirements.

Factors in Parent Participation

In our practice we come across a spectrum of participation among parents. They can be put on a continuum from "actively participating" parents to "non-participating parents". In between we find the parents who are passive participants. Based on experience and empirical analysis (Narayan, 1993), the participation of parents can be succinctly presented as below.

		Knowledge and management know-how	
		Low	**High**
Acceptance	**Low**	**L-PP**	**L-PP**
Positive attitude	**High**	**Passive PP** **H-PP**	**Active PP** **HH-PP**

Fig.7.2: Paradigm of parent participation

In general we come across these following four types of PP:

1. Parents with low levels of knowledge and acceptance, and low levels of PP (To equate, LK+LA= LL-PP)
2. Parents with low levels of acceptance and high levels of knowledge, and low levels of PP (LA+HK= L-PP)
3. Parents with high levels of acceptance and low levels of knowledge, and passive participation (HA+LK= H-PP-passive)
4. Parents with high levels of knowledge and acceptance, and high levels of PP (active), (HK+HA= H-PP).

On closer examination, we learn that high level of acceptance leads to better PP than high levels of knowledge alone. Therefore, knowledge binding cannot be aimed at the neglect of positive attitude and acceptance. The implication is that either both should go side by side or acceptance may be given precedence. Our aim is to promote the fourth group of PP. This paradigm gives the direct clue to promoting PP *viz.*, adequate knowledge and management skills, high level of acceptance and positive attitudes.

We may also find that the non-participating parents manifest their responses to professional interventions in various forms. Some of the parents may be very difficult to work with. The stance to be taken is although parents are considered as experts of their children, professionals are experts in various disciplines. Some conflicts are bound to arise as a result of this. This does pose a great challenge to professionals, although these difficulties are overweighed by the potential benefits. The implication is that, the parents' participation should be carefully planned to minimize these conflicts.

Professionals must accept that, it may be difficult to work with some parents as listed below:

- Un-supportive parents;
- Uncooperative parents;
- Hostile, complaining, threatening parents;
- Abusing and neglecting parents;
- Parents with personal, family, marital problems, or overworked;

- Vulnerable parents;
- Parents who expect too much or too little; and
- Parents with a different cultural background.

It may also be noted irrespective of the type of parents, a host of conditions cause parents to behave in negative and non-productive ways and prevent them from contributing positively towards development of their children. Very often we observe the symptoms manifested in them, as aggression, indifference, demanding, abusive, neglect, uncooperative, non-supportive and so on. Very often our unempathetic, stereotypic interpretations tend to reinforce their negative behaviour, instead of inspiring them to increase their positive behavior. This mainly happens because, we as professionals do not take time or make effort to understand these parents, and enable them to come to terms with their problems. If we really try to understand them, we come to realize that all of them are basically 'good parents' that love their children and want the best for them. So too every parent is capable of PPP. What is essential is 'preparing' and 'equipping' them for PPP. Family intervention becomes imperative in order to prepare, enable and empower parents to offer the expected participation, as it is one of the very effective strategies in this direction.

Family Intervention (FI)

> "If you can help parents convert their problem into good for mankind, their agony into a harmonizing melody, their life-shaking experience into a life-making one, you will find the precious jewel in your professionalism that you can ever think of..."

In the midst of society's misconceptions, negative attitudes and discrimination, is the child with a disability; and with him is his/her family. How can he be helped? What reinforcements would she/he need to survive adequately, realize her/his potentials, be able to contribute according to his/her abilities? What reinforcements do the family need? And how can these be provided? Some parents are faced with the reality of CWDs as persons living in a family group and if they do not act positively, the child is doomed.

The role of parents is a critical factor in children's success throughout their developmental years and the family climate surely improves or impedes the development of the child However, a very frequent complaint of professionals and educators (general and special) is that the parents they most want to see seldom turn up or participate in children's programs. On the other hand, parents are critical of professionals' attitudes and behaviour. They often feel that professionals do not try to understand them, they have 'deaf-ear' to their views and suggestions, and possess the attitude that parents are complete 'ignoramuses' so that any conclusion they reach regarding their own child is categorically ignored. They consider all parents of CWDs as 'disturbed' because their children are disabled. Professional put up a show of 'omniscience and omnipotence'. They put up a facade of professional competence. These feelings create 'distance' between parents and professionals.

In reality, we find that parents are more enthusiastic than professionals to participate in many programs; but they fail to do so, as they are stopped by the 'stumbling blocks' in their lives. We examine these blocks and see whether we can convert them into 'building blocks' towards PPP. We come across 'good' participating parents and 'bad' non-participating parents. This section considers the need for family intervention as a strategy for removing 'blocks' and facilitating effective PPP.

Family intervention, in very simple terms is viewed as a process by which professionals offer therapeutic support to the family in order to enable a family to overcome its stress/crisis, and develop better coping skills as well as enrich the emotional climate of the family, so that the child is accepted, loved, cared for and feels secure. It also aims at promoting the optimum development of the child- be it disabled or otherwise.

FI is not a new kind of intervention, it is only a model that can be applied for any intervention that concerns the family- be it counseling, casework, family therapy, marital therapy, psychotherapy and so on. It is not the purpose of the chapter to deal with these therapeutic models .The details of one form of intervention viz., counseling is however, discussed in the tenth chapter. This chapter would only deal with aspects that are unique to the counseling/ FI of parents of CWDs.

The underlying assumption is that most people deal with

their problems (with greater or lesser success) throughout their lifetimes, that if we can identify what 'obstructions' or difficulties they now encounter, we may have a cogent entry point for help. By this diagnostic question we may find our immediate focus for treatment- to reinforce, to restore, or refashion the client's own problem-solving operations. We assume that as in the past they try to deal with, to cope, and to master their problems, and they continue to do so. But, they would require support now.

Professionals are now dealing not only with the areas of diagnosis and placement, but also with the complex task of helping the family and child live together more comfortably at home. Moreover, the purpose of providing maximum benefits to the child must be interlocked with minimal stress to total parental needs and family functioning as both the children and the family are faced with making adjustments to and in the community in which they live.

A young couple had just heard the diagnosis of retardation for the first time. In the hostile tirade, the mother got agitated with the social worker, she vehemently denied that her child could be retarded, attacked the doctor and blamed herself. Towards the end of the outburst she cried" nothing I ever do is correct. How will I ever be able to raise this child". In this plead for help, the social worker realized the mother's immediate fear and denial of the diagnosis as resulting from her shaken confidence in being successfully able to handle her mothering role with the disabled child.

This could be an area that could be worked with realistically in family intervention, since she was indeed performing successfully in her mothering role with her other two children. The husband's support to his wife was encouraged. With help and attitudinal change the mother was enabled top depend again on her inner strengths and resources in coping with the child, this in turn paved the way towards better understanding of the child's limitations and freed her to work on other aspects of the problem. (Schild, 1970; p. 358).

In contrast to the medical conditions, treatment of CWDs rests primarily with the parents and not with the professionals, even if the younger one attends a center. It usually consists of helping a child to achieve optimal development and maximum use of his/her capacities. To do this effectively, parents need help in working through their own feelings and adjustments as well as practical advise in regard to their everyday problems. Sometimes, it can be deficiency in knowledge that is basic to the futile efforts and frustration of parents in coping with the problem. The supplying of necessary facts and the implication in the context of an emotionally supportive therapeutic relationship is the first step towards re-establishing parental planning and action that is appropriate and productive.

Given in Figure 7.3, is a model for family intervention irrespective of the method we follow, be it case work, group work, counseling, family case work, family therapy, marital therapy, psychotherapy and so on. The basic steps remain the same *viz.*, starting from initial contact, through study and understanding, conflict resolution to the termination of professional relationship. During the initial contact we come to know of the parents and their situation, (ABC-pattern described in the previous chapter on Families of CWDs), that includes their strengths and weaknesses, support resources and problem areas. This should lead to the next process-diagnosis.

To take on the role of parenting is one thing. To find one self as the parents' of a child with a disability is something else. To normal parenting is added a number of additional burdens, such as the physical care and child tending (long after the parents of non-disabled children have been relieved) and from it is subtracted a number of gratification(s); he is realistically worried about what his child can look forward to, what sort of economic and social future can be hoped for, what parent is supposed to do, how he/she is supposed to act in relation to the child's best interest, become troubling questions. In brief, into the roles of this parent has been added an extra load of emotional, economic and social problems needing action.

We have discussed in the previous chapter that the responses that parents make to these common problems differ. Therefore, the nature of support parents need also differs. All parents do not require the same degree or kind of intervention. This is what professionals should design at diagnosis stage: differential intervention. The ABC pattern described in the previous chapter helps to pinpoint deficiencies, and reasons for such incapacity, and family strengths. It also helps us to gauge where the parents are going through 'deviancy crisis' or the 'chronic stress crisis', the daily grind of caring for the special needs. Appropriate guidance can be offered accordingly.

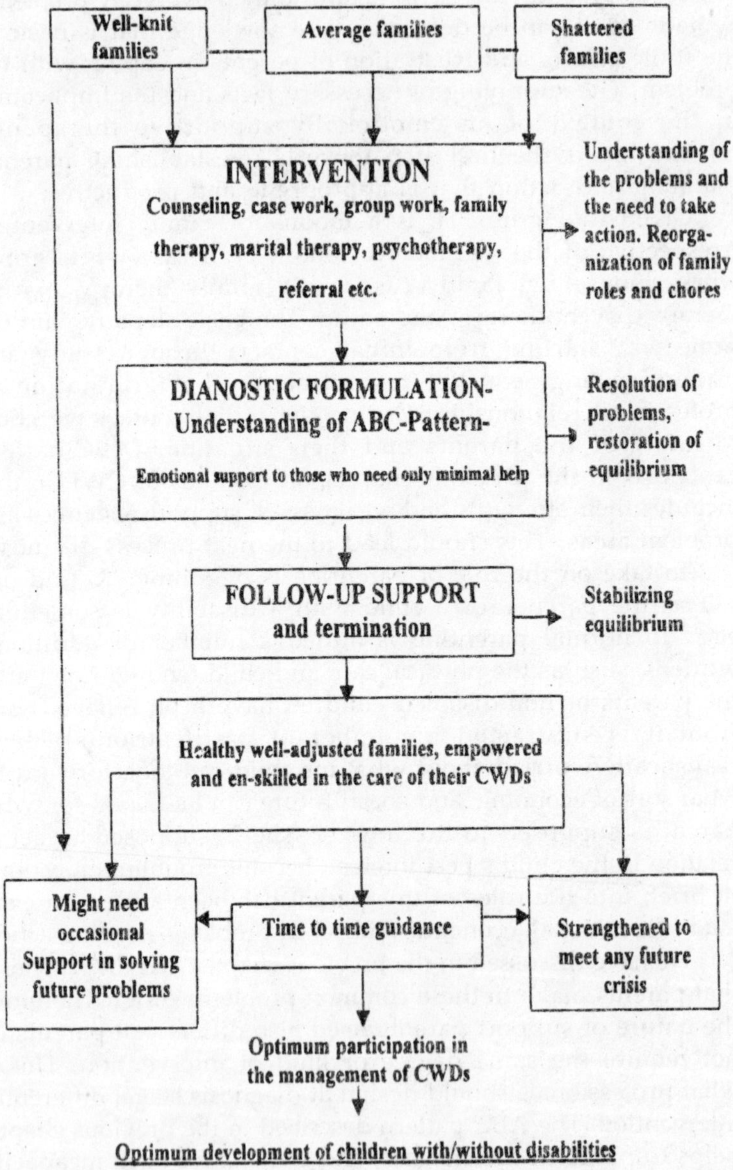

Fig. 7.3: Optimum development of children with/without disabilities

If they are struggling with the 'deviancy crisis', they need to be helped with first aid of psychological support and support in accepting the facts, followed by guidance in management. Those parents who have fully digested the nature of a child's disability may be ready to take necessary steps by which to cope with it- early stimulation, special education and behaviour therapy. But, these services may be non-existent or inaccessible to him/her. Similarly, the mother would need someone to take care of her child for a few hours so that she can attend to some other important tasks issues of deficiency of resources.

We also come across parents with emotional disturbances. The diagnostic question here is to understand whether the current disturbances are triggered by the disability or the resultant of long established conflicts. When the former situation calls for short term and easier solutions, the latter and perhaps more chronic problems would need long term and recurrent interventions. In some cases, it may indicate the need for psychiatric interventions. Long term help with realistically limited goals may be anticipated if the emotional disturbances of the parent are found to be chronic. Likely, various alternate solutions are available for the numerous problems confronted by parents. Professional's duty is to identify these and guide them. Involving the family as a group will have extreme positive effect upon the scope and need for any later intervention.

It may be noted that the termination of therapeutic relationship should be gradual and smooth and never abrupt. The clients must be adequately prepared for termination, with contract for follow-up if indicated. It is not necessary that all parents have to pass through the steps in Chart-7.1 to become strong and capable of managing CWDs. Some parents would only require initial support, and then they can go on by themselves, with or without very little guidance. Some parents would however, would require long-term help. It may also be noted that some parents even after reaching the level of action, may slip back to earlier levels at times, and they need to be supported to pull themselves up.

In case of families which are facing multiple problems for instance, marital problems, depression, non-acceptance of the child, financial crisis as the mother has to give up job, lack of adequate support system and so on, we do not start working with all the problems at a time. The diagnostic formulation guides the professionals to identify the most pressing problems, and deal with that first. It is quite possible once the parents are guided through problem-solution of the most difficult problem, they might acquire enough problem-solving skills to handle other problems by themselves or with minimal professional support.

It may also be noted, that even the strongest of families get disturbed on hearing the news of the disability of their children, and therefore, services for them should not be overlooked. "The onslaught of the exceptionality can cast a heavy blanket of gloom over the healthiest, the most solid family" (Buscaglia, 1985). All they need is at times a 'gentle pat' by the professional. But, even an insignificant amount of support as it appears cannot be neglected, as a 'spark neglected can lead to fire'. Such a state of even mild anguish should not be allowed to continue in terms of mental health for the mother and father and all children involved.

Therefore, it is critical that professionals who recognize such a condition work towards alleviating it as gently and as quickly as possible. It is succinctly put as, "Take care of your child with his/her very special needs, reach out for help and direction, but take care of yourself too. Stay alert to the needs of your husband (wife) and other youngsters in the family. More than anything else your child with a disability will benefit from passiveness within the family group. You have asked what you can do to help well, this is one area you can do much. Indeed, only you can do it" (*Ibid*).

Parents are human beings, they want solutions neatly packed and promptly delivered, and they must be counseled that no single approach or discipline or program or school or institution has all of the answers for all children. They must judiciously explore a number of possibilities, using all of the wit and wisdom at hand, perhaps what is expected is an extra counseling session after a cooling-off period.

When Do We Begin FI

FI for CWDs will have to consider the special physical or mental limitations of the child who is disabled, her/his self-concept, total family environment, their present level of integration and their total emotional and social adjustments. It will also be concerned with the cognitive abilities, vocational skills and future of CWDs. As we know, most of the formation of a child's self-concept will occur during his/her early years, and therefore, the best kind of counseling/intervention for CWDs, should always be family counseling or family intervention.

This intervention must begin as early as possible with the family, if possible, immediately after the birth of the child who has a disability continue with them as long as it seems necessary, into adulthood and beyond. Involving the family as a group, early, will have an extreme positive effect upon the scope and need for any later interventions. It may be noted that counseling a CWD and his parents is not a matter of *remaking people.* It is concerned mostly concerned with trying to clarify feelings and issues, which are standing in the way of their 'making of themselves'. It is involved with creating for them a non-threatening, accepting environment where they are encouraged to find, learn, and enjoy new self-affirming feelings, knowledge and behavior and put them into positive action for the good of all (Buscaglia, 1975).

Spacing of FI Sessions

FI can be spaced. CWDs may be 'slow' in responding to intervention, which can be frustrating, if attention is not paid towards adequate preparation, and concentration is on the 'change' in the child. Parents need intensive intervention in times of crisis but in addition they need a continued support. The latter can be less intensive and made available to them over a long period of time. Such counseling/intervention should be properly spaced and educationally focused, to help parents with the practical problems of daily living with their CWD. This is essential in sustaining the mental health of the whole family unit. They may need an 'extra' session after the cooling off period. *"Now I have given you the facts...lets us get together after a week, and explore what possibilities exist for your child. We both can think about it."*

Timing of FI

Much has been written about the importance of the initial informing of parents usually by the physician. In retrospect, parents are much critical of the doctor's failure to discuss developmental and prognostic implications frankly and realistically. They frequently report a callous, perfunctory attitude that intensifies their disturbed reaction to the diagnosis. In such instances, the professional may feel a sense of having failed and may be attempting to deny his own emotional involvement. While the most thoughtful and sensitive early handling can only mitigate that impact of what has occurred, it can help establish a frame work for the family to engage the healthier part of their ego in the first vital stages of crisis response. More details on skills required in FI/counseling is provided in chapter 10.

Need to Involve All Family Members

Research evidences reviewed in chapter 7 are convincing that the father's support can do a lot towards stress-reduction in mothers. Therefore, Both parents need to be pulled along together in their understanding and acceptance. If a balance of responsibility is created from the beginning, the unified effort will profit each other in turn. Further, it has been amply proved that the status of a marital relationship is significantly correlated with family adjustment to disability.

Our most prime goal must be to ensure that the home is a relaxed and pleasant place, a source of strength to the child. It should not shield the child from the outside world, but give the courage to cope with it. This means that the child must feel like an accepted, valued member of the family, sharing plans, decisions, special occasions and concerns. I strongly feel that the home is the child's anchor and that other considerations are secondary.

FI should be directed towards the CWD as well as the other significant family members viz. siblings, grandparents, uncle and aunts, as they all exert influence on the child in some way or the other. FI for the CWDs and their families, then, becomes a cooperative relationship. Each member is expected to examine their feelings and problems towards the CWD and the resultant behaviour. It encourages each family member to gain more insight into their behaviour and others in the family. The goal is towards a better and more comfortable level of action in order to deal with the disabling condition and the unique family and personal problems it may create. Management of the CWD becomes not just the parents' responsibility, but collective responsibility.

Indications for FI

One mother complained about her child's temper tantrums. The disturbance the child was creating was upsetting to the entire household and the mother felt at her wit's end. The parents were beginning to feel that to keep the child at home was almost impossible. Closer examination revealed that in reality the mother, caught up in her own disappointment and her attitude that a disabled child was totally worthless, considered the child not worth bothering to discipline. Also, the father was non-supportive leaving all discipline to his wife. Hence, the mother was responding to the tantrums with anger and helplessness, and was permitting herself to be manipulated by the child. The youngster having no external controls put on his behaviour, became increasingly infantile and difficult. This gave validation to the low value placed on him by his mother.

When the mother gained insight that she was reacting differently to this child than to her normal offspring, she began to cope with the problem. Her self-esteem increased with her more effective management of the child. In addition, the father was helped to participate more meaningfully in the child's discipline, thereby giving his wife emotional support. As the child's behaviour improved, the parents acquired a new appreciation of him. This in turn helped them to evaluate better the considerable potential latent in their son with cerebral palsy and to enjoy a more favorable relationship with him in the home situation. Other siblings too started liking to have him with them and enjoy his company. (Schild, 1970).

Before we discuss the details of FI we just have a look at our main target group- children in general and CWDs in particular. The other indications for FI are:

- Marked delay in progress in the child;
- Poor or nil-follow-up by parents;
- Irregularity to interventions;
- Shows symptoms of 'neglect';
- Symptoms of 'child abuse';

- Disinterest in intervention programs;
- Highly demanding and non-cooperative;
- Visible emotional disturbances in the parents;
- Disagreements of parents during interview;
- Visible emotional disturbances in the child;
- Challenging behavior of the child;
- Negative and unhealthy attitudes;
- Lack of response to parent meetings/invitations;
- Absolute neglect of children with no intervention;
- Opting for institutionalization;
- Resistance to inclusive education or any other intervention; and
- Symptoms of anxiety, depression and other psychiatric problems.

Working in Groups

While FI is useful to work with parents at individual level, various group approaches are available to deal with parents' in-group situations. Group processes are helpful to parents who are basically mature parents whose functioning is temporarily impaired by the overwhelming nature of their problem, to parents with a tendency to projection and intellectualization, to parents with pronounced, though well-controlled feelings of hostility, who can find relief through limited acting out, and to parents with dependency needs which may be met through group identification and support.

Group counseling has advantages for those parents who suddenly feel cut off from the mainstream of the uncomplicated and conventional life around them. They are given opportunity to meet with parents who are struggling with the same trauma.

Various types of groups have evolved in order to cater to the needs of parents and other family members. Self-help groups (MENCAP, CRUSE) and advocacy groups have emerged to support parents of children with a wide range of difficulties. In addition, workshops have been developed to address the needs of other members of the families who have children with various special needs; that is siblings, fathers and grandparents. Also, parent-to-parent schemes aimed at providing guidance and support to parents of children with special needs of various kinds have been developed in several countries. All involve an education focus facilitated by some form of group work.

Strategies to Facilitate PPP

Once parents are ready for PP, a variety of strategies are available for PPP. Informal contacts such as open days, joint sports etc. are useful way of 'breaking the ice' in most forms of human relationships, and is most effective in bringing parents and professionals together in the name of their children, and thereby breaking 'barriers' between them. It can be seen that a wide variety of strategies are available in building relationships between professionals/teachers and parents. The actual methods used will depend on the professionals and the parent preferences, but in general it is considered that a range of strategies available to parents will lead to substantial improvements in the level of PP.

These strategies are briefly presented in the Box 7.2 given below:

Box 7.2: Strategies to promote PPP

- Parent training, and workshops (most important);
- Family intervention, group work, counseling etc. (-do);
- Open days, parent-professional meets;
- Outings, picnics;
- Parents and professionals sports day;
- Debates, seminars, conferences, elocution competitions;
- Invited Guest speakers;
- Written communication such as notes, diary, letters;
- Telephone calls, personal talks;
- Scheduled meetings; and
- Concerts, fairs, family get-together.

Tips for Effective Parent-professional Relationship

Be honest with the nature of problem: Tell them the nature of the problem as soon as possible, and admit it when you yourself is not sure... It also helps them to shift their concentration of energies from fruitless pursuits for why this has happened to them to productive pursuits on how they can better perform in their parental roles in order to benefit their child.

Watch your language—use friendly language, emphasize the strengths of the child, use less of professional jargons that make people get stuck or confused, and do not use emotionally charged words to describe their reactions....Avoid use of implacable statements like "your child is severely disabled, and will not be able to do anything.." Instead say you may be descriptive without slamming the door *"I have just finished understanding John, he has great difficulties in walking, but he can interact so well...But we will try to make some plans, that will help him. You are not alone, I am here. I care."*

Consider the problem as our problem: Help them to see that this is our problem, take parents into confidence, do not thrust solutions on them, provide guidance and support to help them feel competent in making decisions, and ultimately make them to take proper decisions and provide support in adjusting to the common decision.

Keep Pace: Help them to understand the problems. Parents differ in the quantity and quality of information they can absorb during different phases of the problem. They are not super human beings, to assimilate and integrate the complex nature of their child's disability. To take on this inordinate task, parents must be afforded the dignity of an understandable diagnosis. An unprepared professional will fail awfully to do this. For instance, to one distraught mother, a neurologist explained her child's inability to read by saying, "Mrs. Sheela, your child has developmental dyslexia due to minimal brain function." Pause. "Do you understand?" Then he chuckled himself and added gently, "forgive me, how will you understand, I will refer you to a social worker". Do not also flood them with too many facts at a time.

Never condemn or judge: Never put them on the defensive, do not make them feel guilty of their sincere attempts. We do not know whether we would have done any better than them, had we been in their shoes. Every parent is 'good' to the best of his or her ability in understanding the circumstances and they meet as adequately as possible the needs of their children. Be sensitive of the fact that "parents live with their problems for 24 hours of the day, unlike you who spend a few hours with the child for a few weeks, you're not sure, you'd be able to do the job these parents were doing. Do not threaten them with statements such as, "unless you start attending meetings, I will not be able to help you at all". Be neutral.

Be watchful of your attitude: Professional's words and attitudes matter a lot in shaping the perspectives of parents very powerfully. Remember that the parents of CWDs are just people with a great sorrow- but they are jut like others, when the problem of disability is magnified, they in turn create new problems to professionals who must deal with them. *Provide hopeful but realistic views* about the likely progress and eventual prognosis of the children with whom they work. In addition professionals need to communicate the idea that nothing is hopeless and that every situation can be improved, even if perhaps not all of the problems experienced by children or parents can be completely solved. Be objective, but also show 'kindness'.

No deaf-ear: Parents opinion and requests should always be given serious consideration, as it is parents who have long term responsibility for their children.

Be discrete: Remember that they are parents and that you are professionals. They expect you to use your professional judgment, for example, do not in front of them belittle or countermand the opinion of one of your professional partners; make critical remarks about other parents and their handling of the problem; jump into conclusion about our case without adequate clinical study of knowledge of the facts, and trying to do the job that is outside your professional discipline. It does not take long for the parents to pigeonhole a 'problem professional' whose own emotional difficulties are getting in the way of our efforts. In other words, do not worry them with your problems, but be concerned about their problems.

Know your resources: Parents must be told where to find what. They should also be advised 'time-outs' from their difficult days.

Persuade and persuade: Be obliged, to 'feelingly persuade' parents as Shakespeare said, to help them find, 'what we are'.

Be prepared to accept failures: Do not assume omnipotence and omniscience, there are situations that professionals might fail in spite of their best efforts. May be you will have to 'wait' or 'refer' the case to some one else.

The PPP, no doubt is a highly potent reservoir for optimizing abilities of children in general, and CWDs in particular. But PPP does not occur on its own. The tint of participation is embedded in all parents and professionals like the 'trigger' zones for 'kinesiological' (stimulation of brain nerves through physiotherapy) therapy on children. This needs to be triggered to facilitate to get required responses. Various strategies and options are available to make it happen. A major responsibility rests with the professionals to bring out this synergy in the field of rehabilitation and education.

Parents need to be motivated, encouraged, supported, guided, strengthened and trained to become effective in PPP. Keeping parents from participating as full members of the team is to lose the singularly most valuable resource available. *Prepare, prepare, and prepare* parents for this task is the cardinal message. Simultaneously, professionals have to gear up to the needs of the situation with adequate knowledge and skills towards this mission. Great effort and training is called for.

The parents conduct a curriculum called child rearing. The professionals conduct a curriculum called academics, language development, or perceptual training. Both groups seek to advance the learner to greater levels of complexity. PPP is being evolved to profitably mesh the two "professional disciplines". It may be added that trans-disciplinary teamwork that is described in the previous chapter is crucial in the success of PPP. Because of all the life problems, those presented by CWDs, (particularly mental handicap), require the utmost in teamwork within professions, between professionals, lay people and especially the parents. Otherwise, there is an inherent danger that the child is seen only in parts and not as a 'whole being'.

Blessed would be the parents and children who fall under the guidance and gentle tutelage of a caring professional. And blessed is the professional, who with such an approach rises to the summit of a demanding, enervating, but noble profession.

References

1. Baker, P., (1986), "Parents-problems and Perspectives", *American Journal of Mental Deficiency*, 84, 345-351.
2. Buscaglia, L., (1985), *The Disabled and Their Parents: A Counseling Challenge*, N.J: Charles B. Slack, Inc.
3. Diamond, S., (1981), "Growing up with parents of a handicapped child: A handicapped person's perspective", in J.L. Paul (Ed.), *Understanding and Working with Parents of Children with Special Needs*, New York: Holt, Rinehart & Winston..
4. Gallagher, J.J. and Bristol, M., (1989), "Efficacy of early Intervention, In M.C.Wang;M.C.Reynolds and H.J.Welberg, (Eds.),

Handbook of Special Education: Research and Practice, Vol. 3, pp. 295-317.

5. Hornby, G., (2000), *Improving Parent Involvement*, New York: Cassel
6. Narayan, S., (1993), "Knowledge, Attitude and Perception of Parents of Mentally handicapped Children", *Indian Journal of Social Work*, Vol. LIV, No. 3, 437-446.
7. Swap, S.M., (1993), *Developing Home-school Partnerships*, NY: teachers College Press.
8. Schild, S., (1970), Counseling with parents of Retarded Children Living at Home, in M. Schreiber (Ed.), *Social Work and Mental Retardation*, 357-359, New York: The John Day Company.

8

Inclusive Education for Children: The Social Face

There is a child involved
Mainstream, self-contain, integrate, include
How's the wind blow, what's the mood?
General ed., special ed., adapted or not,
Teachers everywhere are put on the spot.
Lighter balls, larger goals, and shorter distance too,
The menu is so large; no one is sure what to do.
These concerns each could be solved
If we'd only remember,
There is a child involved.
(Block, 2000)

Introduction

Inclusive education (mainstream education/integrated education) has come to stay. It is going to be an inevitable reality of the 21st century, where the general schools have to accommodate to the special needs of the children with various types and levels of handicap, and include them as part of educational system. Our age-old negative perspectives about persons with disabilities, and our concentration on their weaknesses led to segregating them from society and educating children with disabilities away in special schools. Currently, there is a paradigm shift in the basic challenge from providing services for children with disabilities to owning up responsibility in restoring their rights as citizens, and not to be discriminated against disability.

Inclusive education, as we know, involves a whole lot of changes in the administration of school system, in the adaptation of curriculum, training of teachers, so on and so forth. Inclusive education is believed as the cardinal step towards helping the disabled to receive all services that enable them to grow with self-esteem and not discriminated. But, we believe that inclusive education does not come about by itself. It must be brought about. One major concern in this process is the attitudes and acceptance of inclusive education by key-actors that play a critical role in the implementation. This chapter is devoted to discuss this key social issue, i.e. the attitudinal changes that need to be brought about in facilitating inclusive education. The various other aspects dealt within here are the inclusion and related concepts, myths about inclusion, its rationale, gains, attitudinal blocks, and facilitation of inclusion through teamwork.

Historical Glimpse

Inclusive education has a long history of how our society in general and how professionals and parents in particular have viewed children with disabilities. In the beginning of 20th century there were no special schools. Children of mild disabilities got admitted in general schools with no special support. As long as they did not pose any problem, the teachers and classmates accepted them. Students who were perceived as a problem or too disabled to benefit from education were excluded from school and sent home. As a result, almost all children who were wheel chair-bound, not toilet trained or those considered uneducable were excluded because of the problems that schooling would entail (Sigmon, 1983).

The manner in which we choose to educate students with disabilities is a consequence of the way we view disability. The shift marked a change from considering the principal limitation as part of the individual to environment. The shift in focus from the individual (and his/her impairments) to the social context was presented by Minow (1990, p: 82) in her analysis of an option facing a school system when educating a child who is hearing handicapped. She has observed that, the school system assumed that the problem was Ann's, because she was different from the other students, the solution must focus on her'. Instead, Minow asserted that one could conceptualize the classroom as a learning community and Ann as a collaborative 'worker' with her classmates. This shifts the focus from Ann, and means that the problem- and the remedy- involves all students. Ann's problem was considered as a situational problem.

Recognizing the social nature of the problem and involving classmates in the solution affords a different stance towards the dilemma of difference: it no longer makes the trait of hearing impairment signify stigma or isolation but responds to the trait as an issue for the entire community. The consequence not only involves the person with difficulties but also has consequences for the learning and perspectives of the students without disabilities. What is required is a paradigm shift in traditional education approaches and curriculum as Johnson (1994) has presented:

Chart 8.1: Shifts from traditional to inclusive education approaches

Traditional	Inclusive
Approaches	
• Education for some	• Education for all
• Static	• Flexible
• Collective teaching	• Individualized teaching
• Learning in segregated setting	• Learning in inclusive setting
• Emphasis on teaching	• Emphasis on learning
• Subject-centered	• Child-centered
• Diagnostic/prescriptive	• Holistic
• Opportunities limited by exclusion	• Equalization of opportunities for all
Curriculum	
• Teacher transmits information	• Teacher as a resource
• Teacher is remote/non-accountable	• Teacher is accountable
• Formal text-book based	• Multi-modal
• One teaching method	• Differential, varied teaching methods
• Homogenous	• Flexible and supplementary contents
• Class focused	• Group and Individual
• Rigid performance indicators	• Different achievement targets

In the 1950s to 1970s, many special schools sprang up all over catering to the educational needs of the disabled children as a result of parental initiatives. The rationale was that the children with disabilities needed to be educated by a trained specialist in a highly structured, intense and unique teaching environment that could not be provided within the general education classrooms (Lewis and Doorlag, 1991). It was also perceived that children with disabilities were not wanted in general schools/classrooms and that their removal would inevitably benefit children without disabilities. As a result, even when special education was housed in general education school buildings, students with disabilities and staff members who served them rarely became 'true' members of the school (Stainback, Stainback and Bunch, 1989). These special schools had special education teachers and therapists who received special education training and used special materials, equipment and teaching methodologies.

Though such services were warranted, the end results were considered as undesirable:

- A rather elaborate dual system of education;
- Exclusion of children with disabilities from general education system;
- Differential treatment that led to viewing students with disabilities as 'different';
- Labeling and separation of children with disabilities led to stigma, ridicule, and poor self-image; and
- Special education facilities did not enable the students with disabilities to move to a general education environment, or to greater independence, rather confined them to special education only.

Out of this dissatisfaction with special education and the realization that the students with disabilities could benefit from increased interaction from students without disabilities, the federal government enacted the Education for All Handicapped Children Act in 1975, now renamed as Individual with Disability Act (IDEA). This landmark legislation guarantees individual with disabilities the right to a free and appropriate public education. Termed *least restrictive environment* (LRE) in IDEA, the provision directed public agencies:

1. To the maximum extent appropriate, children with disabilities, including children in public or private institutions or other care facilities, are educated with children who are not disabled; and
2. That special classes, separate schooling, or other removal of children with disabilities from the regular educational environment occurs when the nature or severity of the disability is such that education in regular classes with the use of supplementary aids and services cannot be achieved satisfactorily.

However, this law does not totally rule out the need for special education at least for some children with severe problems, for sometime. In other words, it recommended a *'continuum of alternative placements'* for intermittent periods at least. The law clearly noted, that all placement decisions need to be made on individual basis, and not on labels. Other influences are: the concept of normalization; UN standard rules; Education Commission Report, 1986 (specific to India); The persons with disabilities (Equal opportunities, protection of rights and full participation) Act, 1995-(specific to India), and so on. Many countries, all over, started enacting legislation in support of inclusive education. United Nations standard rules for persons with disabilities are in tune with what we have discussed:

Box 8.1: United Nations standard rules for persons with disabilities

United Nations advocates:

"Equalization of Opportunities for Disabled Persons' states that: "the education of disabled persons should as far as possible take place within the general school system, and should be the responsibility of the educational authorities. Law regarding compulsory education should include children with all ranges of disabilities, including the most severely disabled".

"Education services for disabled children and adults should be individualized, locally accessible, comprehensive, and should offer a range of choices".

The concept of inclusive education should be reflected in teacher-training programs, both for ordinary teachers and special teachers".

For most people, the 1990s represented a period of gradual familiarization with what the term inclusion actually meant. The new millennium witnessed a matured phase of inclusive thinking and action. Deliberate efforts were being made at international and global level on a consistent basis towards educational inclusion as a major strategy to secure economic and social cohesion (Daniels and Garner, 2000). Schools also encountered new problems such as, the need to get transformed in to learning organizations for all and the challenges of preparing young people for new patterns of communication and learning.

What Is Inclusive Education?

Inclusive education is defined differently by various professionals depending on their main focus---be it democratic principles, normalization principles or benefits of inclusion for children with disabilities, or the key actors *viz.* children, teachers or parents. But, the core message remains the same, that is, promoting the educational rights of children with disabilities.

A comprehensive definition provided by the National Center on Inclusive Education and Restructuring (NCIER), states inclusive education is: "providing to all students including those with significant disabilities, equitable opportunities to receive effective educational services, with the needed supplemental aids and support services, in age-appropriate classes in their neighborhood schools, in order to prepare students for productive lives as full members of society". It is a system that provided quality of education for all children (Lipsky and Gartner, 1997). In other words, inclusive education means welcoming all children, without discrimination, into ordinary schools.

The philosophy of inclusion is perhaps best summed up by the following statement: "although some children, especially those with severe and multiple disabilities, may have unique ways of leaning, separating them from others who learn in a different way is unnecessary and could prevent them from achieving their full potential (Downing, 1996). It simply is physically placing a child in a general classroom.

Levels of Inclusion

Inclusive education does not mean 'dumping' children with

handicap along with other children of ordinary school. Inclusive education aims at possible inclusion of children with handicap with their peers of same age in the classrooms and curricula of general schools. At most we aim at inclusion at all levels including school curricula, and at least functional inclusion in social affairs. In fact, there are different levels of integration *viz.* academic, social, functional and emotional. There are also different types of inclusion such as full-time inclusion, part-time inclusion and special support, neighborhood inclusion and inverse inclusion. Irrespective of the types and levels of integration that we target, one basic principle that underlies all forms of integration is—the preparedness that precedes any integration programs. It involves preparation of the head teachers, teachers, administrative staff members, the parents of groups of children, the children with handicaps and their counterparts in the ordinary schools. Arrangements for special support in the case of children with problems such as speech, behavioral, mobility, etc. must be ensured.

An adapted version of Deno's (1970) range of special education provision is provided in Fig. 8.1, that conveys the realistic model that may be considered for some time to come for children with severe disabilities especially the learning disability. It makes clear, that inclusive education does not mean 'do away' with special education totally. It means do not deny inclusive education or segregate children with disabilities who will benefit in a general education environment. At the same time, it foresees the need for special education provisions to be made available at various stages in inclusive education. The existing special schools may be made use of as resource centers for training and guidance.

Inclusive Schools

An inclusive school is a place where everyone belongs, is accepted, and supported by his or her peers and other members of the school community in the course of having his or her educational needs met (Stainback *et al*, p.3). This notion of bringing services to the general education environment provides continual opportunities for the child with disabilities to interact with, learn from, and form friendships with peers while still ensuring that the child receives an appropriate, individualized program. Based on the various view points and definitions cited above. The characteristics of inclusive education may be delineated as below.

- It is a school-wide approach where all children can learn;
- A sense of 'community' prevails among all;
- Services are need- based than location;
- Natural proportion of children with disabilities and children without disabilities' will be maintained;
- Support systems shall be developed such as teacher collaboration, curriculum adaptation, enhanced educational instructions; and
- Standards and outcomes will be developed, where everybody counts.

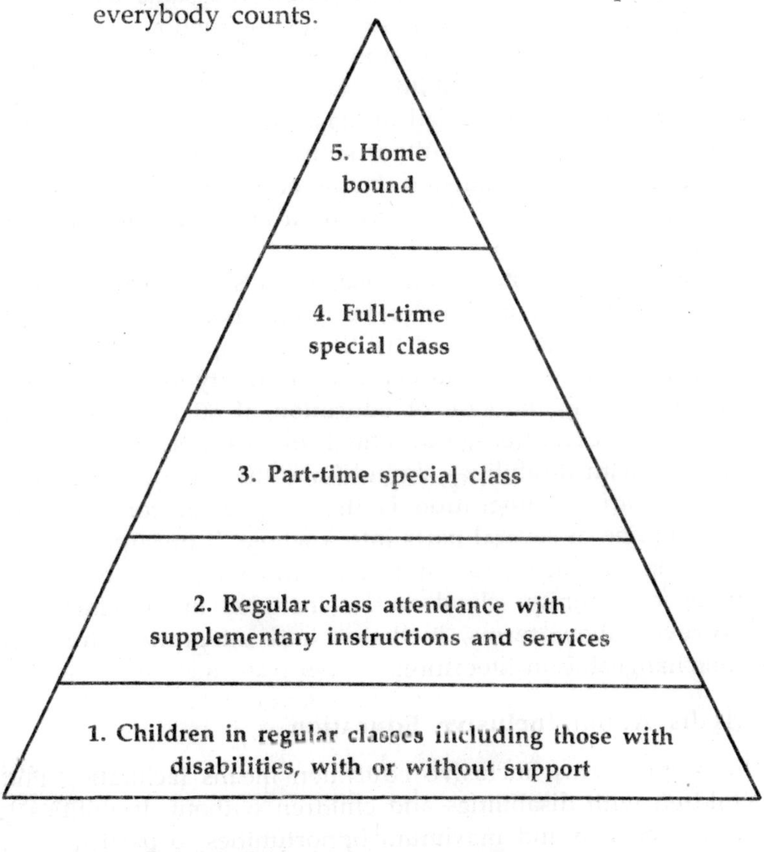

Fig. 8.1: Special education needs-pyramid

At this juncture we may differentiate inclusion from related concepts such as 'mainstreaming', 'normalization' and 'integration'.

Mainstreaming: In an effort to provide some direction as to how to implement LRE, the council of exceptional children (CEC, 1975), coined the term *mainstreaming*. To describe the process of placing students with disabilities into general education classes with appropriate services as determined by the students' of Inclusive Education Programme (IEP). Despite their guidelines, mainstreaming developed into unnecessary "dumping" of students with disabilities into general education classes without support. In contrast to what the CEC suggested, these students with disabilities were asked to follow the same curriculum content, use the same materials and instruction, and follow the same pace as the other students in the class. As a result, many children with disabilities failed in these environments. Mainstream in brief, tended to place students with disabilities into general education without support. Inclusion philosophy suggests that each student's unique educational needs be met through adaptation to the curriculum and with the provision of support.

Normalization: The term normalization is often misinterpreted as the process of making or becoming normal. Instead, the term must be understood as the development of a social infrastructure that provides equal opportunity for all in society. For example in the case of education, if 80 per cent of the non-disabled children go to school, then 80 per cent of all the children with disabilities should have the same opportunity.

Integration: Integration is the process of combining or forming one or several parts into a whole. It presupposes that inclusion has taken place and that each child has a given place in the community school and is included in the classroom. However, these terms, inclusion and integration are used interchangeably in literature.

Myths About Inclusive Education

In simple terms, inclusive education means facilitating both children with disabilities and children without disabilities to have access to and maximum opportunities to participate in all activities of the school environment and outside. But, there are many myths about inclusion as presented in Box-8.2.

Box 8.2: Myths about inclusive education

- Dumping children with disabilities into general classrooms and forcing to learn in general classrooms.
- Pressurizing teachers to strain themselves to accommodate children with disabilities.
- Denying children with disabilities of special education facilities.
- Children with disabilities can be a 'nuisance' and disturb the well-planned teaching program.
- Abilities of children without disabilities may be reduced because of their constant interaction with children with disabilities (those with fewer abilities).
- Children with disabilities may develop 'complexes' and additional problems because of stress to perform at par with children without disabilities.
- Parents will resist integration.
- It is a very expensive program.
- Diluting general educational curriculum.
- Too taxing and difficult for teachers.
- Ignoring special needs.
- Exposing children with disabilities to unnecessary hazards and risks.

Gains of Inclusive Education

The rationale for special education presumably rests on the notion that something distinctive is provided for the students with special education needs in segregated settings. However, this position did not gain its place. Moreover, segregated special education is a costly business, which concentrates relatively large resources on a few children, and which requires the maintenance of a separate infrastructure of schools, teachers and administration.

Wolfensberger (1974) first promoted the concept of inclusive education in the later part of 20th century based on his successful experiments. It has been further observed by many other educational psychologists and today we have a plethora of studies in this fields that confirms to the positive effects of inclusive education and negative effects of exclusive education. Accordingly, there are benefits available in inclusive education environments that are not available in segregated environments. These are presented below:

(i) Benefits for children with handicap:

- Get an opportunity to learn social skills in natural environments- no need to learn to generalize to inclusive environments later;
- More stimulating and motivating environment (ex: the halls, the cafeteria, the recess yard, the bus station, school bus, where much social exchange takes place) improved capacity for socialization;
- Learn appropriate skills (ex: refrain from stigmatizing behaviour, appropriate greetings, wearing age-appropriate dress- better and adaptation to the school);
- Availability of age- appropriate role models without disabilities;
- Opportunities to participate in a variety of school activities appropriate to their chronological age (recess, lunch, assemblies, music, art, and athletic events);
- Has greater potential for new friendship with peers without disabilities;
- More probability for improved scholastic performance and faster acquisition of knowledge and skills;
- Overcome other problems such as speech problems faster;
- Improved interpersonal relationships at home, school and neighborhood;
- Learn useful life-skills, which improve independent living and quality of life;
- Show less mal-adaptive behavior;
- Increased quality and quantity of peer interaction;
- Better self-image; and
- Most importantly, they learn to lead as 'normal' a life as possible and to think of themselves as being the same as others and not as handicapped persons.

(ii) Benefits for children without handicap:

- Improved social adjustment (no bullying, more friendly and helping);
- Positive attitude towards children with handicap, and

elimination of negative mind-sets (ex: fewer starring, fears, and negative comments);

- Acceptance of children with handicap by peers (willing to play, make friends, etc.);
- Increased emotional maturity (able to appreciate 'differences', and see the positive in every one, find strength and weaknesses);
- Ability to understand and empathize with their peers with handicap and a change in perspective: getting a "C" on test is not as devastating when students see a person with disabilities working as hard as he can just to keep his head up and eyes focused!
- Opportunity to share knowledge and skills with their peers with handicaps; and
- Improved interpersonal relationships in general.

Similar positive impacts were also found among teachers, parents and community as well. Teachers learn to be sensitive to the individual needs of children, and accommodate to the differential needs of students. They will have more expectation from students with disabilities and work towards it, resulting in more gains for students with handicap. Parents will be able to accept children with disabilities more easily, and with less stigma or prejudice attached.

Clearly one of the greatest benefits of social interaction is the opportunity for social acceptance and interactions between students with and without disabilities. Inclusion, if done correctly, can promote social aspects, such as how to interact with peers, play cooperatively, take turns, deal with anger, follow directions, listen quietly, stay on task, and behave appropriately. Teachers and ordinary schools can make a difference to young persons' emotional and social development as well as to their cognitive-intellectual development. They can improve pupils' self-esteem, impart self-confidence and prevent learning problems that would graduate to behavioral problems (Falvey and Rosenberg, 1995; Johns and Charltron, 1996; Croll and Moses, 2000 and Munn, *et.al,* 2000)

In contrast, exclusive education which is also known as 'segregated education' or 'special education' is fraught with many limitations and disadvantages (Munn, Lloyd and Culle, 2000), such as:

- Strong negative feelings (rejection, fear, injustice);
- Angry reaction and punishments for parents;
- Missing out on school work;
- Missing out on school time with school friends without disabilities;
- Negative reputation in the community and rejection;
- Negative reaction of peers;
- Negative reputation among teachers;
- Difficulties in catching up with school works;
- Poor prospectus for job in the community; and
- Poor adjustment leading to increased stigmatization.

Therefore, there is no denial of the fact that ordinary schools must cater to the special needs of children with handicap alongside the curricula of ordinary schools.

Attitudinal Blocks and Obstacles to Inclusion

Inclusive education has attracted lot of resistance and criticism. In fact, critics and fanatics were many during the 90's; but their proportion is slowly diminishing as more and more professionals and educationists have put the philosophy on trial ground and met with enormous success. The obstacles to inclusion are given below:

- Resistance from teachers;
- Inadequate preparation of teachers and schools;
- Lack of support services;
- Unhelpful and negative attitudes;
- Misconceptions about the programme;
- Afraid of investments;
- School and children are "not yet ready" with positive attitudes;
- Bureaucracy; and
- Vested interests of those who have invested in 'segregated education'.

We have seen inclusive education as a philosophy, a movement, and an approach that involves radical change in thinking and action process. No doubt, one's attitude is a critical determinant in its acceptance and implementation. How do we deal with this soft side of the process?

Facilitating Acceptance

It may be noted that simply placing a student with a disability into general education, however, does not ensure appropriate and meaningful social interactions and acceptance. Meaningful interaction and subsequent acceptance have to be carefully planned and facilitated. Teachers and parents often unwittingly create barriers to social interactions and acceptance by not telling the students without disabilities that a student with severe mental retardation does not have to learn all the academics, he/she might drool, look awkward etc., because of their condition. In fact, placing students with disabilities into general education without preparing students without disabilities often can lead to feelings such as, "why is he/she in my class?" "Why does she/he has to be in my bench?" "Why does she/he takes long time to understand and keep staring?" "He/she will spoil our class". Hence there is a need to foster social interactions and acceptance.

This section will concentrate on four major players who can facilitate social interactions, acceptance and inclusion of students with disabilities *viz.;* (1) the general education teacher who could promote inclusion during class; (2) the student's classmates who could be prepared to accept and interact with peers with disabilities; (3) the parents; and (4) the children with handicap who play the real roles in reinforcing appropriate social interactions and acceptance, and inclusion attitudes and activities.

Facilitating Inclusion Through Teacher Behaviour

The general education teacher is perhaps the most important determinant in successful inclusion. The teachers can either welcome students with disabilities, or show disinterest, or manifest unwelcome gestures; they can view them as part of the class and their responsibility or as a nuisance forced on them and a 'headache and burden'. The attitude and commitment, a teacher displays affect how classmates without disabilities accept the students with disabilities. In the beginning it is very natural for teachers to feel nervous and even incompetent when working with students with disabilities. Although these feelings are common, these should not be used as an excuse to exclude students or to ignore them when they come to her/his class. They should be willing to try as first step.

In fact, many general education teachers found that teaching students with disabilities to be more rewarding, and "those kids seem to appreciate you a lot and that's a little pat on the back for the teacher" (Janney, *et al*, 1995, p. 435). They also found inclusive teaching not as difficult as imagined. No doubt the teachers should be given proper training and follow-up support as well as the back up support of the school team. But it is important to include teachers who are most receptive to inclusion initially, who later can become models for others (Curry and Bromfield, 1994; Lang 1999, Mosely, 1999 and Mallon, 1998).

Some tips general education teachers can use to facilitate social acceptance and inclusion of students with disabilities, provided by Block (2000, p. 264) are presented below:

- Have a positive attitude;
- Be the teacher for all students in your general education classes;
- Model appropriate behaviour;
- Include the students with disabilities in as many activities as possible;
- Individualize the curriculum and instruction;
- Reinforce positive interactions (while condoning the negative ones);
- Be knowledgeable about the students with disabilities;
- Include teachers throughout the planning process, in order to promote ownership of the plan; and
- Conduct workshop for teachers and provide follow-up guidance.

Preparing Classmates Without Disabilities

Peer acceptance can make the critical difference between successful and unsuccessful inclusion. Experience and research suggests that many students without disabilities have positive attitudes towards including students with disabilities in their class. In a neighborhood inclusive programme implemented by the author, it was noticed that the children of 11-13, both boys and girls eagerly looked forward to the period during which time, their peers with disability joined them. They greeted them with smiles in their faces, and enjoyed as they worked together with peers with disabilities, most of whom were learning disabilities with morbid problems of hearing, speech, gait and so on. Peers without disabilities were eager to help them in their activities, and offered seats just next to them. They were also willing to make modifications to ensure that their peers with disabilities achieved success and were happy.

Several professionals have suggested ways in which teachers could help peers without disabilities develop positive attitudes towards peers with disabilities (Block and Brady, 1999; Jones and Charlton, 1996; Stainback *et al*, 1989;). The key factor is helping classmates: (1) to become knowledgeable about disabilities in general to avoid myths and stereotypes; (2) to learn how to view peers with a disability in a positive manner; and (3) to learn how to interact with peers with disabilities during class hours. There are several ways this could be accomplished. Some of these important strategies are:

- Conduct circle of friends exercise, sociometry;
- Invite guest speakers with disability to speak to the class;
- Role-plays- general and specific to class room behaviour;
- Discuss the concept of rules and handicapping;
- Lead a discussion about disabilities;
- Conduct elocution and competitions and debates about persons with disabilities;
- Talk about famous people who have disabilities;
- Discuss about the specific students who will be included;
- Provide ongoing information, encouragement, and support for acceptance;
- Explain how to interact with specific students with disabilities;
- Encourage and promote peer support practices; and
- Encourage friendship with students with disabilities.

Peer support has been recognized as a very potent aid and of great value in enabling peers with disabilities to benefit from classroom learning as well as in being consistently in producing social, personal and instructional gains, and improving cost-effectiveness. It has helped students with disabilities, (1) to function more fully in school life; (2) to improve academic learning; (3) to maximize some aspects of functioning such as affective, social, physical and cognitive performance; and (4) to overcome difficulties they are experiencing in aspects of their school life. However, it has been observed, that occasions arise when the peer tutor's contribution appears more effective than those given by the teacher (Jones and Charlton, 1996, p. 94). If they are administered properly and carefully, peer support practices can offer opportunities for students with disabilities to experience individualized classroom support of a degree and type, which is not as readily available as they should, and could be. *Children accept their peers with disabilities much more easily and spontaneously than we think, with required facilitation.*

In brief the benefits that could be envisaged for the stakeholders through the inclusive education and tutoring are shown below:

Chart 8.2: Benefits from inclusive education

Benefits from inclusive education

Peers with disabilities

- Improve social, physical, personal and academic competency.
- Boost self-esteem.
- Overall performance.
- Peer counseling.

Teachers

- More free time to concentrate on individu l's learning tasks.
- More need-oriented teaching.
- Balance between teacher and student participation.

Peers without disabilities

- Learning by teaching.
- Increased feelings of worth and self-esteem.
- Helping practice.
- Healthy pro-social attitudes

Preparing Parents

Parents as we have seen throughout, exert an equally powerful influence on attitude formation and consequently the success of inclusion. All work done in the classroom can just be extinguished by the unhelpful attitudes of parents of students with and without disabilities. Hence, no successful inclusion program can afford to overlook and underestimate the role of parents in inclusion. In one of the inclusion projects, a student without disability who showed much interest and helping attitude towards inclusion of peers with disabilities during the first few days was found to be dull, quiet and wanting to sit away from students with disabilities. The class room teacher and the resource teacher was a bit concerned, and called the student aside after the class to find out the reason. The child's tearful response was like this: "I was shouted at by my mother for talking about them at home. She warned me to care my business, and study. I am afraid she will come to school and protest their inclusion as she warned me of".

This sharing conveys the feelings of the mother, her resentment of inclusion, her fear that her child's study may be affected and her difficulty to accept children with disabilities as classmates for her child. These are but common reactions of parents who are not prepared for inclusion. Some parents went almost to the extent of withdrawing their children without disabilities from that particular school and were in search of a school without inclusion. Parents of children without disabilities are usually afraid that by inclusion, the studies of their children will be affected, their children might pick up 'bad behaviour' from them, and that their future prospects might be lost.

On the other side we have parents of children with disabilities themselves getting disturbed and worried about inclusion for fear that, their child might be bullied, rejected and isolated by their peers, they may get more frustrated and inferior as they may fail to compete with their 'normal' peers. These parents may rather prefer to keep their children with disabilities at home rather than sending them for inclusive education. These worries and anxieties are real to any parent who is not prepared adequately. And parents can be real 'blocks' to inclusion instead of being 'building blocks".

Moreover, the gains of inclusive education can be realized fully only if parents participate actively and that follow up activities are carried out consistently at home. Therefore, in the best interest of the children as well as of the parents we need to educate and empower both groups of parents with information on, (1) knowledge about the philosophy and procedures of inclusion, (2) the benefits of inclusion for children with and without disabilities, (3) exposure to successful practices of inclusion and so on. Some of the useful strategies are outlined below.

- Joint orientation programmes;
- Parent meetings to clear out all fears and doubts;
- Training programmes;
- Exposure to successful programmes;
- Involving parents in planning and implementation of inclusive education;
- Discussion in parent-teacher associations;
- Making children speak;
- Arranging guest speakers;
- Developing children's net-works;
- Group co-curricular activities with children with disabilities;
- Workshops; and
- Counseling services.

Preparation of Children with Disabilities

It may be noted that children with disabilities also need to be prepared for successful inclusion. For example, a child with severe speech problem would require the support of a speech therapist or a para-professional to cope with articulation problems and voice therapy. And a child with hyperactivity must be first helped to bring down the excessive restlessness and running around before she/he is sent to an inclusive classroom. This does not undermine the philosophy of inclusion, rather it helps and vitiates the chances of anxious responses by peers. This can be very well compared with the head-start programmes we are very well aware of. The head-start is used as an initial preparatory step to develop the learning-preparedness in children of disadvantaged families who were deprived of it owing to their poor socialization, extremely impoverished living environments and so on. Therefore, they are given a 'push' so that they can learn at par with their counterparts.

"Catch them young" if inclusive education is to be very successful. The earlier children experience being with, working with and playing with peers with disabilities, the easier will be their ability to accept them and accommodate them as classroom peers. This has been successfully tried out in many countries that implemented the early inclusion programme. At younger age they learn to accept their peers with disabilities at par with them as peers with 'differences' and to with 'disabilities'. If they are taught in inclusive set-ups early in their life, we need not waste more resources, efforts and time towards 'later' preparation of peers and parents. However, efforts need to be made towards 'preparing' the key persons involved.

Desired Inclusion Paradigm: It Concerns All

The inclusive education calls for collaborative teamwork, where various professionals are expected to work not in isolation but cooperatively and collaboratively in the development and implementation of Inclusive Education Programme. As shown in figure-8.2, it calls for *a hybrid of transdisciplinary and integrated model* (Block, 2000, p. 42). This means professional boundaries are removed and each professional is willing to share his technical know-how and is committed to promoting the student's overall functional independence and participation in age-appropriate activities and routines.

For example, physiotherapists could share information on positioning that could help a student in the classroom, and speech therapist can show the physiotherapist how to work on language development, while she/he conducts her/his physical therapy. In the integrated therapy model, therapy is conducted/promoted within functional contexts. The collaborative teamwork model allows team members to integrate their programmes into the student's daily routine. In addition, team members are encouraged to work together to help students in various environments. Parents and family members are particularly important because they can practice therapeutic skills in numerous living situations at home.

One critical need of the inclusion philosophy is that children with disabilities are the responsibility of both general and special education staff members unlike the traditional self-contained special education classes in which the special education teacher is solely responsible for their education. The notion of "its not my responsibility" has no place in properly implemented inclusive environment. The inclusion philosophy suggests that only through a merger of resources, knowledge base, and talents of general and special education teachers can both children with and without disabilities receive a comprehensive and appropriate education. Continual support to teachers and use of various co-teaching arrangements is an effective way to facilitate inclusive education (Lipsky and Gartner, 1998).

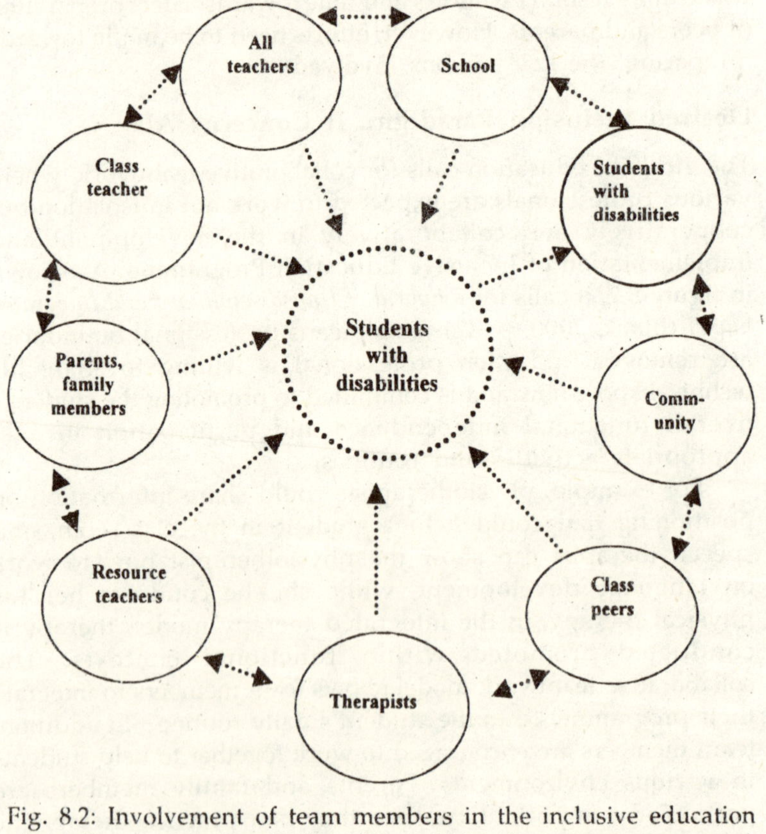

Fig. 8.2: Involvement of team members in the inclusive education (Initially a student with disability will be the center of concern, but it is expected that he/she will soon be part of the team)

With sufficient preparation of students, teachers and parents; adequate provision of support services and collaborative teamwork, inclusive education is bound to meet with success. It may be noted that though we discussed only about four key actors in this chapter, we do not undermine the need to orient and sensitize the school authorities and administrative staff members as these members also play an important role in facilitating and contributing to the success. We need to prepare and involve the school principals, administrators, and other staff members. So too other family members especially the siblings, do play a very significant role in strengthening inclusion process. The cumulative effect of the social preparation is captured through the Johari-window presented below (Fig. 8.3). It is also presumed that reorganization of school administration, adaptation of curriculum and teacher's training about the inclusive methodology (that are critical components of inclusive education system), are also addressed properly and adequately.

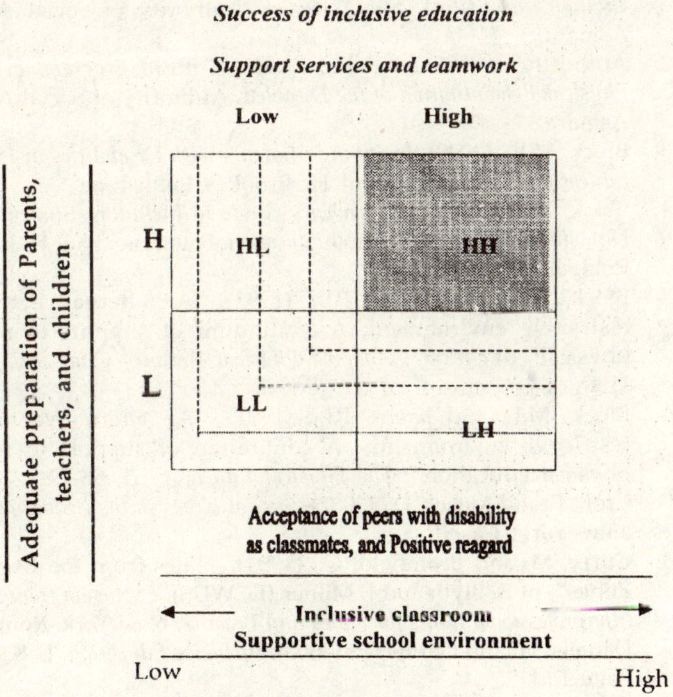

Fig. 8.3: Desired inclusion paradigm

It may be concluded that creativity and flexibility, together with willingness to change and improve educational opportunities, are the key factors for building a new educational concept that will eventually lead to schools open for all children (irrespective of their disabilities). The change of attitudes and values is an important component in inclusive education process, as it involves sharing of school lives and education, and its implementation is totally dependent on these. Attitudes can change and when attitudes change, behavior changes follow.

"I was too overwhelmed by the disability that I failed to see the child.... Today, I am too overwhelmed by the child that I fail to notice the handicap" (Told by a Headmistress, based on her experience of inclusion, who earlier refused admission to a child because of the child's disability).

References

1. Authority of Social Affairs, (1992), *A National Survey of Disabled Civilians in Eritrea, Study Report*, Authority of Social Affairs, Asmara.
2. Authority of Social Affairs, (1993), *Eritrean Programme for the Physical Rehabilitation of the Disabled*, Authority of Social Affairs, Asmara.
3. Block, M.E., (2000), *Including Students with Disabilities in Physical Education*, Baltimore: Paul H. Brookes Publishing Co.
4. Block, M.E., (1994), *A Teacher's Guide to Including Students with Disabilities in Regular Physical Education*, Baltimore: Paul H. Brookes Publishing Co.
5. Block, M.E. and Krebs, P.L., (1992), "An alternative to least restrictive environment: A continuum of support to regular physical education", *Adapted Physical Activity Quarterly*, 9, 97-113.
6. Block, M.E. and Krebs, P.L., (1991), "An alternative to least restrictive environments: A continuum of support to regular physical education", *The Physical Educator*, 55, 58-72.
7. Croll, P. and Moses, D., (2002), *Special Needs in the Primary School*, New York: Casell.
8. Curry, M. and Bromfield, C., (1994), "Tales from the Exclusion Zones", in E. Blyth and J. Milner (ECWDS), *Exclusion from School: Interprofessional Issues for Policy and Practice*, New York: Routledge.
9. Daniels, H. and Garner, P., (2000), *Inclusive Education*, U K Kegan Page Ltd.
10. Falvey, M.A., and Rosenberg, R.L., (1995), Developing and

fostering friendships, In M.A. Falvey 9th Ed.), *Inclusive and Heterogenous Schooling: Assessment, Curriculum and Instruction,* (pp. 267-284), Baltimore: Paul H. Brookes Publishing Co.

11. Fiseha, G. and Eyassu, G., (1995), "The Disabled in Eritrea", Report, Alfred Sen, E., (Ed), *First National Conference on Rehabilitation of Disabled in Eritrea,* ASA, Asmara.
12. French, S., (1993), *What's So Great About Independence, Disabling Barriers, Enabling Environments,* London: Sage Pub.
13. Goytom, A., (1995), "Disability Among Women and Children—Its Special Implication", *op. cit.*
14. Johnson, T., (1994), *Inclusive Education,* UNDP Publication, THPI, India.
15. Jones, K. and Charlron, T., (1996), *Overcoming Learning and Behavioural Difficulties,* London: Routledge.
16. Kunc, N., (1992), "The need to belong: recovering Maslow's hierarchy of needs", cited in Daniels and Garner, *Ibid.*
17. Lang, P., (1999), "Counseling Skills and Encouraging Pupils to talk: Clarifying and addressing Confusion", *British Journal of Guidance and Counseling,* Vol. 27, no.1, pp. 387-407.
18. Lewis, R.B. and Doorlag, D.H., (1996), *Teaching Special Students in the Mainstream,* 3rd Ed., New York: Macmillan.
19. Lipsky, D.K. and Gartner, A., (1997), *Inclusion and School Reform: Transforming America's Classrooms,* Paul H. Brookes Publishing Co. Baltimore.
20. Malton, B., (1998), *Helping Children Manage Loss: Positive Strategies for Renewal and Growth,* London: Jessica Kingsley.
21. Mosley, J., (1999), *More Quality Circle Time,* Wisbetch: LDA.
22. Munn, P., Lloyd, G. and Cullen, M.A., (2000), *Alternatives to Exclusion from School,* New Delhi: Sage Publications Ltd.
23. NCERI, (1995), *National Study of Inclusive Education,* "New York: the city University of New York: NCERI.
24. Radda Barnen, (1996), *Towards Inclusive Education, The Vietnamese Experience,* Swedish Save the Children.
25. Ramsey, E., (1993), "Foreward' in R. Slee (Ed.), *Is There a Desk With My Name On It? The Politics of Integration,* London: Falmer Press.
26. Reddy, S.N., (1992), *Give Them an Opportunity to be One Amongst You,* Hyderabad: THPI Publications.
27. Sigmon, S., (1983), "The history and future of educational segregation", Journal for Special Educators, 19, 1-13.
28. Stainback, W. and Stainback, S., (1991), A rationale for integration and restructuring, In J.W. Lloyd, N.N. Singh, and A.C. Repp. (Eds.), *The Regular Education Initiative: Alternative Perspectives on*

Concepts, issues and models, (pp. 225-239), Syncamore Press.

29. Stainback, W., Stainback, S. and Bunch, G., (1989), *Educating All Students in the Mainstream of Regular Education*, (pp. 1-14), Baltimore: Paul H. Brookes Publishing Co.
30. UNICEF, (1994), *Children and Women in Eritrea*, UNICEF, Asmara
31. United Nations, (1986), *Manual on the Equalization of Opportunities for Disabled Persons*, United Nations, New York.
32. Wolfesberger, W., (1972), *The Principle of Normalization in Human Services*, Toronto: National Institute of Mental Retardation.

9

The WIN/WIN Paradigm—A Powerful Technique for Effective Parent-Child Relationship

"If you do not invest in building healthy relationships and unifying and organizing family, you invest more time later trying to influence children who have been powerfully pulled away from parents, and correct the behaviour of those who became deviants".

Introduction

Today we are confronted with an overwhelmingly devastating and ominous destructive process in family life. Wars are raging and diseases are exacting their toll; millions of refugees live in conditions of abject misery; families are breaking apart; children are neglected, suppressed, abused, and abandoned. The powers of science and technology are misused for destructive purposes; political leaders are becoming increasingly incapable; and religions are ceasing to have influence over people. Among such current situations faced by humanity, the most ubiquitous challenge concerns the institution of family and its present plight.

Currently, the most serious concern about the family and 'criticism against' it relates to its vital role in parenting and rearing children. Many researchers have questioned the desirability of having children reared by their inadequate parents who are becoming destructive forces to individuality and human growth. They viewed family as an institution that is characterized more by control, dominance, abuse and violence against its weakest members especially, women and children (Covey, 1997, Danesh, 1995; Muncie *et. al*, 1995, and Buscaglia, 1975).

In the contemporary society, though we confront varying opinions as to the efficacy and value of family system, it continues to play an important part in determining human behaviour, building personality, influencing the course of moral, mental and social evolution and shaping culture and its institutions. Irrespective of all criticism, and technological advancements and influences of modernization, family still remains the basic social unit that lays the foundation for development of children. For better or worse, all of us have experienced and will experience a family and feel its influence. Therefore, the biggest challenge that we face today is building up strong families, and more than that, maintaining it as a healthy, happy and growth-stimulating unit.

A plethora of studies is available today, that has tried to establish the correlation between healthy family climate and interactions, and healthy social, intellectual and emotional development of a child. We have extensively reviewed these issues, including the significance of interpersonal relationships, in the earlier chapters; while here we shall discuss, the possible mediating factors that can influence this family system and relationships, so that the positive influences can be preserved and strengthened and the negative influences can be nullified or replaced with positive ones.

This chapter is based on the premise that the quality of each person's life *vis-à-vis* family climate is directly linked to the quality of interpersonal relationship one maintains, which in turn is dependent on the quality of communication one experiences. It means that the behaviour, which leads to poor interpersonal relationship, is socialized in early childhood, that is, it is learned. Secondly, that the problem involved in the effects of poor communication and interpersonal relationship is a lack of cognitive meaning in the parent-child communication system. And thirdly, that the growth of cognitive processes is fostered in family control systems which offer and permit a wide range of alternative actions and thought, and that, such growth is constricted by systems of control which offer predetermined solutions and few alternatives for consideration and choice.

Relevance of WIN/WIN Strategy

As we know, family is basically an interacting unit and the family system is characterized by a whole lot of interactions between parents and children, between father and mother, between children themselves and so on. One most powerful conduit therefore, that builds or wrecks families/communities is interpersonal relationships. The relationships confront us everywhere be it family, school, office, neighborhood, play ground, friends circle and society at large. With some persons we relate more intimately than with others; with a few it is out of obligation; it is purely functional, and with a few others it is out of our own choice and interest.

In this chapter we have argued, that the WIN/WIN communication, language and behaviour proposed by Covey (1997) shapes the interpersonal relationships and that interpersonal relationships shape thought and cognitive styles of problem solving. The WIN/WIN philosophy consists of four paradigms, *viz.*, win/win, win/lose, lose/win and lose/lose. The win-win paradigm is a frame of mind and heart that constantly seeks mutual benefit in all human interactions. It involves interactions, decisions and agreements and solutions that are mutually beneficial.

Assume that the emotional climate of two homes is approximately the same; the significant difference between them is in the style of communication employed. A child is playing noisily in the kitchen with an assortment of pots and pans when the telephone rings. In one home the mother says, "be quiet," or "shut up," or any one of several other short, preemptory commands. In the other home the mother says, "would you keep quiet for a minute? I want to talk on the phone." The question our study poses is this: what inner response is elicited in the child, what is the effect upon his developing cognitive network of concepts and meaning in each if these two situation? In one instance the child is asked for simple mental response. He is asked to attend to an uncomplicated message and to make a conditioned response (to comply); he is not called upon to reflect or to make mental discriminations. It is a non-WIN/WIN situation.

In the other example, the child is required to follow two or three ideas. He is asked to relate his behavior to a time dimension; he must think of his behavior in relation to its effect upon another person. He must perform a more complicated task to follow the communication of his mother in that his relationship to her is mediated in part through concepts and shared ideas; his mind is stimulated or exercised (in an elementary fashion) by a more elaborate and complex verbal communication initiated by the mother. He is called to respond to a WIN/WIN situation.

Communication as Base to Interpersonal Relationships

Before we go into description about these paradigms, we may differentiate between the concepts, 'communication' and 'relationship'. Communication is the information/message (content) that is transmitted from one person to another. It is, interaction between two persons, which is interpersonal communication. The content aspect of communication is the information, the facts, and the data in the message. (The difference between "shut up" or "keep quite" and "would you keep quiet for a minute? I want to talk on the phone" is a difference in communication content). But there is a relationship aspect that has to do with the way people communicate and relate with each other.

The difference between the three instructions, is a difference in relationship of communication: *how I perceive myself, how I see you, how I see you seeing me, and vice versa*—how you perceive yourself, your perception of me, and how you see me seeing you. So when the information makes up the content aspect, the relationship aspect refers to the quality or kind of contacts that are occurring between the communicators. And the quality or type of content can *be small pebbles that can split or make and strengthen relationships and hence we need to be cautious in our selection and use of words and expressions.*

The author is not trying to say that the quality of our interpersonal relationships is the be-all and end-all of our life; but would like to assert that it is of vital importance. This interpersonal relationship does not occur just like that. Certain factors are involved to convert an ordinary interaction in to an extraordinary 'quality interaction' or an unhealthy interaction in to a healthy interaction. This quality/healthy interaction happens when a person/family makes a conscious choice to improve relationships and make efforts towards achieving the win/win synergy.

The WIN-WIN Paradigm

The win-win is a frame of mind and heart that involves interactions, decisions, agreements and solutions that are mutually beneficial (Covey, 1989). The "my" interests, feelings and decisions give way for "our" common interests and decisions. It is rooted in the belief that there is plenty for everybody and we need not 'snatch' or 'compete' with anybody. It also affirms that every individual is of worth and dignity as much as anybody else. It is a fundamental belief in *a third alternative*—it is not my way or your way, but a better way, a higher way.

This requires a paradigm shift in our thinking and behavior and roles, from 'controlling' to facilitating, from the feeling of supremacy to feeling of oneness, from 'I know it all, you learn' to 'let us learn', from 'criticizing', 'complaining' and 'condemning' to 'acknowledge', 'accept' and 'appreciate'. It means, *live and let live*. It means win for every one concerned. There is no hurt feelings or room for ill feelings, A sense of cooperation prevails. It calls for a greater deal of empathy and maturity of mind too. This indeed is an extremely difficult challenge; people—parents, teachers, children, leaders, are not necessarily born with that, but *it is something that can be cultivated* in all of us with commitment, constant practice and perseverance.

Sandra (a win/win mother) describes her experience with the youngest of her children thus:

Sean and David were only eighteen months apart in age. Sometimes, there are competitions and rivalry. When David was learning to read, for example, Sean would often mimic him and make him cry. Slowly and haltingly, David would stumble on the words, "Mary...went...to ...the...store". Sean would crawl out from his hiding place and repeat it in the same slow manner, "Mary...went...to ...the...store", teasing and laughing and making fun of David until he started crying.

We would interact with him: "Sean, David is trying to learn to read. You also have to learn to read. It's hard at first. Stop teasing him. He's your little brother, for heaven's sake! Don't make him cry just leave him alone".

This went on for some time until we finally came up with a better solution. Taking Sean aside, we visited with him. " Sean, how would you like to take an assignment? You are older than David. Do you think you could teach David to read? That would be nice. Sit down with him every day for half an hour and see if you can help him to do better than we were able to do".

Sean thought about it and decided to do it. After a few days he brought David by the hand and presented him to us with this exclamation: "Listen to David read. I've been teaching him every day, and he sounds really good". David would open his book and proceed to read, "Mary...went...to ...the...store", sounding slow and unsteady, just as he had a few days earlier.

We said, "Congratulations, Sean! You've taught David how to read". Sean was beaming, full of pride for being the master teacher. David was happy too, knowing that his brother, though he sounded great. It was win for both of them. Sean had become the teacher, bringing his student for approval. David has become the student proud of his accomplishments (Covey, 1997:187).

Win/Lose

It means 'if I win, you lose', there is no question of both winning. I get my way but you do not get your way. It is mere competition. There is no effort to understand and cooperate. This can be compared to 'autocratic rule', instances are many, the power-relationships in families and communities, competition in scoring marks, sports and athletics and proceedings in the courts. It also appears in other ways, such as unilateral decision-making, authoritarian decision-making, leader-centered decision-making and domination. Win/lose people are prone to use their positions, power, possessions and other credentials to get things done. It originates from their feelings of superiority or insecurity. In all these spheres one person tries to win at the cost of others. Classical examples in family situations are in messages such as these:

"If you are not going to get 1st rank, no video-games for you";
"You must be able to do as well as your brother, otherwise no outing for you";
"If you do not eat your food, you will get beatings";
"If you are not going to listen, out you go, do not enter this house";
"If you respect me, I'll love you, otherwise you will be on streets";
"If you are not going to come in time, you will be punished"; and
"If you play with that boy, no games or ice-cream".

Messages that involve withdrawal of benefits, threats, comparisons, rewards, all these overwhelm relationships in family life between child and parent, between husband and wife, between peers and in organizational settings, between boss and subordinates, manager and supervisor, supervisors and workers and so on. They involve purely conditional relationships. This *conditional love/reward* would have long lasting imprint especially on the young minds and hearts of children, who are extremely vulnerable, and highly dependent on parents for the support and emotional affirmation. As a result the child gets molded, shaped and programmed in the win/lose mentality.

The same logic applies in the case of others too in various social situations and roles. It may appear to be a win for one person, but it is not so, it is a camouflaged-lose for both in the long run. For example, a father may force compliance on a child by caning him, and he thinks he has won, but in that process he has created a psychological crevice in the mind of the child. Win/lose basically overlooks individual potentialities, suppresses your emotions and does not promote growth and cooperation, rather stifles it and perpetuates resentment. Some of the other negative impacts are reduction in communication and sharing, reaction formations, destr ıctive competitiveness and rivalry, submission and conformity, rebellion and defiance, withdrawing and escaping. The effect on children is the cost of defiance, stress and the cost of 'diminishing influence.' It is therefore, considered an unhealthy paradigm for interpersonal relationships. Given below is the author's personal observations put in a slightly different form:

Anne who used to play chess frequently with her mother suddenly stopped playing with her mother. When the mother calls her, she stubbornly refuses to play and moves away. Mother started getting irritated and annoyed. She started withholding from her daughter of some of the privileges such as ice creams on weekends. Still the daughter refused to comply and did not play with her and even started distancing from her mother. Anne was very friendly with her father. Her mother shared her problem with the father and requested him to intervene. The father took Anne for an ice cream and asked her as to why she refuses to play with her mother. With tears in her eyes Anne replied, "my mom will win all the time, and I hate to lose all the time. And I hate her".

Initially Anne used to get up and go with tears when she consistently loses for many times. Anne 's patience stared dropping down gradually till she refused to play, and subsequently avoided being with her mother at all. This is natural for any one. Nobody likes to lose all the time. When the mother was asked about it, she said: "it is a game and one has to be competitive, so she has to learn to lose till she learns how to play". The mother is also right in her own way but what is important is the result. The mother has realized the need to let her daughter win, and she let her win the alternate games to begin with. The results were wonderful with the mother and daughter coming closer and closer and playing not only chess but other indoor games as well.

If the mother had not adopted a *win/win* and continued in her *win/lose* strategy, the results would have been disastrous. This is a typical example that conveys that even in a competitive situation such as games, you can apply *win/win* leading to mutual happiness and growth.

Lose/Win

This is a position of giving up or yielding to. OK you win, let me lose. Go ahead let me stay back. OK you decide; I'll simply listen. This expresses weakness rather than strength. These children also suffer from insecurity and often live to appease and please others. They do not want to displease anyone and feed themselves on popularity or acceptance. They fail to assert themselves or put their point of view across, and can be easily silenced by the ego-strength of others. They want to be "good guys" and in the good books of every one. The danger is that such children have to suppress a lot, and land up in child guidance clinics with behaviour and emotional problems, or end up with psychosomatic illnesses, and exhibit disproportionate rage or anger and cynicism as adults.

The win/lose people just love these lose/win people as they can take advantage of their weaknesses and feed their ego. But when the former produces some results, the latter will create chaos from the outset. In usual life circumstances, we see these people may swing back and forth as a pendulum from win/lose in consideration to lose/win indulgence. When they cannot tolerate discipline, orders and threats, they swing back to win/lose- until guilt undermines their resolve and drives them back to lose/win- until anger frustration overtakes them back to win/lose.

Lose/Lose

"If I cannot get it, you too should not";
"I will see that you will have a miserable time, if you are going to leave me and go";
"I did not pass, therefore I will see that yours too"; and
"If I am not taken to a cinema that is due to me, I'll see to it that none of you will go".

This normally happens when two win/lose people get together, who are equally egoistic, stubborn and self-centered. In the process, both will lose and they are satisfied. Nobody stands to gain. Both become vindictive. We can encounter this situation most often in the modern society where the wife is educated and earns at par with the husband! Two children fight for a toy, and the weaker one who realized that, can no longer hold on to it, as the other child destroys it and throws. No body has gained! Instances are plenty in organizational conflicts and divorce cases. Husbands sells off the property to a much lower rate so that the equal share to be given to wife will be 'too less an amount', even though he too stands to lose.

Such mind-set leads you to nowhere except harming yourself and others, and is dangerous to human relationships. In fact many broken homes are the reincarnation of this longstanding lose-lose interaction! Given below are few illustrations of the above four paradigms. Interactions in day-to-day life need not follow the same sequence. Also it is not necessary, a win/win approach will fetch a win/win response only, and the like. A win/win can fetch a 'lose-win' response or any of the other non-win responses. Therefore, examples are provided just to illustrate each of the four paradigms.

Though the responses are not necessarily in the same fashion, if you are a person of win/win orientation you can change any of the above undesirable responses in to a positive one as shown above. Through our conscious practice, a 'tit-for-tat' response can be converted in to a positive response. The decision to choose a response is with us. Initially, a win/win response may not evoke a positive response from a person of win/lose orientation or other orientations. But, it is very often experienced that persistence with a win/win approach evokes a more or less positive response from a person of other orientation over a period of time. Persistence with win/win strategy to the other person's unhealthy responses is certain to obtain a positive and workable solution or positive response in the long run. But it may be noted that, in spite of all these, we may fail in a few cases, and that failure may only be transitory if we are to persist with win/win strategy.

Cultivating WIN/WIN Behaviour

A few factors have to get assimilated to facilitate win/win. This win/win synergy has been explained with the help of the following four components that are considered crucial in interpersonal relationships. They are:

1. The family destination;
2. The win-win discipline;
3. "You" to "I"—messages, owning up breaking the punctuating rhythm; and
4. The win/win family climate and type.

Chart 9.1: Illustrations of WIN/WIN Paradigm

	From desired to undesired paradigms			
Home Situation	*Win/Win*	*Win/Lose*	*Lose/Win*	*Lose/Lose*
1. Father to son	"John, these days it is not safe to come late, so we get a bit worried when you do not call up and inform us about your late coming	"How many times should I tell you note that you should ring up if you are late" (angry tone).	"I think I have to put up with your irresponsible behaviour"	"There will never be any change in your behavior of coming home late".
Response of son	"Today I did have an urgent work, I forgot to tell you. But I will take care Dad!"	"Ok, I am late, I am sorry!" (Abrupt response).	"You better do it".	"Ok, if that is the way you think, let it be so".
2. Elder sister to younger one	"I find it difficult to locate my books when you displace things on my table, why don't you please play down on the floor...."	"You just don't touch my table any more...."	"All I can do is put up with the mess you create on my table...."	Sister throws her toys from the table.
Response of younger one	I am sorry, next time I'll play on the floor.	Ok, you don't like me... (and starts weeping...)	Yes, I enjoy playing on your table only...	She throws her sister's books.
3. Mother to daughter	"Darling, why don't you give your toy to your friend for sometime, meanwhile you can help me with this task. Your friend will also feel happy. happy.	You selfish girl, can't you lend your toy for your friend at least for sometime... Why do you make her feel bad like that... it is not good on your part...	You will not spare that toy, is it?	Mother beats her.
Response of daughter	Lends the toy with a smile and moves to help the mother.	Leaves the toy and move away with resentment.	Takes the toy and walks away...	She breaks the toy... and flings it off.
4. Husband to wife	"I was a bit worried about my office, I should not have spoken so rudely to you, I am sorry".	"Is there any occasion that you refrain from irritating me and provoking me".	"I better give up...after all who am I".	"I have problems at office, here, there, everywhere, and no body tries to understand me".
Response of wife	"It is alright, I can understand, let us forget about it".	"Ok, if you think so, I only have to keep quite..."	"You better learn to to behave, I cannot take this nonsense any more..."	"If this is the way you behave, no one will ever come near you".

It is this family destination, win/win discipline, "you" to "I" to "we"—messages, and the required family type (not necessarily in this order) which brings out the synergy that we need to maintain effective interpersonal relationships. What is desired is a balanced blend of all four realms. They are briefly discussed in the context of communication as a powerful base in forming and maintaining relationships.

The Family Destination—The Key to Win/Win

Good families and even great families are off the track 90 per cent of the times, says the eminent psychologist Covey (1997). But they continue the journey and reach their destination. Covey compares it to the flight of an airplane. Before the plane takes off, the pilots have a flight plan. They know exactly where they are going and start off in accordance with their plan. But during the course of flight, wind, rain, turbulence, air traffic, human error and other factors act on the course of the flight. They move it slightly in different directions so that most of the time the plane is not even on the prescribed flight path. But barring anything too major, the plane will arrive at its destination. This happens, as the pilot receives constant feedback-from the instruments that read the environment, from the control towers, from other planes and sometimes from the stars. The hope lies not in the deviations, but in the vision, the plan, and the ability to get back on track.

Covey considers this metaphor as the ideal one for family life. What matters is not that families are on track or in a mess, but the vision and the courage to keep coming back time and time again. Now what is the big family vision? It is the vision for a beautiful culture—not of west or east, or of Christian or Hindus, but a culture that transcends all these societal barriers in to something human. A culture where family members deeply, sincerely and genuinely enjoy being together; where they have a sense of shared values and beliefs; where they act and interact in ways that really work, based on the principles of service and justice that govern the society. It enables families to deal with the powerful forces that would throw them off the track-including turbulent weather outside the plane and turbulent social weather inside the cockpit (contention, lack of communication, authoritarianism, and the tendency to dominate, condemn, criticize, complain, compare and compete).

Win/Win Discipline

It may be noted that the family vision has a lot to do with win/win discipline that we adopt, if it has to be part of our system as a lifetime approach. In a win/win parenting, we are expected to 'discipline' children and not 'punish' them. The attitude that supports this paradigm is accepting our inevitable need to relate to our children, the need to value and accept children as children, and the imperative for maintaining healthy parent-child relationships. The more committed we are to the successful family vision, the more of win/win response we make use of as a disciplining strategy.

Whenever a child misbehaves, it is important to remember the family vision, the end, and to be clear what you are trying to do. Your *end in mind as a parent is to help the child learn and grow, to nurture as a responsible person.* The objective of discipline is to help the child to develop internal discipline—the capacity to make right choices even when there are influences to do otherwise. When parents strive to move in this direction, there is little chance that children reject your values and go astray. The key to WIN/WIN discipline is creating *win/win agreement.*

Win/win agreement helps to create shared vision; clarifies expectations, builds trust and provides a *win* situation for every one involved. A sound win/win agreement involves five cardinal elements: setting desired results, guidelines, resources, accountability and consequences.

From I and You Messages to We

This win/win discipline necessary calls for a paradigm shift from "you-messages" to I-messages" and we-feeling. *You and I* dichotomy is fixing responsibility on 'myself' (internal) and on 'others' (external), in other words problem-ownership. We are addicted to using you-messages such as:

I messages (owning up)	*You messages (blaming others)*
I get irritated	"You irritate me"
I get easily provoked	"You provoked me"
I get disappointed	"You disappointed me"
I get hurt easily	"Your behaviour hurts me"
I feel rejected	"You are rejecting me"

'I messages' are honest, clear, confessional. "I messages" own my anger, my responsibility, my demands without placing blame on others and probably seeking for the support of other person to solve the problem ending in we—the family. 'You-messages' are most often attacks, criticisms, devaluation of the other person, labels or fixing the blame on another person for your behavior which you fail to own up. In you-messages, we are basically communicating that the other person is responsible for our problem and expect the other person to change. This is a very common feature in parent-child relationships, marital relationships, and other social relationships. We cannot always try and change a child's behaviour to our liking.

Therefore, the change has to be in you, from 'blaming' to 'owning'. This change so simply stated as it is, is not an easy shift to make like changing dresses. It involves tremendous efforts and thinking—a real paradigm shift in "locus of responsibility from you to me", a change in the driver's seat and 'shifting of gears' as Gordon (1987) has rightly put it. It also means a change from 'active blaming' to 'active listening' and from a sending posture to receiving posture. And this shift will result in the most phenomenal magic process of creating we-feeling that is basic to a happy family.

The result will be " I am getting irritated at your behaviour, shall we sit down and discuss as to how we can work with my irritation". It involves a shift from "you are responsible for family unhappiness" to "I have an equal responsibility in creating family happiness" to the third and most desired level of "let us work together to create family happiness". In fact, this monumental shift is essential in promoting collective family feeling from self-centered orientation. This we feeling is the base and seed for family success (Fig. 9.1). The necessity of this paradigm shift is made very clear with the need to break the *punctuating rhythm.*

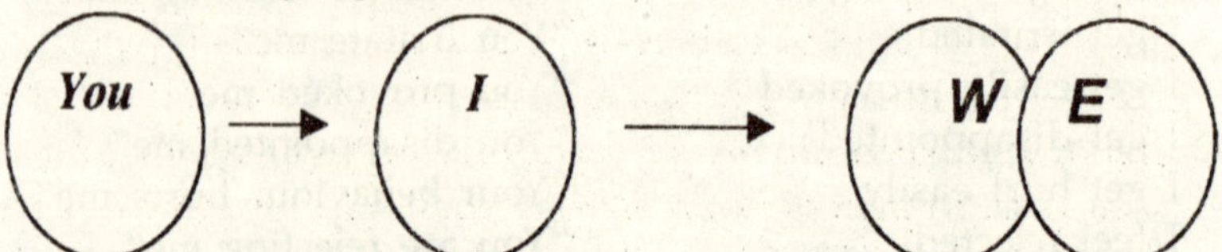

Fig. 9.1: Transformation of you/I in to we

Break the Punctuating Rhythm

Given below is a method of everyday situation in life that punctuates the sequence of an interaction. It is elaborated by Watzlawick, Beavin and Jackson (1968) and relies on fault finding that leads you nowhere. Assuming those two children of your family come to you with a problem as given below. A and B are brothers. A tells you that B always ignores him and insults him. B complaints that A is always poor at play and never tries to learn and do well and that is why he ignores him and not for any other reason. Now this is the symptom, fixing responsibility on the other. Their interaction is punctuated as below in Fig. 9.2.

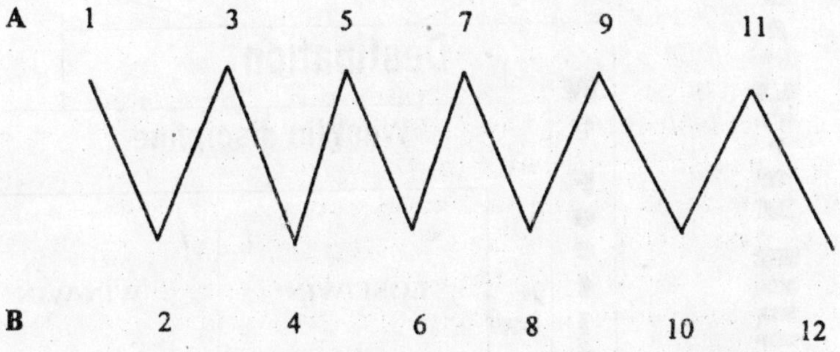

Fig. 9. 2: Interaction pattern between parent and child

B sequence goes 1-2-3, 3-4-5 and so on. He believes that A starts the pattern. It is his fault and he is just being reasonable. A sees it differently. His sequence goes, 2-3-4, 4-5-6, 6-7-8 and so on. He thinks it starts with B, and he's just responding the way any normal brother would by ignoring. The point is both try to define the relationship, depending on the way they perceive and organize or 'punctuate' reality. In one way, both are right and wrong. *This sequence leads them nowhere.* What is important is how to help them break this sequence, and enable them to deal with what goes on in between—anger. The above paradigm works wonders to end this sequence and bring them together. But it may be noted, in serious situations they would require the support of professionals in application of the suggested method of owning up responsibility.

A break in this rhythm leads to accepting responsibility for individual actions too. "You make me get irritated," parents used to say. Wrong! Absolutely untrue! No one can make another person angry or get annoyed. If I become angry with you, I am responsible for it. (Anger or getting annoyed as such is not wrong; it may be the most appropriate and loving response that I am aware of at that moment). The message is that owning up responsibility is one powerful link that can stop this punctuating and in opting for a win/win way of strengthening and re-building parent-child relationships rather than breaking. *Owning up helps to break this punctuating rhythm and to build bridges than walls in human relationships.*

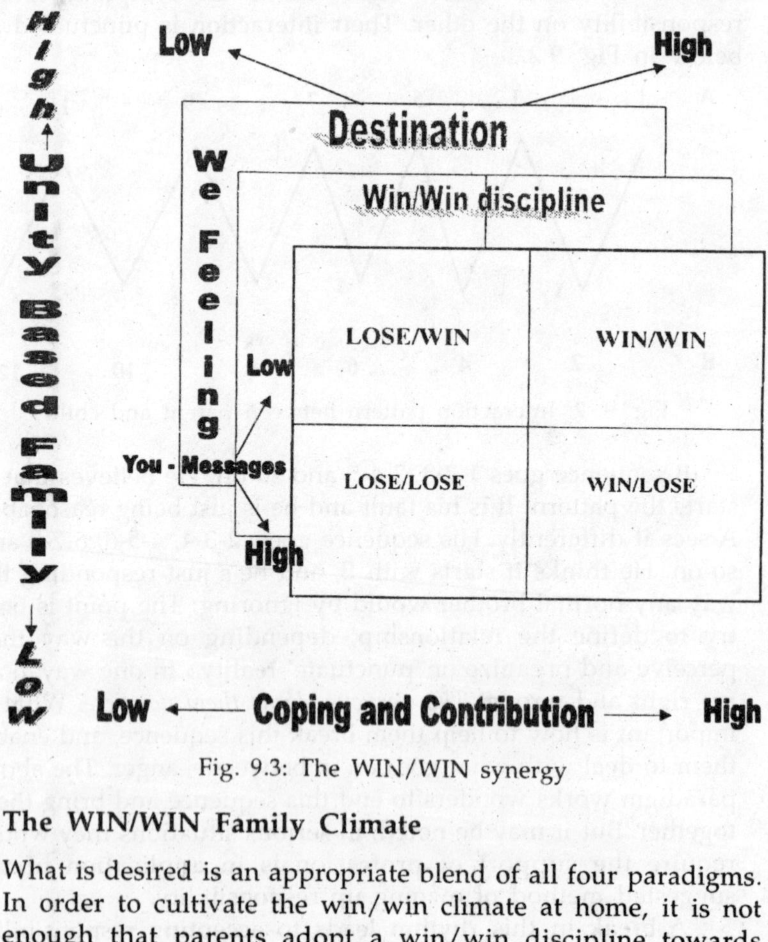

Fig. 9.3: The WIN/WIN synergy

The WIN/WIN Family Climate

What is desired is an appropriate blend of all four paradigms. In order to cultivate the win/win climate at home, it is not enough that parents adopt a win/win discipline towards children. They need to practice win/win between themselves, as husband and wife, as mother and father. Children do observe the behaviour of parents very closely. If the mother and father interact on win/lose or other non-win/win paradigms, the children will get confusing messages, and they may try out similar patterns. Hence, consistency in the win/win behaviour with the same person as well as with the other members in the family is absolutely necessary if we expect children to assimilate a win/win orientation as shown in Fig. 9.4.

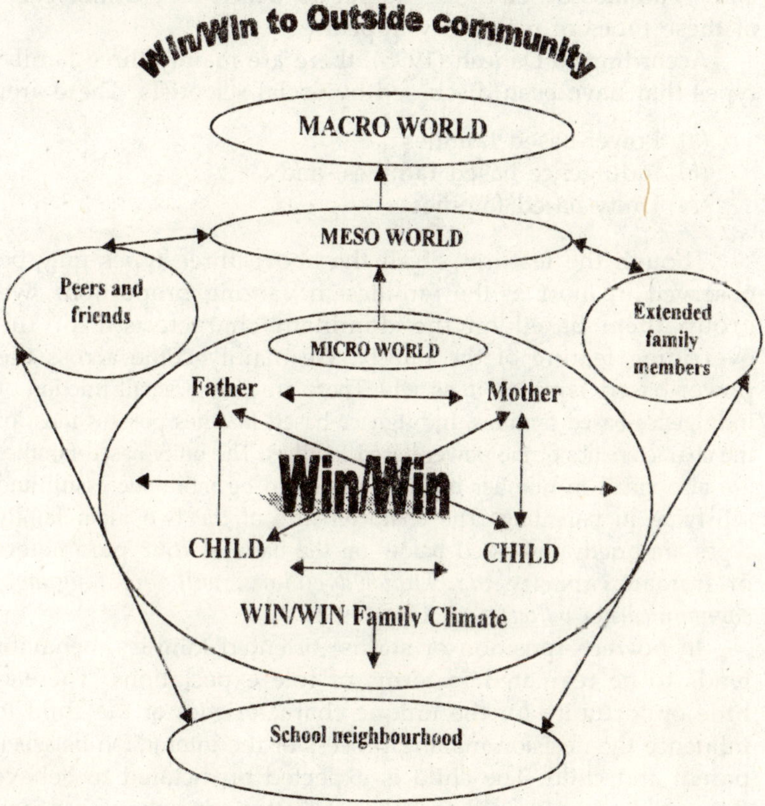

Fig. 9.4: The WIN/WIN family climate

Win/win should become the very spirit, culture, environment and the base of the family and family relationships. It should permeate in to the very structure and family systems and break 'barriers'. It implies that unhealthy and dis-empowering systems must be replaced with empowering ones. Two types of families have been mainly identified *viz.* the power-based families (status-based families) and the unity-based families (person-based family) by Danesh (1995) and others. In his view the type of family structure and conditions what the child learns and how he/she learns, setting limits within which future learning may take place. The interlacing of social interaction and language is illustrated by the distinction between two types of family control. One is oriented toward *control by status/power* appeal or ascribed role norms. The second is oriented toward *persons and family unity*. Families differ in the degree to which they utilize each of these types of regulatory appeal.

According to Danesh (1995), there are mainly three family types that have been discussed by social scientists. These are:

(a) Power-based families
(b) Indulgence based families, and
(c) Unity-based families.

Though the features of all the above three types may be observed in most of the families in varying proportions, we group them based on the dominant characteristic or the overriding feature of the family. We mainly come across the power-based families in society. There are only a small fraction of indulgence-based families. Indulgence-based families possess most of the characteristics of the power-based families. The unity-based families are also small in number but these seem to be more successful and satisfying in parenting. The characteristics of the two main family types are briefly discussed below on the basis of four parameters of human capacity *viz. knowledge, love, will and language/ communication patterns*, in Chart 9.2.

In power—(position or status) oriented families, behavior tends to be regulated in terms of role expectations. There is little opportunity for the unique characteristics of the child to influence the decision-making process or the interaction between parent and child. The child is expected or dictated to behave the way he/she is told to behave: "listen, do what I say and do as I say". Norms of behavior are stressed with such imperatives as, "you must do this because I say so" or "girls don't act like that," or other statements which rely on the status of the participants or a behavior norm for justification (Bernstein, 1964). In the family, as in other social structures, control is exercised in part through status/power appeals. Respecting the position—head of family is important disregard of the fact whether it amounts to trampling on the needs, emotions and requirements of its members.

Chart 9.2: Family types on the basis of four parameters of human capacity

Characteristics of power-based families	*Characteristics of unity-based families*
Knowledge	
• Family suffers from varying • Disorders of knowledge. • Access to knowledge is unequal, and women who are the basic caretakers of children, and who would require more education are denied of it. • Family is suffused with a lack of truthfulness and trust in their interpersonal relationships. • Conditions of intimacy, and sharing elude marital and family interactions.	• Acquisition of knowledge is a right and responsibility of all the family members including women. • Conditions of equality and mutuality removes lack of truthfulness and trust that plagues families' male-female relationships. • It replaces family with conditions of intimacy, and sharing.
Love	
• Suffers from disorders of love. • Authoritarian parenting. • Love is contingent upon one's willingness to confirm. • Father expects obedience and submission from wife and children. • Parents are more interested in controlling and molding children. • Rigid boundaries of conformity are drawn and nonconformity is punished. • Love-ambivalence prevails.	• Expression of love is unconditional, growth inducing, unifying, and marked with tenderness and openness. • Pace and pain of growth is not dulled by set rules and regulations. • Universality, creativity, curiosity and search for truth are actively encouraged. • Love is unifying and all encompassing, and children are helped to love themselves and others.

(Contd.)

Characteristics of power-based families	*Characteristics of unity-based families*
• Curiosity, originality and creativity are discouraged. • Diversity becomes a threat, and uniformity takes precedence. • Seeds of prejudice, suspicion and exclusivity are shown in the minds of children.	• A creative cycle exists: unity creates love and love creates unity, resulting in more love and unity.
Will	
• Ill-equipped to help children develop will power in a healthy manner. • Considerable amount of resentment, fears and anxieties are cultivated among children. • Life is rigidly structured and made much simpler, albeit less fulfilling. • Personal freedom is exchanged for social security. • Individuals engage in disunifying acts of seeking personal justice that often deteriorate into revenge and violence. • Qualities of true freedom are not valued and are usually dismissed as unrealistic and utopian in nature. • Conducive to creating undue dependency and self-preoccupation. • Concentrates all energy on survival and feeling safe.	• Fundamental expressions of maturity and human will—service at the individual level and justice at the societal level. • Practices of control, competition and excessive individualism and independence give way to those qualities or cooperation, universality, and inter-dependence. • Finds noblest expression of free will by creating conditions of justice. • Individuals endeavour to their utmost to serve one another, while the family makes it certain that justice will be the modus operandi of the group.
*Communication codes or styles**	
• Restricted	• Elaborated

(* See appendix)

In contrast, in a person-oriented family system, the unique characteristics of the child modify parental (status) demands and are taken into account in interaction. The decisions of this type of family are individualized and less frequently related to status or role ascription. Behavior is justified in terms of feelings, preference, personal and unique reactions, and subjective states.

Indulgence-based families possess most of the characteristics of the power-based families, and in addition they give primacy to gratification of personal needs. Pursuit of knowledge and truth has relevance only for personal gains. Love is viewed as identical to gratification, and human will is expressed in promiscuous and anarchic ways. Children in these families grow up to be immensely self-centered, intolerant, and indisciplined. They demand immediate need gratification and when their demands are not met, they often resort to violence and crime. These individuals are highly prone to develop addictions and relate to others as though they have unlimited powers. At times we come across family situation that oscillates between the tow types- power-based and the indulgence-based. The power-based and the indulgence-based families are not suitable to promote win/win climate.

Benefits of the Win/Win Method

It has to be emphasized that this method involves trade-off: while it is easy enough to conceptualize, it is not easy to acquire competence in applying this method. However, the benefits of the win/win method are immense:

(i) Wholesome family climate in which the principles of mutual respect, mutual understanding, and creative cooperation govern. A related benefit is a peaceful and happy family climate; when problems crop up they get solved through participation; when conflicts are resolved, they stay resolved.

(ii) Higher-quality decisions, as it is the resultant of the participation and working together of both parents and children, that is better than any individual member could ever come up with a quality decision alone.

(iii) Warmer relationships, one of the most predictable outcomes of this approach is that the parties involved end up feeling good about each other, and a positive feeling of liking/

loving each other. The resentment that usually follows the other approaches gets extinguished and is not seen in this approach.

(iv) Better parenting, parents will be less and less concerned about their 'power' and 'positions' and in 'clinging on to rigid roles', and more and more concerned in loving nurturing 'better children' as against 'conformists'.

(v) Transformation from power-based families to unity-based families, it will be an inevitable outcome of the above; and

(vi) Children of win/win orientation, who would become win/win adults and parents, become building blocks of a better civilization.

Facilitating Tips for Win/Win

The important tips in successful win/win parenting as explained will always remain:

- — Letting children win in the little things and interact around big things;
- — Making win/win agreements; and
- — Letting win/win agreements govern.

A few other tips that are very helpful are:

- — Minding your words-psycholinguistic changes;
- — Touch;
- — The pause; and
- — Refusal to revert to the other three paradigms—*no going back.* These are briefly explained below.

Minding Your Words

Words are powerful tools in human interactions. In fact they are the most consciously used torms of contact. When we are angry we commonly use non-win words like 'get lost', 'go to hell', 'damn it', 'throw it', 'you are stupid', 'you are silly', 'you are unreasonable', 'you are this and that'—all negative naming and accusation etc. These are disempowering words and the win/win would demand a replacement of these with empowering words like: 'You are different', 'you are simply honest', 'you are great', 'your attitude is incredible', 'your idea sounds good', 'common let us look in to it',' 'it is interesting', 'it is exciting', and so on.

The first category of words simply does not promote win/win contacts. They just hurt and create scars in the child's heart. Whereas, you can also encourage, help and inspire your child with your kind and good words -empowering words that heal, soothe, unite and create win/win for all! Once you go for win/win you cannot afford to indulge in the use of dis-empowering words.

Touch

Touching behaviour can have significant impact on interpersonal relationships. Our touches and tactual expressions when applied appropriately and tactfully can carry with them warmth and companionship. It tends to improve interactions and communications. They also cement our social and personal bonding with those people who are special to us (Hardison, 1896 and Buscaglia, 1975). From early childhood, we begin to learn how much we can trust people by the way they touch us. We affix a supreme trust to our parents as we feel their tender and caring touch in feeding, bathing, clothing and rocking us. Our trust in them stabilizes in proportion to how often we are touched and how often their contact comforts and satisfies. Gentle and loving touch in our communication to children has a very profound impact and supports win/win than harsh touch and punishments.

Touch may be used as often in interactions with children along with win/win communication. For example, a few kind words to a child with a gentle touch, when she/he is upset about low marks in spite of hard work, will work wonders in healing the child of the hurt feelings of failure and in encouraging/equipping her or him to do still better. The gentle touch instills more confidence and trust. It can be used in the day-to-day win/win discipline, during problem solving, conflict resolutions and numerous other situations. It helps children to be warm and kind when they grow up as adults.

The Pause

Pause is a unique capacity of human beings to be silent for sometime amidst various external stimuli, and in this moment to modify our response. The significance of the pause is that the rigid chain of cause effect is broken (May, 1986). It comes with disciplining our mind to withhold immediate reactions. Such discipline involves the attempt from our side to withhold responses catering to the unhealthy paradigms, and consciously trying to modify and bring it out as a positive win/win response. For example, when someone hurts or insults us, the instinctual response is to hit back, if possible in greater intensity, as per the respondent conditioning theory of the prominent behavioral theorists Pavlov.

As Covey has beautifully put it (1989), this stimulus-response pattern is common to both animals and human beings, and what distinguish the human beings from the animals is our basic ability to pause and think before we respond to a stimuli, the stimulus-response and paired learning of Skinner (1974). The more we exercise this capability, the more we get nearer to being human, and farther from animal behaviour. So too in problem solving, conflict resolution and decision-making situations in any other set-ups the more pause-button we apply, the more it enables our children to exercise caution in their behaviour towards others.

No Going Back

Even under the best conditions parents will run in to problems using the win/win paradigm. While win/win do protect children from becoming unhappy, it does not guarantee that the children can become happy right away. Seldom does it work without a hitch. At times parents feel frustrated because it will take more time and effort than expected. Or they may fail to find to initiate a win/win situation right away. They may come across situations where others failed to understand them. Sometimes, they will be tempted to chuck the whole process and revert to win/lose approach. On occasions they may get angry or irritated when the children are too stubborn to respond positively, or too demanding, or refuse to cooperate.

To stress again, it is only natural to expect that the win/win paradigm involves trade-off-costs that go with the benefits and problems that go with the rewards. No matter how committed we are to win/win paradigm, occasionally we are tempted to fall back on one of the other three paradigms when a mutually satisfying response or acceptable solution to a conflict is not forthcoming. Becoming frustrated and impatient or getting exasperated with a child who will not come around to their expectation, parents sometimes get to the point where they want to say, "all right, damn it, if you cannot agree to anything. I'm going to decide what's to be done."

However, Covey and others who used win/win in various spheres of their life are convinced of the fact that commitment to win/win in interpersonal relationships especially, in resolving conflicts would eliminate our option in going back to the authoritarian approach. Perhaps it is like a "point of no return"—once others get accustomed to having a parent, partner, sibling, friend or leader or colleague who is respectful of their needs. They will not tolerate a return to a previous condition of lesser need satisfaction. On occasions, when you happen to revert to unhealthy paradigms, there are constructive actions that you can take afterwards to undo it. These are:

- Explaining the circumstances to the child which will certainly be accepted (for example, time pressure, win/win attempt has failed, imperative need of the hour, stress etc.);
- Active listening to demonstrate your understanding and acceptance of their negative feelings;
- Initiate problem-solving to prevent similar situations from arising in the future; and
- Apologizing (if you genuinely feel like doing so).

Children are seldom influenced by the experience and wisdom of parents whose use of power has made the kids dislike or hate them. And we have plenty of first hand experiences of our own of the failure of other methods. At the same time, experiences are plenty where such owning up led to remarkable changes in human relationships- at home, at office, in friend's circle, just anywhere. Can we consider its incorporation in our personal life, so that we succeed in living a much happier and healthier life as well promote the same in our families? Can we start it with small steps in everyday dealings? Success is sure if not immediate, in the long run and as a final result.

Win/win may be begun with by taking baby steps. But one must start with the end in mind—the flight plan. One step will lead to the other, till we reach our destination. We may go off the track, but once our destination is clear, it is easy to get back to the track and keep moving forward. Win/win steps are presented in Fig. 9.5.

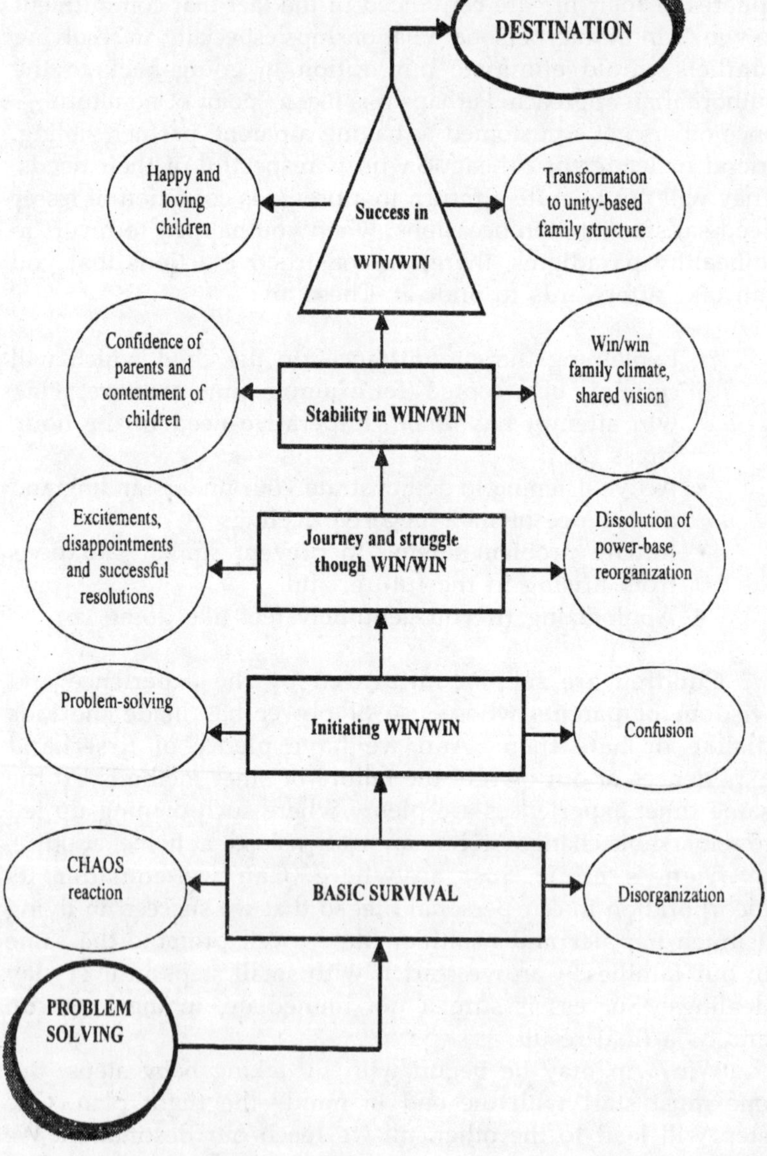

Fig. 9.5: The WIN/WIN family destination pyramid

Therefore, we need to aim at family destination *i.e.* higher realms of quality interpersonal relationship between parents and children from mere problem-solving level at family set-ups and all other social set-ups. One may start nevertheless, at problem solving level. But it is only our beginning steps and we need to move from there if we have to reach the higher levels of the destination pyramid. Otherwise the family may have a crash or a grinding halt with dangerous implications or may never take off, and continues to groan in confusion upbringing children who are vulnerable to all kinds of anti-social behaviour and emotional problems.

The suggested approach is a powerful tool in reaching family destinations. The key to success is in 'sticking to the right track'. If practiced consistently, it would produce positive results be it family, school, training center, work place, organizational set-ups, building leadership qualities, neighborhoods, and other social and official circles—in all realms of human relationships and set-ups. It works wonders in day-to-day ordinary situations, not necessarily problem situations, in achieving targets and actualizing family's goals for optimum success-unity based win/win families to promote better quality of life/climate for children and those around them. In other words, win/win upbringing works to nurture healthier and happier children who alone can withstand the rigors of modern society that is fraught with stresses and challenges.

References

1. Bernstein, B., (1964), "Family role systems, communication, and socialization," in A.H. Halsey, J. Floud and C.A. Anderson (Eds.), *Education, Economy and Society,* Glencoe, III: Free Press.
2. Buscaglia,L., (1986), "Together with Leo Buscaglia", in Stewart J., *Bridges Not Walls,* (4th Edition), New York: Random House.
3. Covey, R.S., (1989), *The Seven Habits of Highly Effective People,* New York: Simon and Schuster.
4. Covey, R.S., (1997), *The Seven Habits of Highly Effective Families,* London. Franklin Covey Company.
5. Danesh, H.B., (1995), *The Violence-free Family,* Ottawa: Bahai Studies Publications.
6. Duck, S. and Wood, J.T., (1995), *Confronting Relationship Challenges,* Vol. 5, New Delhi: Sage Publications.

7. Gordon, T., (1987), *Leader Effectiveness Training*, USA: Wyden Books.
8. Hardison, J., (1986), "Touching for Improving Interpersonal Relationships", in Stewart, J., *Bridges Not Walls*, 4th Edition, New York: Random House.
9. Klinger, E., (1977), *Meaning and Void: Inner Experience and the Incentives in People's Lives*, Minneapolis: University of Minnesota Press.
10. Maslow, A.H., (1973), "A Theory of Human Motivation", *Psychological Review*, 50, 37-396.
11. May, R., (1986), "The significance of Pause", in Stewart J., *Bridges Not Walls*, 4th Edition, New York: Random House.
12. Muncie, J. *et. al* (Eds.) (1995), *Understanding the Family*, New Delhi: Sage Publication.
13. Powell, J., (1969), *Why I am Afraid to Tell You Who I am?* Chicago: Argus Communications.
14. Skinner, B.F., (1974), *About Behaviourism*, New York: Alfred A. Knopf. Inc.
15. Stewart, J., (1986), *Bridges Not Walls*, 4th Edition, New York: Random House.
16. Watzlawick, P., Beavin, J. and Jackson, D., (1968), *Pragmatics of Human Communication*, New York: Norton.

*Appendix-1

Restricted and elaborated codes

Bernstein (1964) identified two forms of communication codes or styles of verbal behavior: *restricted and elaborated*. Restricted codes are stereotyped, limited, and condensed, lacking in specificity and the exactness needed for precise conceptualization and differentiation. Sentences are short, simple, often unfinished; there is little use of subordinate clauses for elaborating the content of the sentence; it is a language of implicit meaning, easily understood and commonly shared. It is the language form often used in impersonal situations when the intent is to promote solidarity or reduce tension.

Elaborated codes, however, are those in which communication is individualized and the message is specific to a particular situation, topic, and person. It is more particular, more differentiated, and more precise. It permits expression of a wider and more complex range of thought, tending toward discrimination among cognitive and affective content.

The effects of early experience with these codes are not only upon the communication modes and cognitive structure—they also establish potential patterns of relations with the external world. As such, language is used by participants of a social network to elaborate and express social and other interpersonal relations and, in turn, is shaped and determined by these relations.

10

Interventions Through Counseling

Introduction

Development is the aim of counseling: All human beings have immense potential for growth, yet there are many who are stuck, immobilized, and unable to meet developmental challenges. Counseling is all about how to facilitate another person's development. Clients come to counselors to solve problems, to find answers, to discover reasons for patterns of behaviour, but always to develop their own unique potential.

Stress and unhappiness may be caused by various problems, sometimes the problems may be long standing involving family disputes, injuries caused by accidents, abuse, domestic violence, victimization etc. Stress and trauma in children may be caused due to coping problems with studies, because of fear of punishment by teachers, because of discrimination shown by others, because of teasing or because of war related experiences such as, bombardments, abuses by soldiers on family members etc. Refugees often experience enormous amount of stress, due to loss of property, loss of family members, hunger and distressing environment. Stress could be caused due to long-term illness such as T.B, leprosy, HIV/AIDS etc.

Many a times elders in the family solve such problems at home, and teachers at school, but they may be very authoritative in their approach. But a counselor will listen to the client attentively, supports and helps the person to find his/her own answers to whatever is troubling. The counselor empathizes with the client with an equal relationship. Working this way, the counselor will focus on how the client can live effectively in this society, knowing and honouring his/her own needs and wishes.

The major aim of counseling is to make people more responsible for themselves and for the society. In this chapter, we shall briefly discuss the counseling process, techniques and approaches and applications of counseling in finding solutions to some of the social problems that children, adolescents and parents are encountering in their day to day family life.

Why Counseling is Needed

Counseling consists of a series of problem solving purposeful conversations; a process and a method of exploring and identifying personal problems and solutions leading to personal growth and development. Counseling is a more intensive and personal process, generally concerned with normal people to cope with normal problems and opportunities. In counseling we use interviewing skills and while interviewing we may also counsel the client. Interviewing skills may be adapted for use in a variety of settings ranging from social work, nursing, management and other fields. The most important skills involved in interviewing are observation, listening, questioning and recording skills.

Counseling whether formal or informal, is expected to make people more responsible for themselves and for the society. There are several situations when counseling may not work or when counseling should not be used. The following are a few such instances, where counseling may not yield results:

- Counseling should not be used as a habit or for recreational purpose and time pass.
- Counseling relationship should not be misused for immoral purposes such as sex and black mailing; for instance, group counseling to pick up women.
- Counseling should not be used in case of persons needing material changes, such as money, job, house

etc. These kinds of things can not be solved easily through counseling.

- Extreme distress and disastrous situations are not congenial for counseling. However, people would need counseling soon after they recover from the state of shock.
- It is also not advisable to counsel those who are closely attached, but suffering from other stressful relationships and problems.

Good Characteristics of a Counselor

The word characteristics include both qualities and behavioural skills of a person. We could identified several good characteristics of a counselor from the available literature on counseling. There are about 35 characteristics ranked in a study cited by Philip Bernard (1999). However, fifteen characteristics, considered very important are given below:

- A good listener
- Non-judgmental attitude
- Empathetic
- Understanding
- Approachable
- Sympathetic
- Caring
- Friendly
- Patient
- Confidential
- Supportive
- Knowledgeable
- Honest
- Trustworthy
- Experienced

Some of the most important characteristics are further explained here.

(1) Good listener

Good counselor listens to their clients. People often begin to feel better simply because they are given the opportunity to talk and begin to listened to. Trying to suppress feelings and speak about them can cause emotional and physical discomfort and stress. Other symptoms such as constant worry, depression, aches, and pains can result from feelings, being held in and not expressed. Counselor must be a good listener to encourage the client to express such feelings in order to bring relief to clients.

A counselor must listen carefully, make observations, get the message behind the words and capture the feelings of the client. Patience is involved in listening as you have to give your time up to the client. Intense listening involves a certain lack of ego and a disinclination to offer our own opinions and judgement (Philip, 1999). During the listening process, the counselor must avoid distractions and note down the body language (non-verbal communication) and expressions of the clients.

Basic Listening Sequence (BLS) includes skills of questioning, paraphrasing to encourage reflection of feelings and summarizing. BLS forms the foundation of effective counseling.

(2) Non-judgmental attitude/acceptance

The client's beliefs and values may be different from those of the counselor's. While counseling suspend your opinions and attitudes and assume a value of neutrality, indicate neither approval nor disapproval. The client should not be judged or evaluated; simply accept the persons with all their weaknesses and actions as they are.

Do not form any opinion about the client till he/she completes his/her story. Some client's intentions may be submerged due to the nature of their problems. A client may say one thing, when he actually means another. Hence, you need to listen to your client's full story and don't judge him \her as bad, good, done wrong etc. Such an attitude will not be of any help to the client.

(3) Empathy

For building up quality relationship with clients, the most important quality of the counselor is to be empathetic. This means moving to client's frame of reference (Rogers, 1975), or putting yourself in the shoes of the client. Gerald Eagan (1986) explains it, as entering the private perceptual world of the client and being sensitive to his/her feelings whether good or bad. Dimensions of empathy include positive regard, respect and warmth concreteness, self-disclosure, non-judgmental attitude and authenticity and congruence (Ivey, 1998: 159). Use of attending skills, particularly paraphrasing, reflection of feelings and meanings are very important in building empathy (Ivey, 1998).

The counselor must convey to the client that he was understood. Respect their situations and avoid imposing your values on them. Self-disclosure helps the client to talk about problem situations more concretely.

Positive regard is the ability to communicate personal warmth and make the client feel free and foster self-respect. Show understanding and caring on your part as a counselor. This reflects honesty, transparency and trust in the counseling relationship (NTISD, 2000).

(4) Understanding

Attending skills such as, listening, paraphrasing, reflecting, body language etc., are basic to helping a client feel that he/she was understood. It becomes easy to free the client for further development (Ivey, 1988). Each individual has his/her own frame of reference, meaning, the perceptions, beliefs, feelings, values and culture influencing his/her personality. Empathy bridges the clients and counselor's frame of reference so that the counselor is able to reflect the feelings of the client and engage in next stages of exploration.

However feelings of pity and sympathy must be avoided while counseling. Other wise, the counselor may become deeply involved with the client's feelings. We may feel sympathetic, yet at the same time have to harden ourselves. If we can not distance ourselves from sufferings of others, we are in danger of becoming emotionally exhausted (Stewart and Martin, 1999).

(5) Confidentiality

Keeping the disclosures of the client as confidential is a basic element in trusting. Unless the client trusts the counselor, he/she may not communicate frankly. Therefore, it is important that the client agrees for disclosure of certain information with others in a specific context. For example, issues such as, abuse by a relative or a teacher may arise in the counseling relationship; in that case, there may be need to disclose certain facts to others, in order to bring justice to the client.

Similarly, suicidal tendencies revealed to the counselor, may require alerting the client's close relatives or friends, with whom, the counselor can work to come up with coping strategies. In any case, the client must not distrust and disrespect the counselor for doing so. In that case, counseling may not work to solve problems of an emotional nature.

(6) Knowledgeable

The counselor must be professionally trained. Through professional training he/she acquires the knowledge and skills related to various issues of counseling. The counselor must have knowledge of human behavior, personality constructs and frames of reference of individuals. The counselor must posses various skills that are being utilized in the process of counseling, must be aware of various approaches such as, psychodynamic, behaviour therapy, cognitive therapy and person/client-centered approaches to counseling. Only then the counselor can be able to use appropriate skills and techniques from different theoretical perspectives, according to the needs of the client at a specific moment.

The counselor must also be self-aware and willing to explore. He/she must know his/her limitations. In many cases, knowledge about other services, such as, health specialists, psychiatric services, economic support agencies and other sources of help is necessary in referrals and rehabilitation work.

(7) Experienced

As the saying goes "experience makes man perfect", counselors become perfect through experience. An experienced counselor will be mature and can handle problems in a different way than the beginners. An experienced person will be conscious and alert in handling his/her own feelings and emotions. Then only he/she can be objective, wise and supportive.

With beginners and inexperienced, the client may try to dominate in the counseling relationship or may direct the counselor what to do, or the counselor may over impose his/her will on the relationship. Such conflict may become a block in the process of counseling.

Abilities such as, listening, patience, logical analysis and understanding including the capacity to keep oneself under control improve, because of life experiences and hence an experienced counselor will be more effective in the process of counseling.

Counseling Skills

There are a variety of skills and approaches to adapt according to different personalities and situations in counseling. The counselor must remember, "if something you try doesn't work, don't try more of the same.... try something different" (Ivey, 1988: 11). Another aspect of using skills is that, the same skills may have different effects on people with different individual and cultural backgrounds.

In counseling, several micro-skills are used, which are communication skill units and provide alternatives to use with client. Micro-skills form the foundation of counseling.

There are four well-known categories of micro-skills, These are:

- Attending skills
- Focusing skills
- Confrontation skills
- Influencing skills

Each of these categories has a group of skills which are explained below:

Attending Skills

Attending, listening and responding skills are inter-related and form the foundation skills of counseling. It means that the clients you are guiding must be attended to and heard properly. You have to communicate this to the client through your attending behavior. Attending behavior consists of the following elements as shown by an acronym "SOLER" outlined by Egan (1986).

- S = Sit facing the client
- O = Adopt open and positive attitude
- L = Lean towards your client
- E = Eye contact with the client
- R = Relax and don't be anxious

During the initial stages of counseling, the following points should be kept in mind:

- It is not advisable to give premature advice and suggestion-suspend judgment;
- Don't search for a single "right" response and rush through the interview;
- Avoid distractions and be attentive; and
- Observe body language of the client and respond appropriately.

Attending skills are also described as Basic Listening Sequence (BLS). These consist of:

- Questioning
- Encouraging and paraphrasing
- Reflection of feelings and meanings
- Summarizing

Questioning

It is a skill of initiating discussion between the client and the counselor. Usually, questions comprise of two types: open ended and closed questions. Open-ended questions are used when the counselor wants more and more information from the client. The client can go on narrating. For instance,

- How are you feeling?
- What happened then?

Closed ended questions usually seek 'yes' or' no' answers or factual information in short, such as:

- How many children do you have?
- Are you suffering with boredom?
- How old are you?

Usually open-ended questions help the counseling to move along and encourage the client to elaborate on his/her feelings and thoughts.

Closed questions may be useful in the beginning to enable counselor to understand the characteristics of the client. There are various purposes of questioning, such as, questions seeking examples, seeking specific information, questions focusing on points of discussion and questions seeking suggestions or plans for change etc. Depending on the situation, the counselor is required to use the questioning skills to get more and more information from the client (Philip, 1999).

Encouraging and Paraphrasing

Counselor encourages the client to talk, but that is not enough. The client must know that he/she has been heard correctly. Encouraging and paraphrasing by the counselor communicates to clients that they have been heard. Counselor puts the client's ideas in his own words and clarifies to the client. For instance, the client may say, "I can not do math's". The counselor may paraphrase this as, "Are you saying that maths is too difficult for you?" This will help the client to focus on the difficulty or the concern. Encouraging the client through your responses and giving feed-back to client through paraphrases help the clients to explore their feelings and thoughts more completely (Ivey, 1988). It also gives the client the confidence and trust to reveal more.

Reflection of Feelings and Meanings

A mirror reflects the sun on to a wall. Similarly, the counselor can make the client to see how others experienced similar conflicts. It is also called echoing, which means echoing back to the client the last few words spoken by the client. For instance,

Client: I started to feel things were going wrong when I changed my job... my husband started keeping distant.

Counselor: Your husband started to get distant... You may also reflect selectively on what your client said during the counseling, for instance: "Let us look at what you have said a few minutes ago. You said...

The purpose of reflection of feelings is to make the implicit, sometimes hidden, emotions explicit and clear to the client. The counselor can also help the client to sort out the complex feelings and thoughts and get free from ambivalent feelings (Ivey, 1988).

Summarizing

Summarizing is simply summing up all the conversation that took place between the counselor and the client. The counselor tries to identify the important issues, a sort of recapitulation. This takes place usually at the end of the interview or as a transition to a new topic or to clarify lengthy and complex client issues. The client in turn will correct any incongruities and agrees with the counselor.

All of these skills-attending, listening, paraphrasing, encouraging and summarizing encourage the client to talk freely and enable the counselor to understand the client accurately. These skills bridge the communication gaps between the client and the counselor.

Experiences of counselors reveal that it is wise to combine these skills and use according to the need and situation in the counseling process. It is not necessary to apply all skills, but the counselor can be more successful, if he is aware of all the skills and use them effectively.

These skills of attending, listening, observation, paraphrasing, encouraging reflection of feelings and summarizing are also considered as basic micro-skills and these are foundation skills for the counseling relationship. Next, we shall examine advanced skills such as, focusing and confrontation skills. Then we shall move on to the influencing skills or action-oriented skills.

Advanced Skills

Advanced skills include focusing, confrontation and influencing skills. Focusing is a skill that enables the counselor to direct client conversational flow to the areas/issues that the counselor wants. This helps the client to focus discussion on important issues and facilitate to concentrate on critical problems. It reduces, "beating around the bush", and can directly come to the point. Thus focusing adds precision to client conversation through selective attention to certain aspects of client's talk (Ivey, 1988).

Sometimes clients are aware of the complex issues surrounding them, but they are unable to focus on any single issue. The counselor can enable the client to focus discussion on particular issues that are relevant to his/her problem and reduce their scattered thinking. Deliberate focusing is helpful in problem definition and assessment.

Confrontation is one of the advanced skills, considered as the most important agent of change in an interview. Ivey (1988) considers it as the most powerful of the micro skills, but it rests on effective listening and observing. It is not independent, it is used in combination with the attending skills such as, questioning, client observation, reflection of feelings and feed back.

Confrontation has two steps:

- First, identifying mixed messages, conflicts, and inconsistencies, and
- Second, pointing out these issues to the clients and helping them to resolve. The client then feels encouraged talking in more detail. Many clients are unaware of their mixed messages and discrepancies, pointing them out gently but firmly can be extremely beneficial to them (Ivey, 1988). The main goal of confrontation is to facilitate client's development through the resolution of incongruities.

Interpersonal influencing skills attempt to influence the client directly and consciously (Ivey, 1988:241). While the listening and attending skills influence the client indirectly. Influencing skills are also regarded as action-oriented skills, which are useful for coaching, self-directed, self-exploring type of counseling aiming at developmental growth and change of clients. Ivey (1988) has identified seven types of influencing skills. The definitions and functions of these seven types of influencing skills are given below:

Directives

Definition: Indicates clearly to a client what actions the client should initiate.

Purpose: To assist a client in understanding a task and helping to ensure action.

Logical consequences

Definition: presents the probable results of a client action, either negative or positive

Purpose: To make clients aware of the impact of their actions and to facilitate their making a choice for the future.

Self disclosure

Definition: Sharing your own thoughts and feelings with the clients.

Purpose: To facilitate client self-disclosure and provide useful models for behaviour change.

Feed-back

Definition: Provides accurate information on how the counselors view the client.

Purpose: To facilitate self-exploration and self-examination using information on how others view the client.

Interpretation

Definition: provides the client with an alternative frame of reference from which to view life situations.

Purpose: To facilitate the client's ability to reframe life situations and view them from alternative perspectives.

Influencing Summary

Definition: Provides the client with a brief summary of what the counselor said or thought during a session.

Purpose: To enable the client to pull together, remember, and understand the counselor's influencing statements.

Information/Advice/Suggestion

Definition: presents information and ideas of the counselor to the client.

Purpose: To bring new points of view and information to the client's attention.

A common feature of all the above seven influencing skills is confrontation, used in order to facilitate clients' new thoughts and actions. The client is made to think of alternative points of view through application of these skills.

Stages and Steps in Counseling Process

Counseling, as a helping process, proceeds through several stages and steps, which are explained in this section. Formal counseling needs structuring, planning and preparation. The structuring of steps and stages differ according to different writers. However, a good counselor is flexible and open to use these according to the situation and needs of the client. A more logical and standardized classification of stages and steps in counseling is provided by Ivey (1988), who has classified counseling process into five steps as given below:

1. Rapport building and structuring sessions and skills(introduction);
2. Gathering information, defining problems and identifying client assets (problem clarification);
3. Determining outcomes (where does the client want to go);
4. Exploring alternatives and confronting client incongruities(what are we going to do about it);
5. Generalization and transfer of learning (will you do it).

The purpose, steps and skills used at each of these stages are described below:

First stage: Rapport building and structuring skills

Purpose: To build a working relationship with, and enable the client to be comfortable and feel confident to speak, and structuring of sessions and skills to explain the client what the counselor can and can not do.

Skills used: Attending skills to establish relationship with the client, observation skills to encourage the client to speak, and information giving (influencing skill) to the client.

Steps used in the process:

- Greet your client warmly and make her feel at home;
- Open up the conversation on a neutral topic to make the client feel important, relaxed, comfortable and ready to talk to you;
- Respect him/her, remembering that each person is unique, with unique problems, attitudes, values, expectations and experiences; and
- Tactfully encourage the client to keep continuing communication.

It is important to provide the details of what your client can expect in the counseling session, for instance,

- Ask what he/she hopes to get from counseling;

- Explain your helping role and its conditions such as, confidentiality and privacy;
- Mention the amount of time that you can avail from him/her; and
- Agree on the number of times to meet and the consultation fee, etc.

The first encounter determines the flow of the counseling session and even the sessions that follow. It gives your client the first impression about the counselor and whether he/she can be trusted to share information. Hence it is important to keep a warm and cordial relationship through out.

Stage two: Defining problems and identifying strengths

Purpose: Gathering information and facilitating the client to define his/her problems, and to identify the positive strengths of the client.

Skills used: Attending skills including the basic listening sequence, influencing skills such as self-disclosure, feed back and interpretation, and confrontation skills to resolve incongruities.

Steps used in the process:

The client is relaxed and is ready to talk about his/her problem. This stage of the counseling is mostly devoted to information gathering and exploring to establish the core problem that needs attention.

The following guidelines may help you to identify the core problem:

- Listen to the problem;
- Probe as to how long the client is suffering with it;
- Find out the causes of the problem;
- Discuss what the client wants to do further? and
- If the client has many problems, try to focus on core problem; and discuss how the client can change to find relief.

By the end of this stage, you are able to identify the major concerns of the client and be able to move to the next stage.

Stage three: Determining outcomes/(Goal-setting)

Purpose: To find out the desirable situation of the client, to know what the client wants to be, and to set accomplishable goals to reach the desirable situation.

Skills used: Attending skills including the basic listening sequence, confrontation, focusing and influencing skills.

Steps to be followed:

- Once the problems are clear, the counselor must work with the client to resolve the problems.
- Try and project a desirable situation- "preferred scenario", which the client could reach.

Consider the following example to illustrate the sequence:

A troubled married student in the in-service programme is worried about his/her continued poor performance. You could help him/her envisage the preferred scenario, which is better performance.

- The student has three alternatives: no alcohol, better study skills and good relations with the wife.
- Once the alternatives are discussed, the client could be helped to choose the best possibilities and turn them into goals to be accomplished.
- However, the student must analyze the advantages and disadvantages and see which of these are viable to put into action. This is done in the next stage.

Stage four: Alternatives analysis

Purpose: Considering alternative solutions for resolving the problems of the client, resolving incongruities in feelings and thoughts of the client, and prioritizing the problems and goals.

Skills used: Heavy use of influencing skills along with attending skills to balance.

Steps to be followed:

By this stage several problems of the client were clarified and goals were set and alternatives were discussed.

- Encourage the client to choose the best possibilities and goals to be accomplished.

- Consider the advantages and disadvantages of each option and goal.
- Come to consensus with the client on the viable actions.
- Let the clients express their feelings such as dependency, anger, love etc.
- If you (counselor) are uncomfortable, angry with the client disclose it to the client and seek others help or refer the client to other counselor.
- Handle silence and resistance of the client carefully with patience.

As an example let us consider the previous instance of the troubled, married student. The client might decide to reduce drinking alcohol. This option would be best if the excess alcohol consumption has been the cause of poor studies and poor relations with the spouse.

The advantages are, more time spent with family and on studies. The result would be better relationship with spouse and better study skills, which lead to better performance.

By now the counselor has enabled the client to set goals, assess the possible solutions and move to the preferred scenario. In the next stage the client will be able to translate these goals into action and sustain the changes brought about through the counseling process.

Stage five: Generalization/(Facilitating action)

Purpose: To facilitate changes in thoughts, feelings and behaviour of the client, and to help the client to make a plan on how to implement his/her goals.

Skills used: To a large extent influencing skills such as information/ advice, directives, explanation etc. Attending skills used to check out the clients' understanding and self-sufficiency.

Steps to be followed:

- Enable the client to internalize the desirable behaviour, in order not to slide back to the problems again.
- Encourage self-help and appreciate the client's efforts to reach that stage.
- Change doesn't come easily, use behavioural therapy to bring about improvement in the client.
- Have follow-up to observe the clients' capacity to cope with new behaviour.

- Develop a plan of action and write it down for the client to follow.

As an example consider the following plan of action in order to check progress:

Name

Date of next follow-up meeting

Sl. No.	*Problems*	*Goals*	*Improvement*
1.	Daily head aches	To reduce head aches	Relaxation exercises every morning
2.	Loneliness	Make friends	Each day spend at least fifteen minutes with your neighbour or a friend
3.	Daughter behaves aggressively	Improve daughter's behaviour	Watch daughter at play. Show her other ways of behaviour when in difficulty. Enroll her in pre-school.

(*Source:* Peer Counseling, MLHW, 2000, unpublished guide).

- Give a schedule of meetings for regular follow-up, if necessary.
- When the client recovers, appreciate his/her efforts to encourage self-confidence.
- Terminate the contract when the client reaches self-sufficiency.
- Remember that you are only helping the clients to help themselves.

In sum, we may say that it is difficult to describe the most effective skills and approaches that could be used in counseling process. Experience of counselors reveal that the fourth stage and fifth stages are very important ones and more work and application of more skills are involved at these two stages. However, rapport building and attending skills are also considered equally important in the counseling process.

Approaches to Counseling

Ivey stated that there are "over 250 theories of counseling and therapy" (1988:315). Similarly, he has described 28 major areas of skills that a counselor can use. To become an effective counselor, it is necessary to master all these skills, as well as, understand different theories and models of counseling, because different theories use different patterns of skills according to the situation of the client.

Broadly speaking different theories relate to one another. There are four major theoretical approaches widely practiced in counseling. These are:

1. Psychoanalytic approach,
2. Behaviouristic approach,
3. Cognitive approach, and
4. Integrated approach.

The fourth approach is an integrated model of the first three approaches, which is commonly used in counseling. Let us examine the salient features of these approaches.

(1) Psychoanalytic Approach

Psychoanalytic approach is based on Freudian theory and analysis. According to this approach, thoughts, feelings and behaviour are viewed as a manifestation of inner drives. It recognizes the role of the unconscious, and how it influences behavior. Further, behaviour is determined by past experiences, genetic endowment and the present happenings.

According to Freudian theory, personality is a system composed of id, ego and super ego, and the behaviour is determined by the multidimensional conflict between id, ego and super ego and their resolution. The resolution of conflicts involves the use of defense mechanisms by ego.

This approach gives much emphasis on childhood experiences. The unconscious and unresolved conflicts within the psyche of the individual can came in the way of his positive behaviour.

The counselor gets in touch with the unconscious world of the client and tries to understand the causes for internal conflict; accompanied by catharsis or release of emotions, the counselor enables the client to understand problems, origins and influences on his/her behaviour. Stage by stage the counselor aims at reorientation of feelings of the client and helps the client in personality reconstruction. The focus in this approach is more on the person rather than on the problems. The goal is self-actualization (Ivey, 1988; Stewart and Martin, 1999).

(2) Behaviouristic Approach

Behavioural counselors work with the clients to change the behaviour that is beyond ethical limits, by concentrating on the behavioural problems observed rather than dealing with thoughts and feelings. This is also called as behaviour modification approach (Stewart and Martin, 1999).

In this approach, the man is viewed as mechanistic, or responding to an environment over which he has little control, has little active role in choosing his destiny (MLHW, 2000). The salient features of this approach include the following:

- Concentrates on behaviour;
- Believes that behaviour is learned and may be unlearned;
- Believes that behaviour is susceptible to change, through learning methods;
- Treatment goals are set with the involvement of the client, fully committed to change;
- Techniques used include, reinforcement, modeling and desensitization (Stewart and Martin 1999).

Behavioural counseling is extensively used to solve the following problems of clients:

- Anxiety disorders
- Childhood disorders
- Depression
- Interpersonal/ marital conflicts
- Sexual disorders
- Speech difficulties
- Stress management
- Substance/drug abuse
- Tension headaches etc.

The following techniques are used for behaviour modification:

(a) Behaviour reinforcement

The counselor enables the client to identify or visualize positive strengths or behaviour patterns and helps him/her to reinforce that behaviour. The client must understand and be convinced about the positive behaviour, unless he/she is committed to positive change it is difficult to bring about change in behaviour pattern of the client.

(b) Social Modeling

This involves providing your clients with personalities whose behaviour characteristics are positive and exemplary. Example, national heroes, philosophers, sports persons, rank students, truthful persons etc. The client is encouraged to learn from such models and cope with behavioural problems by changing their negative behaviour. This could be done through stories and literature about upright personalities and expose the clients to learn from such examples/models.

(c) Desensitization

Desensitization aims to reduce or remove sensitivity to something that causes a problem or irritation. The counselor will ascertain all situations that generate anxiety and orders them. For example:

- Thinking about flying a long distance;
- Seeing a person whom you hate, etc.

The client is encouraged to confront such anxiety situations by presenting to him/her such anxiety provoking situations in a relaxed atmosphere. The client is encouraged to tackle the next situation, and gradually till all fearful or anxiety-producing situations are tackled by the client. This is also similar to assertiveness training, where the client learns to assert and tackle the situation boldly.

(3) Cognitive Approach

Cognitive approach concentrates on thinking, what and how a person thinks. The assumption is that, what a person thinks influences his/her feelings and behaviour.

Cognitive counseling is particularly useful in dealing with clients who have negative thought patterns, attitudes and beliefs accompanied with depression.

Cognitive therapy works on the premise that thoughts of low self-worth are incorrect and are due to faulty learning.

For example:

- It is not worth living;
- I deserve to be condemned;
- I could not achieve anything etc.

The aim of cognitive therapy is to get rid of faulty concepts that influence negative thinking and encouraging the client to develop creative positive thoughts, feelings and behaviour. Negative thinking and behaviour not only puts clients down, but pulls other people down as well. They tend to compare themselves unfavorably with other people. The counselor can help the client to replace such negative aspects of thinking with positive thinking and attitudes through techniques such as, thought stopping and cognitive restructuring.

(a) Thought stopping

The counselor will help the client to imagine or visualize situations, which provide irrational thoughts and guide them to 'STOP'! such thoughts. For example:

Wear a loose elastic band to your wrist, and when the negative thought comes, snap the band and stop or substitute with positive imagination. Gradually positive thinking can become a habit as negative thinking has been.

(b) Cognitive restructuring

The counselor helps the client to recognize and stop self-defeating thoughts or mental blocks and enables him to substitute with positive coping thoughts. Engage the client to construct positive thoughts and replace them with negative thoughts and practice continuously. Gradually, such an exercise reinforces the positive thinking, attitudes, and beliefs in the client.

(4) Integrated Approach

The integrated approach uses all the three approaches and works with the person-centered principles. Instead of trying to fit the client in to one model, this approach adapts the model that works for the client.

It is believed that people are rational beings with needs,

goals specific to their own life stage and potentialities, which may be developed in either positive or negative directions. Some clients are not capable of developing on their own and need assistance of others to achieve full potentiality. Hence, the goal is to aid the individual in approximation of self-understanding and self-management.

The integrated model of counseling uses any of the following approaches:

- A psychodynanic approach to bring unconscious drives and/or defenses into conscious awareness.
- Behavioural therapy may be appropriate if a particular behaviour pattern is inhibiting the client, for example it the client has a specific sexual difficulty.
- Cognitive therapy could help if the massages from your earlier life are leading to self-defeating or self-destruction through negative patterns of behaviour (Stewart and Martin, 1999).

Per cent-centered core principles used in an integrated approach include the following:

- Every individual has internal resources and potentiality for growth.
- Human nature is essentially social and constructive.
- Persons are motivated to seek truth.
- The client should be the focus of the counseling relationship (Stewart and Martin, 1999).

Counseling Applications in Social Settings

Counseling Traumatized, Displaced and Refugee Children

Psychosocial impact on the children, displaced and refugees may be difficult to assess, but it is an important area needing attention of the doctors, change agents, social workers and the paramedical workers. Child counseling is an essential strategy to help children cope with stress and traumatic experiences. The traumatic stresses in these persons may be due to any of these factors given below:

- Death of a near person,
- Shelling and bombing near school or home,
- Unanticipated displacement,

- Subjection to torture and detention,
- Child abuse in wars and for beggary,
- Sexual molestation or rape,
- Sudden destruction due to floods, war, earthquake etc.

The stress disorders may not occur in all children, and all children may not exhibit signs and symptoms of traumatic stress disorder. However these stressful memories linger in all and they become anxious, depressed and fearful. The duration of symptoms may last for a month or may come and go. The symptoms of stressful behaviour in children could be the following:

- Disturbing intrusions, flashbacks, and hallucinations about the event;
- Anxiety and fear, stuttering, rocking or nail biting;
- Traumatic dreams and nightmares;
- Emotional detachment from parents and friends;
- Little interest in play and other enjoyment;
- Increased state of alertness;
- Avoidance behaviour; and
- Difficulty in concentration.

The psychosocial work focused on children has two purposes:

(1) Prevention of psychosocial problems, and

(2) Provision of special care for those who were traumatized and need to recover.

Psychosocial work should not be confused with psychotherapy, which is aimed at changing a person and his relations, but not of his environment. Psychotherapy is not recommended in temporary situations, as it is a long process. The child interventions aimed through psychosocial work include the following:

- Individual interview and using appropriate skills and approaches of counseling with the children;
- Relaxation exercises, such as drawings, story telling, play etc.;
- Group sessions with children;
- Introduction of kindergarten and schooling as soon as possible;

- Introducing of games and sports for the affected children;
- Counseling parents and guiding them to handle the child in a desirable manner;
- Outreach programmes to train and build up awareness among parents, teachers, medical workers etc.; and
- Reuniting unaccompanied children as soon as possible.

Apart from children, refugees and displaced persons affected by the frightful events also need counseling, as they too can develop symptoms of the same nature. In such cases do the following:

- Ask them to explain you the frightful events that they have experienced;
- Give them all information they want from you about the situation and find out how you can help them;
- Determine if they have any symptoms described above;
- Ask them specifically about the nightmares and dreams that they get;
- When rape or sexual violence has occurred, deal with it as described in the relevant section on rape;
- Offer supportive counseling and encourage family support and reunification;
- If appropriate refer them to religious counselors, priests and traditional healers for help;
- If the person is using alcohol or drugs give necessary therapy to come out of the habit;
- Arrange medical help for treating any physical illness; and
- Do not make promises, which you or the authorities can not meet.

The process of counseling services and guidance for children and young persons must lay emphasis on:

(1) Problem solving,
(2) Stress release, and
(3) Informed decision-making.

Follow these steps to help the children and their families:

- CNSPM can be counseled individually or in groups depending on the problem and situation.

- Parents of CNSPM should also be supported with guidance and counseling to provide for the psychosocial needs of children and in creating a congenial home environment.
- Income generating activities must be encouraged with credit support to improve the economic conditions of such families;
- Where schooling is possible arrange to educate the children;
- Where children can not be entrusted to family members, encourage them to learn skills for some kind of employment;
- Arrange for institutional support, such as group homes, night shelters, non-formal education centers etc., if necessary;
- Provide coordinated service support ; and
- Create a belief in the better future and an opportunity to influence their positive thinking.

(a) Dealing with rape victims

Rape is a form of sexual violence commonly committed against refugee women and girls. It can occur during their flight of displacement or in refugee camps when there is no protection. The experience of rape is so traumatic for the women and her family, and in many cases, they attempt to commit suicide. The following are some of the facts and traumatic experiences about rape:

- Rape is a violent act committed against the will of the women/girl;
- Rape is usually committed to show the power of man or to gain control over the women so that she surrenders to him;
- Rape or any other form of sexual violence is against the human rights of a person;
- Rape is committed on younger girls of age 9 years to elders of age 60 as well;
- Rape has serious harmful effects on the individual, family as well as the community where the person lives;
- Many rape victims end up as commercial sex workers, as they are rejected for marriage after rape;

- Many rape incidents are not reported and hidden because of the fear of humiliation and isolation;
- Refugees may be forced to compromise for sex by the guards, authorities and others who may help them to flee or promise to provide care;
- Depression is common reaction to rape;
- Feelings of shame and disgrace or humiliation, feelings of guilt, anger, and lack of hope for about the future are very commonly experienced by the rape victims; and
- Fear of strangers, inability to sleep and nightmares are common problems among the rape victims.

(b) How to help victims of rape?

- Since it is a very sensitive issue, the clients must be assured of confidentiality and work with the rape victims in privacy. Strict confidentiality is essential to help the rape victims.
- If the rape victim is pregnant or has contracted a STD, immediately arrange for professional medical help;
- Don't force her to talk, allow her to narrate the story only when she feels like and do not force her to take decisions against her will;
- Show your full emotional support to her and do not make any judgments about her;
- Find ways to end isolation and reduce stress among the rape victims;
- Organize support groups to take up group activities or productive activities;

(c) Four important steps to be followed

Step-1. Explain the woman that what has happened is not her fault and she should not blame herself. This is especially important to those women who, because of their culture or religion, believe that the tragedy happened to punish them for something bad they had done in the past. Deal with the victims sympathetically and skillfully.

Step-2. Seek the help of religious leaders and elders to perform certain rituals and ceremonies of cleansing the women victims in order to remove the blot that they are "unclean". Educate the family and community members to change their beliefs and cooperate with the victims by not blaming her.

Step-3. Encourage the victim to express their anger on the rapists, so that the victims do not blame themselves. Organize support groups to tackle the issue in an effective manner.

Step-4. Educate the victims to prevent further rape incidents. After darkness, they may move in groups and never alone. Report any suspicious movements and any attempts of rape by the men to proper authorities.

Social Support and Counseling for Adolescents and Youth

Experiences have shown that it takes a longer time for behavioural change to occur among the affected persons. Adults must therefore be good role models to provide positive influence to teenage behaviour. Determinants of behavioural change include education and awareness, knowledge, moral values and norms, and perception of consequences and negative aspects of problems and positive aspects of change of behaviour.

A powerful tool to improve the awareness and knowledge about these problems is the *peer group education,* to involve adolescents in a participatory manner to identify their problems and search for solutions through the help of a facilitator. An action research study undertaken to involve adolescents through Information Education and Communication (IEC) based interventions showed that, it was very effective and useful to involve teenagers to analyze their problems, spread messages of negative consequences of STDs and unwanted pregnancy. They had improved their knowledge, over a period of two years, on sexuality, use of contraception and safe methods when required, and made consistent efforts to mobilize community support for the programme (Kinoti, 1995).

Apart from the above the *preventive measures* may include the following:

- Improve knowledge on reproductive biology among adolescents;
- Identification of risky behaviour and counseling to change such behaviour;
- Recreation facilities as a viable alternative;
- Education on the magnitude and consequences of the major problems that the adolescents are facing;
- Formal and informal education on the mechanism of

transmission of STDs and HIV infections and ways and means of protecting one self;
- National policy on illicit drug trafficking and use with provisions for severe penalties for the recalcitrant; and
- Public education awareness campaigns on the dangers of drug abuse, AIDS and other social problems.

Community counseling is ideally carried out through volunteers selected by the community and are trained by the medical team. Such insiders are expected to work more effectively than the outsiders who are less familiar with community attitudes and beliefs. The community counselor can sustain the commitment of the whole community to care of the affected persons and their families. The counselors can do the following in the community:

1. Promoting respectful and confidential sharing of information within the community and groups;
2. Linking community with the Government health services and other NGOs providing rehabilitation services;
3. Helping to implement community specific strategies and activities;
4. Referring patients to health care givers; and
5. Counseling in bereavement and other stressful times in the community.

Counselors need to understand local beliefs and customs and the difficulties faced by the poor in getting proper treatment. In dealing at the community level, the counselor must play the role of an effective educator, since they have to work with the public. An effective educator must have clear concepts and objectives and a clear statement of what the learners or listeners should be able to think, feel and do (behaviour).

It is imperative for the counselor be a good communicator, as most of his/her work depends on effective communication. Activities such as awareness building, education and counseling all depend upon good communication skills, which include:

- Ability to enable the client to involve in listening or receiving process;
- Effective speaking;

- Questioning and explaining doubts;
- Effective listening; and
- Using effective methods of communication.

Once the learner internalizes the message, there is a greater chance for behavioural change to occur. However, behavioural change is also strongly influenced by cultural beliefs, attitudes and values (Esther, M. and N.K. Stephen, 1995). Clear understanding of these attributes and their consideration in preparing education messages will have a positive impact on the programme.

The methods of communication are also very important when we deal with the public. Most of the rural population is illiterate. It is difficult to retain their attention to lectures and print material. Hence, it is appropriate to use one-to-one communication, individual and group counseling and audio-visual methods to retain their interest in listening. We must remember the Chinese proverb, *"what I hear, I forget; what I see, I recall; and what I do, I know"*.

Community counselor can also undertake the following activities to bring about sustained behavioural change in the community:

- Organizing youth groups, who take interest in helping the affected persons in educating, guiding them to service points and mobilizing support for the persons affected by the diseases such as AIDS, Malaria and TB.
- Involving religious, political and influential leaders in mobilizing support, changing community attitudes and accepting persons affected by the AIDS, Malaria and TB.
- Mobilizing local resources and organizing campaigns;
- Supporting the medical staff who visit the villages for their work;
- Identifying target groups for providing community education through discussion and counseling to change behaviour;
- Identifying suspected cases of persons with AIDS (PWAs) and guiding them to take necessary medical care;
- Supporting families that are affected by these diseases to cope with their treatment and survival needs by

setting up community self-help groups and home-based care;

- Promoting social marketing, use of condoms and safer sex methods; and
- Liaisoning with the health workers and providing facilities and assistance for community health programmes, such as malaria bed-net programme, IEC programmes for educating people, promoting positive attitudes in the community, preventing harmful practices (FGM) and getting supportive programmes for these disadvantaged families such as credit, housing etc.

References

1. Egan, G., (1986), *The Skilled Helper* (3rd Ed.), Springfield III: Charles C Thomas.
2. Florence, H., (1966), *Casework: A Psychosocial Therapy*, Kegan Page: London.
3. Ivey, A.E., (1988), *Intentional Interviewing and Counseling*, Brooks Cole Publishing Company: California.
4. Kadushin, A., (1983), "The Social Work Interview", cited in Radda Barnen, *Social Work and Administration: Methods and Techniques*, Radda Barnen: Sweden.
5. Lankester, Ted, (1994), *Setting up Community Health Programmes: A Practical Manual*, Macmillan India Ltd.: Delhi.
6. MLHW, (2000), *MLHW Training of Peer Counseling and Para Counseling*, (Unpublished manual): Asmara.
7. MOH, (1997), *Five Year Strategic Plan to Prevent and Control HIV/AIDS in the State of Eritrea*, Ministry of Health: Asmara.
8. MOH, (1999), *Five-Year Action Plan for the Control of Malaria*, Ministry of Health: Asmara.
9. NTISD, (2000), *Skills in Guidance and Counseling*, (Unpublished manual) Nsamizi Training Institute for Social Development: Uganda.
10. Philip, Burnard, (1999), *Practical Counseling and Helping*, Routledge: London.
11. Philip, Burnard, (1993), *Counseling Skills Training: A Sourcebook of Training Activities for Trainers*, Kegan Page: London.
12. Rogers Carl and D. Stevens, (1975), *Person to Person*, New York: Pocket Books.
13. Stewart, W. and A. Martin, (1999), *Going for Counseling*, How to Books Ltd.: London.
14. Werner David, (1987), *Disabled Village Children*, The Hesperian Foundation: Palo Alto, USA.

11

Conclusion and Some Imperatives

Scope of the Book

Children need to be grown up healthy and happy to become economically productive, socially useful and contended adults. To give them this happy childhood, the various stakeholders, such as parents, families, communities and the State apparatus have to play their roles effectively with sincerity and commitment. We must first understand the problems associated with these actors and then could find some possible solutions to minimize or eradicate those problems. Contextually, the authors have considered illustrating the roles and responsibilities of different stakeholders in shaping the childhood and managing childhood problems.

The book falls under the category of family impact studies, which are valued in providing inputs to virtually every government programme, such as social security, foster care, employment, taxation etc. The need to understand the impact of changes in family relations on the social policies and programmes of government is more pronounced due to the deteriorating family bonds and withering care and decaying support systems of the traditional family.

We have unraveled some of the untouched issues, and those issues that seem to have an impact on rehabilitation and development of the disadvantaged children and their families in need of special protection measures. The various factors, interventions and support strategies that contribute to care, protection and development of children in society were delineated.

We have reviewed how the changing family environment, value systems and increasing social, communal and political conflicts in society could have endangering effects on childhood development. On the one hand family relationships and bonds for care and protection of children were deteriorating; while, on the other hand, materialism is pervading modern and western families resulting in erosion of family bonds and cultural values. At the macro-level, political instability, racial and communal tensions, armed conflicts, terrorist activities and separatist movements were increasingly driving children and families to vulnerability and distress. The alleged rise in child abuse, childhood crimes and disorder in society, all reflected on the physical insecurity and moral ambiguity of our society.

In the contemporary society, attitudes, beliefs and cultural values of people have been changing at a rapid manner, especially towards parenting and childhood. Currently, nuclear families, a fewer children, more financial and emotional investments for longer duration on children has been the trend. Children are no more the exclusive possession of parents. The rights of children have become paramount in society.

Several factors contribute to care, protection and development of children in society. Proper socialization of childhood depends to a large extent on parents and teachers, whose social and moral value systems play a key role. Family relationships and social environment also contribute to a greater extent, in shaping children's cultural orientation. The economic capability of parents is also a key factor, to the extent that they can meet the basic needs of children and reduce their relative deprivations.

Practically, the burden of managing childhood is so enormous that, even well-intentioned parents find themselves wondering whether they are getting it right. Sometimes it goes out of hand may be due to ignorance, lack of neibourhood support or lack of accessibility to services; and that is time when they should turn to professional advice.

Apart from these, some new areas of concern, such as sexual abuse of children, use of children as soldiers, trafficking of children for sex trade and child labour have become demanding issues for greater intervention of the State machinery and allocation of new resources. There is a need to address policy reforms and development needs within this backdrop of perceived problems.

The various issues that were analyzed in this book could be classified in to four major groups as mentioned below:

- Family and social environment in shaping childhood;
- Quality of family life, culture and value system and the parent-child relationship in enabling the future adulthood of children;
- Categories of children in difficult circumstances and roles of various stakeholders in managing childhood problems; and
- Professional services, ethical considerations and parents involvement in meeting the challenges.

Let us discuss the above issues one by one here.

Family and Social Environment in Shaping Childhood

The chapter on "Families and Social Environment in Childhood Development" illustrated as to how family and social environment could support and enhance or, alternatively, undermine happy and healthy childhood development and how parents and children could experience emotional competence in the process.

The importance of family relationships and their impact on childhood socialization has been variously described. Family is the basic unit for cultivation of interpersonal and intrapersonal interactions and sociocultural orientation to children, apart from the school and their neighbourhood. It provides a network of relationships that connect together children, parents, aunts, uncles, grandparents, friends, neighbours, communities and professional caregivers. Much of what makes us human beings are the social networks and relationships; while families and society provide these for us.

Children completely depend on parents and families in their

first few years of life, and this biological fact necessitates protection, nurturing and teaching of children. Family is also described as "headquarters" for human development (Garbarino, 1982: 62). It is a place for love, care, learning and socialization of children. Children, parents and the lifelong kinship make up the family concept.

Families mediate between individuals and society through socialization and social relationships. Families, individuals and society are thus intertwined. However, the balance of power, individualization and meeting of family goals differ across time and culture. For instance, individual freedom is more in "open families" than the traditional "closed" type of families; while the "atomic" family represents an excessive swing away from the domestic closed type. As family bonds weaken, individualism grows or vice-versa.

Family is basically an interacting unit and the family system is characterized by a whole lot of interactions between parents and children, between father and mother, between children themselves and so on. One most powerful conduit therefore, that builds or wrecks families/communities is interpersonal relationships. Therefore, our basic childhood training is of profound importance. Failing to get that, the outcome will be 'constricted growth'; unable to cope adequately with the outside world as well as within the family resulting in behaviour problems, emotional difficulties, addictions, and other deviant behaviour. Other coping demands of the modern society will compound this. The implication is that, families need to prepare children with adequate interpersonal and problem-solving skills to cope with the external demands.

However, some parents of disadvantaged families are either ignorant or are not capable of providing basic needs for their children; while the 'under class' category of families representing 'undeserving poor' are culpable of creating a culture of deprivation and crime among many modern families. They can not properly structure the processes of childhood due to several disadvantageous factors affecting their livelihood, which include:

- Poverty and deprivation of basic needs such as, food, clothing, housing, water and sanitation, health care and education facilities;

- Nutritional deprivation, resulting in lack of immunity for infections as well as low physical and mental growth;
- Burden of sharing parents' work to sustain families, depriving child's educational development;
- Increased number of children in families, resulting in less attention for children due to heavy burden of meeting survival needs;
- Cultural factors affecting proper parenting of children (control, dependency syndrome, lack of competence, patronage, over protection, etc.).

In modern society, it is very difficult to balance between various needs of life-material needs, esteem needs, social needs and intellectual needs (Maslow, 1954, cited in Clare, 1998). Every one has to confront a highly competitive situation, winning and excelling at the profession may take priority rather than being at peace with themselves and their conscience. Thus one has to sacrifice one area of life to achieve excellence in another area. However, an emotionally competent adult can actively develop well enough to achieve and maintain considerably successful balance in most areas/aspects of life.

Another important aspect is that, the priorities of children keep changing and growing as the circumstances change around them. Parents have to be flexible to the changes in needs and priorities of children through different ages. It is an essential life skill, which is in most cases learnt, in the process of experiencing and understanding life. The most difficult experiences are usually our best teachers, and they are essential to continuing growth and advancement in terms of development of self-knowledge (Clare, 1998).

In this process, sometimes parents make mistakes and the outcome may not be as expected and it can make it harder for the child to be successful. However, it is a part of the learning process. Some parents may not show much importance to the growing child, as they may be busy with their professional obligations or may be away from child; or they may voluntarily neglect and abuse because of family disharmony and breakdown.

In any case, parents must know how important children are for them? In life priorities, where do they place children? How much time and energy they are able to devote for their agrowing children? These are some of the pertinent questions parents must comprehend in the child rearing process. It is in this context that the quality of parent-child relationship, strong family background and the cultural heritage that the child carries to his/her adulthood are so important, which we shall examine in the next section.

Before that we shall briefly mention what the government and community can do in this regard to help the disadvantaged families to cope with their problems. First and foremost is to tackle poverty situation, as most problems arise from poverty and deprivation. Government must consider giving financial help at the time when the child is ready to go to school; establish day-care centers with the partnership of parents themselves; and provide income-generating assets for very poor families. Midday-meal scheme in schools is one such good programme. Next, the pre-school play groups, pre-school day care centers could be established within the niebourhoods as self-help ventures by parents themselves. This kind of programme will be a boon for the working women.

Quality of Family Life and Parent-child Relationship

Currently, the most serious concern about the family and 'criticism against' it relates to its vital role in parenting and rearing children. Many researchers have questioned the desirability of having children reared by their inadequate parents who are becoming destructive forces to individuality and human growth. They viewed family as an institution that is characterized more by control, dominance, abuse and violence against its weakest members especially, women and children (Covey, 1997, Danesh, 1995; Muncie *et. al*, 1995, and Buscaglia, 1985).

There are intergenerational factors that influence parental attitude and behaviour more so in developing societies like India. There are also larger cultural groups like extended family, church, relatives, friends, community, political systems etc., which influence the family dynamics either directly or through the other social systems. The interventions by professionals and change agents in matters of family counseling and childhood issues have been on the increase. It is not limited to medical professionals, but the media, politicians, religious leaders and community play key roles in passing judgments and modifying social behaviour of people in society.

However, the family as a basic unit, serves as the first significant training and nurturing ground for the newborn infant. The key to growth process depends on opportunities that the family affords the child as a safe place to find him/her and others in this world. The main actors are the immediate family members *viz.* the mother and father, brothers and sisters and then the other extended family members. These persons have their strengths, weaknesses, fears, attachments, needs, desires and dreams. But there are other actors too viz. the professionals or teachers the child may come in to contact with, neighbours, peers and the community around. All these persons exert some kind of influence on child directly or indirectly, though it begins its first relationship with the mother.

If the family members as a group will respond positively, he/she is likely to see himself/herself in a positive light. He/she may learn that he/she is beautiful, capable, alert, and that he/she has great hope for the future awaiting outside the family. On the other hand, if their responses are negative, he/she may learn that he/she is limited, unattractive, embarrassing, dull, and that his/her future is dim.

The quality of life in a family depends to a large extent on its resources and the coping mechanisms of its members. Mothers of children who reported adequate support from their spouses reported fewer depressive symptoms, happier marriages, and received higher scores from ratings on quality of parenting (Bristol and Schopler, 1984). Mc Cubbin and Patterson (1982) defined resources for family adaptation as, "the psychological, social, interpersonal, and material characteristics of individual members, the family unit, and the community that may be brought in to play in reducing tension, managing conflicts, and, in general, meeting demands and needs". Such resources might be added, strengthened, developed or depleted in response to the situation. These resources will also mediate with the adverse effects of demands made.

In case of families with disabled children, more than the internal resources, the availability of other facilities and services had marked difference in the stress level of parents. The parents who were availing day care and other services reportedly had much lower level of stress and higher levels of marital integration than those who were not availing such services.

Availability of affordable 'formal services' like early intervention services, home-based management, inclusive education, vocational training, therapeutic services were of great importance and provided palliative support for the affected families. Other aspects that could be counted were the availability of right professionals, counseling services, affordable services, concessions and scholarship for children with disabilities and so on.

As regards children in families of the "under class" and those that indulge in family violence, it is essential to suggest behaviour modification for various reasons such as these. It is a fact that the growth of cognitive processes is fostered in family control systems which offer and permit a wide range of alternative actions and thought, and that, such growth is constricted by systems of control which offer predetermined solutions and few alternatives for consideration and choice. The behaviour which leads to poor interpersonal relationship, is socialized in early childhood, that is, it is learned. Also the problem involved in the effects of poor communication and interpersonal relationship is a lack of cognitive meaning in the parent-child communication system.

We have suggested a few strategies for this, among which the win/win communication, language and behaviour proposed by Covey (1997) could be considered with seriousness; and that is very useful in shaping the interpersonal relationships, thought process and cognitive styles of problem solving in disorganized families. The win-win paradigm has a frame of mind and heart that constantly seeks mutual benefit in all human interactions. It involves interactions, decisions and agreements and solutions that are mutually beneficial.

This requires a paradigm shift in our thinking and behavior and roles, from 'controlling' to facilitating, from the feeling of supremacy to feeling of oneness, from 'I know it all, you learn' to 'let us learn', from 'criticizing', 'complaining' and 'condemning' to 'acknowledge', 'accept' and 'appreciate'. It means, live and let live. It means win for every one concerned.

It has to be emphasized that this method involves trade-off: while it is easy enough to conceptualize, it is not easy to acquire competence in applying this method. However, the benefits of the win/win method are immense, such as: wholesome family, higher quality decisions, warmer relationships, better parenting, transformation from power/control based families to unity-based families and children acquiring win/win orientation to become building blocks of a better civilization.

Categories of Children in Difficult Circumstances

Children in difficult circumstances needing special protection measures are those children whose basic needs such as food, shelter, medical care, educational opportunities, security and psychological well being are not met (Bwibo, 1995). These basic needs are not met because of increasing social, economic and political problems. As far as African countries are concerned, the single most important cause for this situation has been the political strife and armed conflicts leading to displaced families and refugees. Poverty, malnurishment, famines, girl child neglect and commercial sex exploitation are some of the other causes for the increasing number of this category of children.

Apart from economic reasons, there are other social and cultural causes for increase in their number, which include, joint families transforming in to nuclear families, lack of earning male member at home, incapacity to provide for basic needs because of large number of children, growing indiscipline among children and care free atmosphere among parents. The children in difficult circumstances may be categorized into five groups, *viz.* abused and traumatized children, orphans, street and working children, child prostitutes and children with disabilities. Each of these groups of children was discussed in great detail in chapters four to six. Various programmes and strategies to ameliorate their problems were also included there.

Here we shall briefly discuss a comprehensive and coherent set of interventions that the stakeholders could initiate in order to provide an environment, which fosters democracy and stimulates emotional, psychological, social and cognitive growth of children in our society. Full realization of the goals of the Convention on the Rights of Children and empowerment of children, parents and communities is a responsibility of each and every one in society.

All action programmes to alleviate general problems of these groups of children in difficult circumstances could be classified into five main components: education and training, welfare provisions, protection, advocacy/public awareness and regulation and enforcement. At each of these levels different stakeholders may have to contribute for the success of these strategies differently. For instance, government must take lead role in providing welfare services and regulation and enforcement, while parents and community have roles to play at every level. A typology of these interventions are given in the Chart 11.1 on next page, which is self-explanatory:

Professional Services and Parents Involvement

It is a well-established fact that parents are the single most critical factor as well as a potent resource in promoting child development. Although, professionals play an important role in crisis situations in making the disturbed and disorganized parents understand their situation realistically and help in alleviating negative impact on their family relations, without parents participation in the process, they could end up paying heavy price at a later stage.

Either in the counseling process or at any stage of the rehabilitation process of the physically or mentally challenged children, it is imperative to involve parents. Parents could play a range of roles *viz.,* as parents, co-therapists, first-hand information providers, resource persons, advocates, assistants, decision-makers, catalysts and as partners. While executing these roles, they can be a 'buffer' or 'trigger', promote or impede development, and can play supplementary or complementary roles. Most importantly, the whole process of rehabilitation of children with disabilities (CWDs) has to do with 'interpersonal' relationship—human interactions, be it speech therapy, physiotherapy, behaviour therapy and nerve-stimulation. Nobody is more blessed with this 'humane touch' than the child's own mother and father.

Various steps in the process of rehabilitation and ways and means of meeting new challenges were illustrated in the seventh chapter. Similarly, various characteristics of professionals that are of significance in the process of counseling or therapeutic rehabilitation have been discussed in greater detail in both seventh and tenth chapters. Professionals are now dealing not only with the areas of diagnosis and placement, but also with the complex task of helping the family and child live together

Chart 11.1: A Typology of Interventions and Roles of Stakeholders

Strategy/ type of intervent	*Levels of intervention and roles of stakeholoders*			
	Children	*Families and Community*	*Service providers*	*Government and NGOs*
I-Education and training	• Access to basic education; • Non-formal schooling; • Vocational training; and • Apprenticeship with firms	• Educating parents on the value of it; • Adapting school hours to family needs; • Facilitating children to attend school; and • Provision of community centers to provide vocational training and employment	• Sensitizing service providers to the special needs of these groups of children and the disadvantaged families.	• Ensuring basic education facilities; • Providing incentives to girls and these groups of children; • Reforming educational policies in favour of these groups.
II-Welfare provisions	• Supplementary nutrition; • Access to basic health facilities; • Universal immunization; • Shelters/group homes; • Provision of work-sheds and credit for self-employment.	• Health awareness; • Attitudes and behavioural changes; • Social security measures; • Neibourhood self-groups/care centers; • Income-generating schemes; and • Establishing of drop-in centers.	• Regular crash courses to orient the service providers and change agents to the new requirements.	• Expansion of basic welfare facilities • Community-based rehabilitation schemes; • Devolving power to local levels.

III-Protection	• Awareness on elements of child abuse and child rights; • Work placement schemes; and • Sheltered workshops.	• Awareness on elements of child abuse and child rights; • Awareness about illegal trafficking of girls and children and abductions to armed groups etc.; • Public action to bring policy changes where required.	• Regular crash courses to orient the service providers and change agents to the new requirements; and • Checklist of services available to these groups of children.	• Government's support for community-based initiatives; and • Legislations in support of these groups.
IV-Advocacy	• Developing awareness of the situation and their rights; • Access to self-representation; and • Media support—news papers, T.V., street plays, mass campaigns.	• Getting informed about the various provisions, do's and dont's; • Establishing citizen's groups; and • Mobilizing support of teachers, workers, religious leaders and other community based groups and organizations.	• Sensitizing civil servants, project coordinators and and service providers to new requirements.	• Designing communication strategies to raise public awareness; and • Mobilizing political support for policy implementation.
V-Regulation and enforcement	• Involving in campaigns to raise awareness; and • Reporting violations in neighbourhood and by unscrupulous elements; • Forming children's groups to tackle specific problems.	• Educating families and public about the laws and responsibilities; and • Cooperating with implementation and regulation machinery to ensure transparency and efficiency.	• Training employers on the various legal provisions and special duties and responsibilities while dealing with child laws and other provisions.	• New legislations in favour of these groups; • Adaptation of laws to local reality; • Expansion of control and supervisory staff and machinery; • Strict enforcement of legal provisions; and • Ensuring transparency and corruption free services.

more comfortably at home. Moreover, the purpose of providing maximum benefits to the child must be interlocked with minimal stress to total parental needs and family functioning as both the children and the family are faced with making adjustments to and in the community in which they live. Hence, an understanding of these professional characteristics and ethics is all the more pronounced.

Main Observations

Finally, we may draw some of the following observations while concluding our discussions:

1. Under any given macro-level scenario and social, political and economic conditions, family as a basic unit continues to function in nurturing and socializing children, in order for them to grow up as socially well adjusted, healthy and economically productive adults. Every parent has this as his/her priority in life. However, the quality of family experiences, interactions and the cultural values that were passed on to children seem to be determinants in shaping children as useful adults or as deviants in society.
2. Proper socialization of children depends to a great extent on the quality of parent-child relationship, support structures available within and out side of families, at school and at neighbourhood; and in this process of interaction with their environment, children acquire good and bad values that determine their future behaviour.
3. At any given period of time, there are some family environments, which are not congenial and are detrimental to the children's growth. These could be the disadvantage and deprivations, those of the 'under class' experiences and those families where violence and abuse prevails. Similarly, refugee status, displacements, concentration camps etc., could play havoc in the childhood period. Due to various reasons, these situations are on the increase, despite national and international efforts to mitigate such circumstances.
4. There are strong evidences, which suggest that childhood deprivations and abusive experiences have negative

impact on the mental health of children and there is every possibility that they may grow up as social deviants or as destructive adults in society.

5. In case of families with mentally or physically challenged children, the positive attitudes, beliefs, responses and strong support structures within the family seem to act as coping mechanisms in accepting the CWD, in reducing stress and improving family relationships as well as the condition of CWDs.
6. In the process of family adjustment and rehabilitation of the CWDs, professional-parent relationship and collaborative efforts seem to be determinants in minimizing negative effects on families as well as the CWDs.
7. In case of children who grow up as social deviants and families that need professional guidance and advise, several methods of behaviour modification are available such as, the counseling techniques and approaches, the win/win strategy to improve inter-personal and family relations and a variety of other methods one could utilize, rather than suffering for longer periods.
8. Major problems at the national level seem to be lack of resources, lack of political commitment and the convenience of using children as child labour, as soldiers and for other purposes of exploitation; and as a consequence there seem to be significant reduction in tackling the problems of the exploited children.
9. Campaigns such as, 'Global Movement for Children', 'Child Labour Eradication', 'Campaign to Stop Child Trafficking', 'Elimination of Child Soldiers', Universalization of Education', Universal Immunization Programme' etc., need to be intensified and spread all over with additional resources that could be generously provided by the developed countries to stop imbalances in society. Wherever, these campaigns take place, make sure that good governance prevails and the resources mobilized for this purpose shall not reach private bank accounts. After all children have to survive and be healthy if our society has to remain.

Finally, as promised, we wish and expect that the book shall be of immense use to a variety of persons and professionals such as, counselors, academics, researchers, trainers, project administrators, students in the field of Family and Child Welfare and the parents too.

References

1. Bristol, M.M. and Schopler, E., (1984), "A developmental perspective on stress and coping in families of antistic children". In I. Blacher (Ed.) *Families of Severely Handicapped Children: Review of Research.* New York: Academic Press.
2. Buscaglia, L., (1986), *The Disabled and Their Parents: A Counseling Challenge,* N.J: Charles B. Slack, Inc.
3. Bwibo, N.O., (1995), "Children in Especially Difficult Circumstances" in *Primary Health Care: A Manual,* (Eds.) Mukelabai, K et.al. Nairobi: UNICEF.
4. Clare, S., (1998), *Raising the Successful Child,* How to Books: Oxford.
5. Covey, R.S., (1997), *The Seven Habits of Highly Effective Families,* London: Franklin Covey Company.
6. Danesh, H.B., (1995), *The Violence-free Family,* Ottawa: Bahai Studies Publications.
7. Garbarino, J., (1982), *Children and Families in the Social Environment,* Aldine de Gruyter: New York.
8. McCubbin, H.I. and Patterson, J.M., (1982), *Family Stress, Coping and Social Support,* (pp. 26-47), Springfield IL: Charles. E. Thomas.
9. Muncie, J., *et. al* (Eds.) (1995), *Understanding the Family,* New Delhi: Sage Publication.

Index